THE SELF ON THE SHELF

THE SELF ON THE SHELF

*Recovery Books
and the Good Life*

Gary Greenberg

STATE UNIVERSITY OF NEW YORK PRESS

Published by
State University of New York Press, Albany

© 1994 State University of New York

For information, address State University of New York Press,
State University Plaza, Albany, N.Y., 12246

Production by Marilyn P. Semerad
Marketing by Dana E. Yanulavich

Library of Congress Cataloging-in-Publication Data

Greenberg, Gary, 1957-
    The self on the shelf : recovery books and the good life / Gary
Greenberg.
        p.   cm.
    Includes bibliographical references and index.
    ISBN 0-7914-2045-0 (alk. paper). — ISBN 0-7914-2046-9 (pbk. :
alk. paper)
    1. Codependency literature. 2. Interpersonal relations—Moral and
ethical aspects. 3. Autonomy (Psychology)—Moral and ethical
aspects. 4. Conduct of life. I. Title.
RC569.5.C63G74 1994
158′.1′0973—dc20   93-38024
                                                                                                      CIP

10 9 8 7 6 5 4 3 2 1

Since this page cannot accommodate all the copyright notices,
the page that follows constitutes an extension of the copyright page.

". . . In order to make the world over anew, people themselves must turn onto a different path psychically. Until one has indeed become the brother of all, there will be no brotherhood. No science or self-interest will ever enable people to share their property and their rights among themselves without offense. Each will always think his share too small, and they will keep murmuring, they will envy and destroy one another. You ask when it will come true. It will come true, but first the period of human *isolation* must conclude." "What isolation?" I asked him. "That which is now reigning everywhere, especially in our age, but it is not concluded yet, its term has not yet come. For everyone now strives most of all to separate his person, wishing to experience the fullness of life within himself, and yet what comes of all his efforts is not the fullness of life but full suicide, for instead of the fullness of self-definition, they fall into complete isolation. For all men in our age are separated into units, each seeks seclusion in his own hole, each withdraws from the others, hides himself, and hides what he has, and ends by pushing himself away from people and pushing people away from himself. He accumulates wealth in solitude, thinking: how strong, how secure I am now; and does not see, madman as he is, that the more he accumulates the more he sinks into suicidal impotence. For he is accustomed to relying only on himself, he has separated his unit from the whole, he has accustomed his soul to not believing in people's help, in people or in mankind, and now only trembles lest his money and his acquired privileges perish. Everywhere now the human mind has begun laughably not to understand that a man's true security lies not in his own solitary effort, but in the general wholeness of humanity."

—Dostoevsky, *The Brothers Karamazov*,
"From the Life of the Elder Zosima," pp. 303-304

Contents

Acknowledgments   xiii

Introduction   1

1. Codependence in Context   11
    Introduction   11
    "Greed is Good!"   14
    Moral Dilemmas of Psychotherapy   15
    Self and Other as Social Constructions   27

2. The Cat's Grin   37
    Prologue   37
    The Problem   38
        Self-Help Psychology   38
        The Codependence Literature   46
    Notes on Method: Rationale for a
        Hermeneutic Analysis   52
        The Necessity of Entering the Circle   52
        Hermeneutics and "Self-Help"   54
        Why the Codependence Literature?   62

3. The Contours of the Codependence Genre   67
    Introduction   67
    The Algebra of "Recovery":
        ACOA + WWLTM = ACDF   68
    The Constituent Texts of the
        Codependence Literature   83
    The Homogeneity of the Codependence Literature   85

4. The Codependence Literature as a Moral Discourse   99
      Codependence as a Strong Evaluation   100
      Strong Evaluation Shapes Moral Space   108
      The Codependence Literature as a Narrative Space   111

5. The Reader's Colloquy with Herself   117
      Introduction   117
      A Walk in the Woods: A Digression
          on the "Space of Questions"   120
      The Narrative Induction: Am I a Codependent?   123
          The Cast of the Net   123
          An Interpretive Framework   129
      The Dimension of Dignity: The "Center" Cannot Hold   132
          Dignity as a Private Affair   132
          Dignity as the Expulsion of Others
              from the Reader's Story   137
          Dignity as the Smooth Functioning of a Machine   142
          The Dimension of Dignity: A Summary   144

6. The Sole Author in the Social World   147
      Good Fences Make Good Neighbors:
          The Dimension of Respect for and
          Obligation to Others   148
          Introduction: Obligation as Crossing Over
              into the Realm of the Other   148
          Obligation as a Serendipity of Self-Love   151
          May I See Your Passport, Please?
              Obligation as Foreign Policy   154
          Laissez-Faire Obligation   158
          The Twelve-Step Group as the
              Arena of Obligation   164
          The Dimension of Obligation and
              Respect: A Summary   167
      The Dimension of a Full Life   169
          Introduction: Horizon as Inescapably Other   169
          The "Higher Power" as the Source of a Full Life 171
          The "Higher Power" as the Divine Within   174
          The "Higher Power" as Santa Claus   177
      Summary and Conclusion   180

7. The Codependence Literature as an Instance of Nihilism   187
    Introduction   187
    The Gordian Knot   191
    Othello and Iago   196
    The Dangling Conversation   198
    "The Triumph of the Therapeutic"   205
    "The Eyes of the World"   218

8. Conclusion: A Reconstitution of Codependence   233
    Introduction: The "Heidegger Problem"   233
    Coda: A Brief Summary of the Argument   236
    A Reconstitution of Codependence   237
    Avenues for Further Research   248

Appendix A   257

Appendix B   259

Notes   263

Bibliography   269

Index   279

Acknowledgments

Many people have helped me along the way to completing this book, and I would like to acknowledge at least some of them. The book has a past life as a doctoral dissertation, and Tony Stigliano was a careful and caring dissertation chair. He used his own erudition and articulacy to correct my deficiencies, delivered spontaneous lectures on Kant and Descartes over the telephone, and was good-natured even in his most challenging criticism. Tom Greening and Charles Webel were both astute and helpful readers, guiding me to a clarity and precision that early drafts of the dissertation lacked. Kenneth Gergen and Richard Addison also provided useful criticism of the manuscript. Jeff Singer has stood as an example of what a psychology scholar can and should be; many of his thoughts and concerns have found their way into this text. Sharon Cooper, Ken Ring, and Lucienne Levy were very helpful in shaping and sharpening the argument of chapter 1. Richid Swanson provided insight and information on the publishing industry. Bill Musgrave, who showed an uncanny intuitive feel for what I was after in this project, was a source of support as well as ideas from the beginning. I am particularly indebted to him for the reading of "The Love Song of J. Alfred Prufrock" which appears in chapter 7, and for sending me the Robert Hunter translation of the Duino Elegies which I used in chapter 8.

Finally, I dedicate this book to Susan Powers, who married me somewhere in the middle of chapter 4. She not only listened to and encouraged me beyond all reason, but, more importantly, she helped me to understand what is, in the end, so sad about the codependence literature. It eclipses the possibility of getting carried away into the realm of the Other; it makes rapture pathological. Susan is an Other who has carried me away, and if this rapture is a "disease," I am content to remain sick for the rest of my life.

Introduction

Something exciting is happening across the land. Let's take a
look.

—Mellody Beattie, *Beyond Codependency
and Getting Better All the Time*

Pick up a newspaper, turn on a televison or radio talk show, or read
a celebrity-oriented magazine, and you will likely find support for
Mellody Beattie's enthusiasm. For you are bound to encounter a story
about someone who is "in recovery," or to hear reference to the
"recovery movement." This phenomenon is not a "movement" in a
political sense, not an upheaval against prevailing social practice, nor
a revolt in the streets against some oppressive State. Rather, it is an
uprising against an inner state, against the private demons that thrive
within a "diseased" psyche. "Recovery" is the establishing of a pristine
state of selfhood lost to a "dysfunctional family." It is the restoration
of the Inner Child who, according to "recovery" advocates, lives
within each of us, awaiting only our discovery. Upon our discovering
it, taking possession of it, and caring for it, that pristine self cannot
help but lead us out of misery and into peace, prosperity, and
happiness.

Once a word that referred primarily, if not solely, to the
rehabilitation of an alcoholic through the Twelve-Step program of
Alcoholics Anonymous, "recovery" now stands as the treatment of
choice for an enormous range of human suffering. It is common to
hear of people "in recovery" from "rageaholicism," "sex and love addiction," "codependence," and so on. It is common to hear this, in part at
least, because it seems to be part of "recovery" to make a public state-

1

ment of one's condition: what was once the cause for shame and concealment is now the occasion for open confession. What were once understood variously as weaknesses of the will, psychological problems, spiritual impoverishments, or moral defects are now understood as morally neutral medical conditions, "addictions" from which to "recover." Even amorphous existential conditions, such as being the "adult child of an alcoholic," are to be seen as states from which to "recover."

The set of ideas captured in the word "recovery" might be understood as what the biologist/philosopher Richard Dawkins (1976) has called a "meme." Arguing that the gene is not the only unit of replication with which humans ought to be concerned, he speculates that ideas travel through a culture, and from generation to generation, through a process analogous to natural selection. The gene's analogue in this scheme—the unit of cultural transmission—is the meme. Memes take hold when an idea spreads like wildfire, replicating itself in such cultural phenomena as popular books and songs, as well as in the minds of those who hear and read them. "Recovery" is such an idea, at least to the extent that it has quickly moved out of its confinement in addiction treatment circles to its current household familiarity. If Dawkins is right, or at least if he gives us a useful way to understand the manner in which ideas seem to spread like wildfire, then somehow conditions must be favorable for the successful replication of the "recovery" meme. What follows in this book is a consideration of the cultural conditions that give rise to the notion of "recovery," and, in particular, to the "phenotype" found in its presentation in books about "codependence."

This kind of analysis, which leaves aside empirical questions of the validity of "addiction" as a universal diagnosis and "recovery" as its treatment, will perhaps be unfamiliar to the reader. It hinges on what might be seen as an antediluvian approach, for it understands what are generally considered "clinical entities"—the range of difficulties from which to "recover"—as moral problems—difficulties in our understanding of the Good. Accordingly, my interpretation hinges on understanding "recovery" not so much as a cure but as a proposal for what actually constitutes the good life. In searching for the resonances that help to explain the popularity of the meme, I will be interpreting it as the expression of a set of ideas about our moral lives that is widely prevalent in contemporary American society. The difficulties that give the the meme its relevance, and those that it raises, will be seen as difficulties inherent in that set of ideas.

This focus on the moral dimension of "recovery" helps to explain the particular manner in which I have chosen the data that I will subject to analysis. It is virtually impossible to address in a rigorous fashion a field as unwieldy, amorphous, and shifting as the "recovery movement." Every day, it seems, there is a new Twelve-Step group to address a problem that is newly conceived as an "addiction," a new confession of a public figure's fall and promised rehabilitation, a new group of victims in need of "recovery." As with so many other cultural phenomena, the sheer quantity and range of information available is overwhelming.

But there is one place in which information is fixed, at least relatively so: in texts. It would be possible, of course, to transcribe the latest Oprah Winfrey show, and thus turn it into a text, or, for that matter, to follow Ricoeur (1971/1981) and interpret all of human action as text. But what I have in mind by this word is the intention of an author to inscribe a set of ideas in a more or less permanent way. And there is no end of books about "recovery;" indeed, it constitutes a genre, at least from the point-of-view of book retailers, almost all of whom now have substantial sections under the heading "Recovery."

Books about "recovery" thus comprise a fertile field for an expedition into the cultural determinants of the meme. By choosing to focus on texts about codependence, I have further narrowed this field, for reasons I will detail in chapters 2 and 3. But here let me confess that I have chosen my data in part because I have a certain axe to grind. As I noted above, I am concerned with the moral dimensions of "recovery," with what their elucidation can tell us about current understandings of the Good. And this concern, in turn, is not only about the abstraction undoubtedly conjured by this capitalized word. For the moral, to me, also has to do with our relations to one another. If it is a worthwhile endeavor to figure out what constitutes the Good, and what kind of life is a good life, then this is because it can guide us in, and help us to reflect upon, our treatment of one another.

The question of our relations to one another is the central concern of the codependence texts. As the word implies, codependence is a "disease" of relationship, a disordered—or, to use the texts' jargon, a "dysfunctional"—approach to being-with-others. To "recover" is to learn how to be in relationships, or as the subtitle of one of the best-selling books puts it, "how to stop controlling others and start caring for yourself." Because books about codependence address this central moral question, they can provide us with a view of the Good toward which "recovery" aspires, and thus give us an idea of the moral determinants and ramifications of the "movement."

Of course, the danger looms that I am embarking (and asking you to embark) on an empty intellectual adventure, doing battle with a straw man. But the codependence literature is a worthy proxy for the "recov-

ery" field, if for no other reason than that the field itself holds codependence to be a universal disease. Over and over again, "recovery"
books remind us that codependence afflicts "96 percent of us." It is, as
John Bradshaw (one of the leading "recovery experts") says, "the most
common family illness because it is what happens to anyone in any kind
of dysfunctional family" (Bradshaw, 1988a, p. 164). Notice that he does
not say "*almost* anyone (or some people) in *almost* any (or some certain)
kind of dysfunctional family"; neither is Bradshaw modest in his claims
about the prevalence of family dysfunction: it is the predominant kind of
household in this country, the result of "our parenting rules" (not *some*
families' rules, or *some* rules in *some* families, but "our" collective and universal rules). There are no exceptions. Even if you are not addicted to
love or sex or drugs or power or money or gambling or rage, you are
unlikely to have escaped the ravages of "codependence." And if you *are*
addicted to something or someone, then, as Wendy Kaminer (1992)
archly puts it, "Chances are you're codependent too" (p. 9).
Codependence, I am arguing, can go proxy for the "recovery" field
because the field itself has appointed it.

   In understanding the success of the "recovery" meme, then, I have
turned to the codependence literature for three reasons: first, because
ideas are relatively fixed in books; second, because I am concerned with
the moral dimensions of that success, and codependence texts concern
themselves specifically with the central moral question of how we are to
be with one another; and third, because codependence is held by the
proponents of "recovery" to be a universal disorder, that from which all
of us need to "recover."

   The means by which I will carry out this analysis is the method
known as hermeneutics. I will discuss this choice of method, why the
codependence literature is highly suited to it, in chapter 2. Here, I only
want to point out that this is not a straightforward means of analysis; it
is an interpretive method, one that takes the data and tries to understand them in terms different from those in which they present themselves. As a result, my method might seem maddening to the reader, for
it rings its subject in concentric circles. The premise of hermeneutic
analysis is that a phenomenon can be illuminated by indirection, by
detailing the horizon against which it shows up. In some ways, then,
the subject of interpretation (the codependence texts, in this case)
becomes the background while its background becomes figural. While
the texts themselves will never drop out of this analysis, in some places
they will figure less strongly than others.

   This indirection might be perceived as my slowness in coming to
the point. It is not, after all, until chapter 5 that I take up the codepen-

dence texts in great detail. I explain this in advance by reminding the reader that hermeneutics is (or at least hermeneuticians fancy it to be) a rigorous method of interpretation because it is self-consciously interpretive. When an empirical scientist sets out to investigate a phenomenon, he or she generally does not need to explain his or her method. Neither the history of statistical theory, nor the reasons for looking at the phenomenon in terms of quantitative measures, nor the prejudices that come to bear on such a method need to be explicated. This is not necessarily because empirical methods are without the kind of problems that would require such explanation, but rather because they are methods that claim to have gotten around that requirement by having discovered procedures that ensure "objectivity" (another term that is generally taken for granted in empirical research), and thus allow for an ahistorical consideration. The empiricist assumes that his or her lens is clear and nondistorting, and also that his or her audience shares this assumption.

I do not have the luxury of these assumptions. In order to justify my claim to have made a valid interpretation, I must demonstrate that I have picked a valid sample and viewed it through a lens which, if not nondistorting, is at least reasonable. The assumptions and prejudices of the approach must be made clear, and this requires a great deal of exposition. Nothing can be taken for granted; this is both a means and an end. Hermeneutics seeks to uncover what lies hidden in the taken-for-granted in everyday life (in the case of this book, in the notions of codependence and recovery). To do this adequately requires the laying of a substantial groundwork, and this is my concern of the first part of the book.

It might be helpful at the outset to think of this book as a leisurely (and, I hope, interesting) drive through the countryside of codependence. We will not be hurtling on the empirical superhighway to some destination of certain and quantifiable conclusions about these books. Rather, we will be stopping at various points by the roadside to consider the contours of the land, and to wonder how it got to be that way. In the course of this trip, we will perhaps learn what it is in that landscape that allows the "recovery meme," the replicating pattern of information that tells us that "96 percent of us" do not know how to be with each other, to take such firm hold and to spread with such vigor.

While this journey may de-emphasize destination, and may prove to be somewhat disorienting, it is not without its road map. To carry out my analysis, I will be following the broad outlines of hermenutic inquiry as described by Packer and Addison (1989).

The first phase is that of entering the hermeneutic circle in the right way: discovering an appropriate workable perspective from which interpretation can proceed. The second is the conduct of inquiry within that perspective. The third phase is one of critical reflection upon and evaluation of the interpretive account that is the outcome of inquiry. (p. 3)

The first chapter will begin our entry into the hermeneutic circle by taking a look at one of the larger contexts in which the codependence texts are embedded: the practice of psychotherapy. This is a fitting place to begin, I will argue, because the notions of "codependence" and "recovery" are undoubtedly therapeutic ideas. In our consideration of some case material from my own practice, we will see some of the taken-for-granted assumptions that lie "behind" therapeutic practice. In particular, we will see that therapy begins with a certain kind of understanding of the human self. I will show that this understanding is particularly problematic in its moral dimensions, and I will propose that these problems should shape the questions that we ask of the codependence texts.

In the second chapter, I will continue the "discovery of a perspective" by spelling out why hermeneutics in general is well-suited to the material at hand. We will visit the field of self-help psychology books in order to see what happens when we attempt to understand their claims both with and without taking a hermeneutic perspective. I will discuss the reason that codependence books both invite and make difficult an interpretive analysis. I will spell out what I understand the hermeneutic method to be, and how I intend to employ it in this book.

In chapter 3, I will prepare the way for the elucidation of a more specific critical perspective by describing the contours of the phenomenon I will be interpreting. I will give a brief history of the codependence literature, locate its place in the "recovery" genre, and argue that its roots can be found in certain books within that genre that took up the concerns of the codependence literature prior to its emergence. I will then provide a rationale for choosing certain texts as exemplary ones for this study: the exemplars are the best-selling of those books which announce themselves, in their titles, as addressing codependence. This rationale hinges on an argument that the books which comprise the codependence literature are homogeneous, that is, that they take up the same questions in largely the same way, that they offer the same account of suffering and palliation, and that they conceal, minimize, or otherwise suppress any differences which might emerge among them. My argument, in addition to providing a rationale for the sample, will also illuminate the seamless nature of the authority of these texts. This will in turn strengthen my claim that these books are particularly well-suited to a hermeneutic analysis and its capacity to penetrate the given meaning of a text.

In chapter 4, I will begin to specify what my interpretive approach will be and how the texts invite this approach. I will argue that the code-pendence literature can be understood as a moral discourse, that is, as a body of texts that purport to tell their readers about a certain understanding of the good life. This concern shows up despite the texts' explicit denial that they are telling anyone about how they "ought" to live their lives. The rhetoric of sickness and health encoded in "codependence" and "recovery" will turn out to conceal what is really a language of good and bad, right and wrong, sin and redemption. And I will show that the reader encounters this proposed good life in what can be understood as a narrative space; the codependence literature helps its readers to fashion a story about their lives. It is in that story, I will argue, that we can glimpse the moral claims of the literature. My interpretation, then, will be a reading of these books as stories about the good life.

The next two chapters, the "conduct of inquiry," will be an investigation of that narrative space. They will take as an interpretive framework the suggestion made by Taylor (1989) that moral discourses necessarily take up three major concerns: the dignity of the person, the obligations one has to others, and the question of what makes a full life. I will use these categories to illuminate the claims the literature makes about the good life. This interpretation will show that narrative space to be one in which the reconciliation of what Krestan and Bepko (1990) have called the struggle between the "integrity of separation" and the "need for relatedness" to others is to be carried out by an obliteration of the otherness of those others. The good life is achieved, as we will see, when a person enters a narrative space in which he or she is the sole author, and others—which include not only other people, but also the codependence texts and other artifacts of the culture at large—are to be held under his or her authorial sway. I will suggest that this understanding of the good raises certain disquieting possibilities, particularly given its open eschewing of any standards which are not author-ized by the reader him- or herself.

Chapter 7 will be a "critical reflection upon and evaluation of the interpretive account" given in chapters 5 and 6. I will place that account in conversation with other moral discourses which have taken up the questions raised by the struggle between integrity and relatedness, or what might also be called "autonomy" and "community." I will show that this struggle itself bears witness to a rupture inherent in modernity's understanding of the self as a sovereign sole author of its own story. This rupture will in turn be seen as pointing to an apprehension of being which is nihilistic insofar as it levels all meaningful distinctions. The codependence literature will then show up as a concrete instance of that nihilism, a dream about the possibilities of the modern self that might be best understood as a nightmare.

In the concluding chapter, following a brief recapitulation of what has come before, I will offer a reconstruction of codependence based on my interpretation of the texts. I will sound a cautious note of optimism regarding the possibility of the restoration of the rupture between self and other, an optimism that can be derived from certain aspects of the codependence books themselves. Finally, I will discuss some of the implications of that argument for further research. I will suggest that other psychological discourses—both academic and popular—are open to the same critique that I have made here and describe some of the ways in which future research might avoid those pitfalls.

Before we embark on this trip, I must point out two peculiarities about our textual vehicle. The first has to do with the use of gender-specific personal pronouns. I have used gender-neutral language throughout this book. When there is no contextual reason for referring to a subject as him or her, I have used both, despite the encumbrances this places on narrative flow.

But a problem arises in this attempt to purify the language of the traces of patriarchal hegemony. Codependence books, like most "recovery" books, are largely directed at women. I know of no studies that prove this, but it is a reasonable guess that the majority of their readers are women, as the majority of psychotherapy patients are; and it is quite clear from the concerns of the literature that codependence can be understood as the encoding in a "disease" of the traditional woman's role in our culture. This point will be explored in more detail in chapters 2 and 8. I make it now in order to explain why I have, in my interpretation of the texts, referred to "the reader" as a woman: she most likely is. My use of the female gender is intended to keep one of the many prejudices embedded in the codependence texts in plain view, and *not* to accuse women of being codependent. I apologize in advance to any whom this practice offends.

The second matter I need to explain is my widespread use of cautionary quotation marks. The codependence literature is almost entirely jargon; that is, it is filled with words like "self-esteem" and "boundaries" that are presented as if their meaning were not in question, as if "we" all know what "we" are talking about when such words are used. But, as will become clear, the authors have in mind particular meanings for these words which may not be the everyday meaning known by the reader; they may not even be the stated definition of the author. I have tried to ferret out the "definition" of many of these words by their context, but I do not continually reiterate these meanings. The quotation marks are intended to remind the reader that these words are jargon, and that their meaning cannot be taken for granted.

The one exception to this practice is the word "codependence," which is, in these books, the mother of all jargon. I have now placed it in quotations for the last time. The premise of what follows is that its meaning is not to be taken for granted.

1

Codependence in Context

Greed is all right, by the way. I want you to know that. I think greed is healthy. You can be greedy and still feel good about yourselves.

—Ivan Boesky, addressing graduating MBA's
at the University of California, 1986

INTRODUCTION

I heard a joke recently.

Q. What did one codependent say to the other after they had sex?
A. That was good for you. How was it for me?

I retell this joke in order to give the reader who may have been spared exposure to it a quick introduction to the claims of the codependence literature. These claims, which I will take up in detail later on, have to do with the way people try to take care of, or otherwise look after, one another. Codependence, it is held, is a "disease" of relationship. Those who suffer this "illness" (according to the literature, 96 percent of us) are afflicted with "self-esteem" which is so low that they repeatedly enter into relationships in which they take on the role of "caretaker." Such people are thought to sacrifice their own fulfillment and happiness in order to uphold that of the other, and hence might well be more aware of their partner's sexual experience than their own. Codependents apparently

11

know of no other way to secure a good life for themselves, so they continue their ill-fated efforts to take care of others, which only worsens their "disease." To "recover," codependents must learn to take care of themselves before others, strengthening their "self-esteem" so that they are no longer dependent on those others for the achievement of a good life. As the title of one of the most popular of these books (Beattie, 1989) puts it, once the reader is "beyond codependency," he or she cannot help but to be "getting better all the time."

These simplistic claims, as we will see, are laden with some of the most invisible and pernicious prejudices of our times, and this will be the subject of what follows. I am concerned in this book not with questions about the "validity" of the concept of codependence or of the "clinical" claims advanced by the books that take up that concept. Rather, I am concerned with the culture in which those books are popular, with the way that the books capture, articulate, and (unwittingly) reproduce some of the central problems of that culture. In particular, I will argue, the notion of codependence and its counterpart "recovery" speak of our culture's understanding of the human self, and show it to be impoverished in important respects. This poverty, I will show, can only be deepened by the understanding of disease and cure that is advanced in these books.

These concerns may seem, at first glance, out of keeping with what is likely to be an ephemeral popular culture phenomenon. But the codependence literature makes vast claims for itself. Its texts announce themselves as describing and ameliorating what they hold to be a nearly universal "disease." Schaef (1986, 1987) writes about the codependent society, and Whitfield's (1991) book about codependence is subtitled "Healing the Human Condition." The books' popularity gives some indication that consumers accept their diagnosis of what ails our society. The relative ease with which the notions of codependence and "recovery" have been accepted by the psychotherapeutic community also indicates that the books' impact is not trivial.

Behind this apparent acceptance seems to lurk the assumption that the books have faithfully described, and advanced a cure for, a genuine epidemic. But it is possible to question this assumption, as some authors (to whose work I will turn in the next chapter) have already done. This possibility takes on a certain urgency if we consider the texts' central claim that people in contemporary U.S. society do not pay sufficient attention to themselves, but rather are too concerned with caring for others, as if an epidemic of altruism had descended upon us. Some would disagree with this claim, and with the idea that an increase in attention to the self is in the interests of that self and the society it lives in. Critics like Bellah, Madsen, Sullivan, Swidler, and Tipton (1985) have suggested that a loss of communal values and the concomitant arising of "hyperindividualism" characterize American society, bearing witness to an already excessive concern with the welfare of the self at the expense of concern with others. The current decade has already been character- ized in the popular press as the "morning after" the eighties, a coming to terms with the excesses of that time. The 1980s seem destined to go into history as a decade in which greed and selfishness, as the epigraph for this chapter indicates, went from being venal sins to being institu- tionalized virtues. Public phenomena like the systematic pillaging of savings and loan institutions, the increasing homelessness and poverty of our cities, and the widening gap between rich and poor, each of which can be seen as a manifestation of a pursuit of self-interest to the exclu- sion of concern with others, call into question the claim that we are too preoccupied with others.

Given critiques and concerns such as these, it is possible that these books might be seen as prescribing the "pathogen" as the "cure," and in so doing, be giving to their large audience a legitimation for practices that ought to be questioned, if not eschewed entirely. To investigate this possibility is to attempt to find out how a dominant form of public discourse which claims that we do not love ourselves sufficiently can arise in a culture that has been criticized as already too self-involved. It is to question how our social order affects and is affected by the account of human suffering and palliation that is offered in the books. It is to ask what kind of self is being helped, and what kind of help is being offered to it by these self-help books.

This book raises these and related questions by carrying out a hermeneutic analysis of the codependence literature. In this interpreta- tion I will argue that the codependence literature—whose constituent publications have sold millions of copies and claim to be addressing a problem that affects 96 percent of us (Schaef, 1986, p. 14)—can be understood as a moral discourse, as a body of literature that offers its readers, perhaps unintentionally, a particular understanding of the good life. Read in this fashion, the claims of the texts about the "self" and how it can be "helped" can be critically interpreted in the light of other understandings of what constitutes a good life. My interpretation will show this popular public discourse to be a concrete instance of certain problems that have perplexed Western moral thought at least since the Enlightenment. These problems largely arise from the question of how the individual, autonomous agent that we Westerners have come to understand as "the self" is to find its way into relationship with other such selves, or, to put it another way, the question of community. The breakdown in our relations with one another that these texts call code-pendence will be seen as an example of a breakdown which long pre-cedes the advent of the literature; and the proposed repair ("recovery") will show up as a furthering, rather than an overcoming, of that break-down. This analysis will thus allow us to see how the "self" that lives the proposed good life is implicated in certain practices, which them-selves disclose some of the critical problems of modernity.

"Greed is Good!"

I am concerned with the cultural determinants of a phenomenon, and, to find the particular cultural vicinity that I wish to explore, it will be helpful to consider the excerpt from Ivan Boesky's speech that is the epi-graph for this chapter. Boesky, the careful reader will note, was not only concerned to encourage his audience of future investment bankers and stockbrokers to be as successful (and greedy) as he had been. His intention was also, and perhaps more crucially, to assure them that, as Gekko, his alter ego in the film *Wall Street* exclaimed, "Greed is good!" And he justified the aspiration to greed not with axioms about the inevitable public benefits of the pursuit of individual self-interest in a free marketplace, let alone to a theology or a cosmology. Rather, Boesky told his audience (and he spoke with the authority of his notorious suc-cess), the important question is one of "health"—in this case a kind of *mental* health. The proof that greed is good is that it is healthy, and this in turn is the case because "you can be greedy and still feel good about yourselves." And, as James Stewart (1991) tells us, something about this chain of reasoning buoyed the graduates in a way that the rest of Boesky's "excruciatingly dull" speech did not: "The crowd burst into spontaneous applause as students laughed and looked at each other knowingly" (p. 223).

This reaction might be understood as the acceptance of Boesky's words as permission for the graduates to enter the designer-suited world of leveraged buyouts and junk bonds, and to do so not as criminals or scoundrels, but rather as people in pursuit of a good life. Greed, in Boesky's formulation, is no longer to be considered a venal sin, nor even the occasion for pangs of conscience about its possible moral ram-ifications; it need no longer be the dirty secret of the practice of "capital accumulation." Rather, because it is possible to be greedy *and* to feel good about oneself, the pursuit of lucre can now be openly held up as an important constituent of the kind of life about which a "healthy" person can feel "all right."

Rather than trying to debunk this notion by asking such questions as whether or not greed is actually "healthy," or if it indeed facilitates a sense of well-being, I wish to focus here on the understanding of ourselves by which such an utterance is possible and intelligible in the first place. Boesky's speech stands as an example of the way that we can, and often (if not always) do, assess our lives' value by how we feel about ourselves. It thus points the way to an ontology of the human, to an understanding of what a human being is: in this case, the kind of being for whom this kind of assessment is meaningful. This book turns to the codependence literature as a document of that ontology in order to show one way that it comes to presence in popular culture. By examining our self-understanding as people who can evaluate our own lives in terms of how we feel about ourselves, I hope to point out some of the problems that proceed from that understanding.

Boesky articulates something important about our moral lives. In doing so, he points us to the practice which in our culture has staked out the vicissitudes of our feelings about ourselves as its special domain, and which, sometimes explicitly and sometimes from concealment, encourages us to adopt how we feel about ourselves as the magnetic north of our moral compasses: the psychotherapeutic. I am taking a liberty here by stating baldly what I will argue later is an important, if often overlooked, aspect of psychotherapy: that it is a *moral* practice insofar as it orients and directs our aspirations to the good. In therapist's offices, in academic and "popular" psychological writings, in the manifold ways that the psychotherapist's voice is heard in mass culture, what is under discussion is not only "mental health," but also the good life, and the way that the understanding and reorientation of our feelings about ourselves can help us to achieve it (see Taylor [1985, 1989] for an account of the entanglement between understandings of selfhood and of morality). This particular account of the good takes for granted an understanding of the self as an agent whose well-being is best derived from purely private considerations, without any necessary entanglement with or mooring in a social world.

MORAL DILEMMAS OF PSYCHOTHERAPY

I will have much to say in later chapters about the problems inherent in this kind of self-understanding. I raise them now in order to help set the context for what follows. This book is a foray into what is generally understood as a "psychological" realm, but its intent is to illuminate aspects of that realm which are often left in the dark.

My context is the social world in which psychotherapeutic discourses, such as the codependence literature, are a possibility, and I am arguing that such a world poses unique moral difficulties. It may seem like sophistry to rely on a known scoundrel like Ivan Boesky for an articulation of our moral problems. So let me turn to some dilemmas that have arisen in my clinical practice in order to detail further the problems that lie in the ontology of the human that underlies the therapeutic turn to the inner as a moral source.

A 35-year-old woman, let us call her Cheryl, came to my office for the first time. She was an attractive, well-dressed woman, whose intelligence was evident from the moment she began to speak. She had, she told me, been depressed on and off for the last three years, a "blackness" that descended and lifted "like a storm." "I thought about seeing someone the first time this happened," she said, "but I kept thinking that it would go away. And it did. But it's come back a couple of times, and this time it's even worse."

Cheryl told me that she first experienced depression after her parents both died in the same year. She found herself confused, because for the first time in her life she was aware of acute feelings of resentment toward them. Where once she had felt grateful to them for a stable, middle-class upbringing, now she was plagued by the sense that all had not been well in her household, that the stability was a veneer covering a miasma of pain and isolation. Her mother, she was beginning to think, was a bitter woman, stingy with her love, who did not hesitate to let her four children know how much of a burden they were to her. As the years went on, she began to drink excessively and to withdraw from the role of nurturer. Her father, who was a salesman, was gone from the home for long periods of time. Even when he was present, he remained emotionally absent, evidently more comfortable with the sons with whom he could share his interests in cars and home improvement projects than with his daughter.

This dawning of her awareness about the hitherto concealed emptiness of her life with her parents was not a welcome enlightenment for Cheryl. "What was really confusing was the way I would think these things and then feel guilty. It was like, what right do I have to feel this way? They provided for me. I always had a roof over my head and food on the table. They paid for me to go to college. I honestly think they did the best they could and had the best intentions. I couldn't get rid of the feelings about them. But I couldn't stop looking around and seeing all the people that come from broken homes, poor people, people who didn't have parents at all, thinking, 'What do I have to complain about? How can I be so ungrateful?'" This conflict—between what she was inescapably feeling and what she thought she ought to feel, between how she found herself and how she thought she ought to be—seemed to me to mirror the discrepancy between the way her family held itself up to be and the way it had actually been in her experience. The loss of her parents, it appeared, had somehow removed the necessity of her maintaining the illusion that things were as they ought to have been, and had awakened her ambivalence. The resulting confusion weighed heavily upon her, literally depressed her.

The cloud eventually lifted, but it returned, sometimes because she was preoccupied with her confusion about her parents, but other times for no apparent reason. And this last period of darkness, the one that brought her to my office, came upon her inexplicably: "I just don't understand why I feel this way. I have a good life: my husband treats me well, my children are all healthy and happy, I have a good job, a nice house. It just doesn't make any sense. I ought to be feeling good about my life. Instead, I walk around the house moping. I'm irritable with Ron and the kids. I don't want to get out of bed. And I don't want to feel this way."

I responded to Cheryl's story with what has become a therapist's bromide. I told her that we can't really help the way that we feel, that the heart has its reasons, which are often unintelligible, inconvenient, and contrary to what we think of as good reasons, that what is important is to tell the truth, to look honestly at what is rather than to limit herself to a consciousness of what ought to be. I told her that it sounded to me as if her depression arose out of a disappointment that she felt with herself about her heart's inclinations: that they led her to feel things she "shouldn't" feel, to be someone she "shouldn't" be. I suggested that her current melancholy might be the result of the way that this discrepancy was showing itself in her life right now, and that we might do well to explore this possibility.

This approach was not immediately fruitful, at least not in terms of understanding the current determinants of her depression. Cheryl filled many therapy hours with a wholehearted effort to explore her dilemma by discussing her feelings about her parents. As time went on, the object of her disappointment shifted from her own failure to feel the way she should to her family's failure to be what it ought to have been (and claimed that it was). The discussion was punctuated less and less often by her saying something like, "I can't believe I'm saying these things about them. I feel like they can hear me and I'm going to get into trouble." She became more comfortable with the idea of facing the feelings that came her way, regardless of their "moral" implications. But despite these insights and changes, her depression did not lift, nor did its current determinants become significantly clearer. Indeed, her depression deepened, and Cheryl told me, after about three months, that she was considering ending therapy with me because "it doesn't seem to be making things any better."

The session after she told me this, Cheryl came in and said, "I thought about not coming back here, and it just made me feel worse. I need this place, I need to come here and have some room." Then there was a long silence, which she ended by saying, "You see, the problem is I don't think I love my husband. And I don't think I ever did. And, worst of all, I'm not sure I even want to. He's not the kind of man I could love. And I feel terrible for that. Because he is a good man. He treats me well. He helps with the kids and the house and he's always there. He's so loyal; he'd rather spend time at home with me than anything else. But sometimes, most of the time now, I just want to get away. I think about just walking out and leaving them all behind. But then I think about how they would feel, how he would feel. I just can't hurt him like that."

I was not surprised by what Cheryl told me. Her descriptions of her home life had made it sound somewhat stultifying; her husband sounded like a man not unlike her father—well-intentioned, but emotionally unavailable and uncomfortable with intimacy. Her depression was intelligible now as a melancholy growing out of her increasing awareness, undoubtedly sharpened by her experience in therapy, that, in her current experience as well as in her history, a crucial part of her life ·was not as it should be. While she clearly held her husband in high regard, respected and indeed loved him in many ways, still she felt bereft of a certain kind of intimacy and passion with him. Perhaps more important, she lacked the desire to feel this way toward him; she did not want Ron, but could only wish that she did. And so she felt the dreadful weight of an existential choice: to disrupt all that was familiar, all that she felt she ought to do and to be, or to continue to live in a way that failed to make her feel good about herself even as it was congruent with that ought. The discrepancy between what she ought to be feeling and what she actually felt, a conflict she was first aware of upon the death of her parents, was showing up in her marriage. It placed her uncomfortably on the horns of a dilemma perhaps best captured in J. Alfred Prufrock's question to himself: "Do I dare/Disturb the universe?"

Therapy, in my experience, often leads to this overwhelming question, and seems well-suited to help a person make the decisions that it forces, to take the dare or to decide that the mermaids will not sing for him or her. But my empathy with Cheryl as she wrestled with her indecision felt unusually burdensome to me. For I wondered with her about the implications of her self-discovery. Hanging in the balance seemed to be a web of relationships that had been spun over the course of a 15-year-long marriage, a web that encompassed an immediate family, a circle of more distant relations, and friends, held together not just by love and passion and intimacy, but also by respect, by common history, by economic security, by the manifold everyday bonds of shared lives. There was a time, in our not-too-distant past, when these bonds could not so easily have been called into question. How one felt about a practice so crucial to society as marriage was immaterial compared with the weight of the obligation to uphold the practice. Of course, this is no longer the case. The web was threatened; in Cheryl's life, as in our own social history, there was no turning back. A divorce was not inevitable, but things would never be the same; and much depended on the fate of the questions that had been raised in her therapy with me.

I was uneasy with this situation, and as it is my duty to be as honest with myself as I urge my patients to be with themselves, I pondered it. Was I feeling burdened by a responsibility that wasn't, after all, mine? Perhaps I was bowed not so much with concern for Cheryl as with the weight of my own narcissism, which took "credit" for her "breakthrough," but couldn't live with its own delusional grandiosity. Considering the problem further, however, I began to think of how I understood Cheryl's difficulty. It had been formulated as an ongoing conflict between her sense of how she ought to be and how she found herself. And her willingness to identify and to speak about the latter clearly hinged on a willingness to question, if not to overthrow, the former. The premise of our therapeutic endeavor was that concerns about how one ought to be can, and must, be questioned; that the realm of the individual's feelings about herself and her world is to be given precedence over those "external" concerns. Even to take up the question of the "ought" as we had is to take it up as a question of one's *feelings* about that ought. Faced with the difficult prospect of finding her way through the conflict between the "inner" and the "outer," between desire and duty, between daring to disturb the universe and daring only to eat a peach, we would commence an exploration of Cheryl's inner world in order to answer the question of what she ought to do.

Of course, her choices were not necessarily this stark, as most dilemmas in therapy are not. It was possible, for instance, that she could begin to bring her actions into line with her feelings, and that her husband's response to her would arouse in her surprising feelings of passion and love. It was possible that an increased authenticity on her part might help to transform her marriage from a burdensome source of depression to a source of joy. Reducing the discrepancy in this fashion would have been a most desirable outcome.

But my discomfort was not so much with the choices she had available to her, with the question of what the next chapter would be in her story; rather, it was with the way the dilemma had come up in the first place, and particularly with the way our therapeutic project had formulated it. For it was clear to me that, while much had been revealed, our conversations had also left some important concerns concealed. What was implicitly put out of play, what all the soundproofing and promises of confidentiality and encouragement to be open are designed to deemphasize, if not devalue, is the "ought."

The sine qua non of my conversations with Cheryl is the background understanding that her sense that she ought not to hurt Ron (or ought to uphold her marriage vows) must, at least potentially, take a backseat to the question of her own authenticity. The very idea of sitting and talking as we do in therapy is absurd without the premise that if there is a conflict between the world of the ought and the world of the heart, the latter must at the very least be listened to carefully; the way must be opened to the possibility that the heart's reasons will prevail and the universe be turned upside down. The ought that says Cheryl should stay with her husband and somehow reconcile herself to her feelings must, at least must be able to, give way to the ought that says that Cheryl must listen to her own heart.

All of this may seem so obvious that it is hardly worth mentioning or making problematic. After all, the idea that the inner world provides a source for oughts that is on a par with, if not superior to, the outer world is a prejudice that not only underlies all of psychotherapeutic practice; it is, moreover, a wellspring of the liberal individualism that we take for granted in our contemporary world. Where would we be without the freethinking Tom Paines or Patrick Henrys, men who took a stand against the public oughts in favor of their own sense of what was right and wrong? How different would the world be today if such freedom of thought and expression had been exercised in Nazi Germany? It is no accident that totalitarian governments always seek to stifle this freedom, or that the authors of the U.S. Constitution sought to secure it for the new republic. Clearly, one of the prejudices that we share (and, for the most part, cherish) is this valuing of the inner over the outer, of the individual over the collective. We are, it seems, to listen to the stirrings of our hearts before the commands of duty imposed from outside. If we can reconcile the inner with the outer, find our way to "feel good" about what we ought to do, then so much the better. But for Cheryl to decide to stay with Ron simply because it is what she should do, for her somehow to will herself back into the benighted state which kept her doubts about her love for him in the dark, is anathema to the psychotherapeutic perspective's imperative to proceed from the inside out.

But Cheryl was not so quick to submit to this imperative as some of my other patients have been. Her inner and outer worlds, perhaps, could not be so easily parsed as they sometimes can be, and this difficulty made the imperative itself surface as an anxiety-provoking question to me. This is a question about the moral world in which psychotherapy stands as an exemplary practice, in which the "inner" is understood as the best guide to achieving the Good. This question, or, more accurately, set of questions is: is this necessarily the case? Is the prejudice toward the inner, without which psychotherapeutic practice is unintelligible, truly in service of the Good? Because therapy always already reveals the "inner" even as it conceals the "outer" as a guide to what one ought to do, an ambiguity arises in the therapeutic background, one which deserves discussion if for no other reason than that it is rarely discussed.

The importance of this ambiguity might be grasped if we think of psychotherapy as the practice of revealing the hidden aspects of the everyday world of the patient. It raises the mundane to the level of the problematic. As Freud's (1901/1966) work on parapraxis shows, meaning precipitates in the most trivial aspects of everyday life, "psychopathology" showing up in the tongue's tripping or the hands' fumbling, in what we forget or foul up. Any utterance or action on the part of the patient is potentially "grist for the mill," to use a therapist's cliche. But I do not interrogate just any utterance or action. I choose to attend to, and thus to make problematic, those issues that seem "clinically" relevant. I am, of course, not always fully aware of why I choose what part of the everyday to question. But the bias I have been discussing here clearly gives a shape to those choices: what needs to be interrogated, and relied upon, is the inner world, the world of private memory, desire, emotion, judgment, and thought.

Therapy doesn't make sense otherwise; there are already professions aplenty that help people negotiate their way through the maze of everyday pressures from the outside: attorneys, clergy, financial advisors, and so on. The profession of psychotherapy, alone among the professions we know, must take as its starting point the notion that the inner is more important than the outer, that we must be able to feel good about ourselves before we can, in a "mentally healthy" way, commit ourselves to a given action.

The inner becomes the point of reference, what I called earlier the magnetic north of our moral compasses. Before the therapist makes his or her carefully considered choice of what aspect of the everyday to interrogate, he or she has already (most likely without knowing it) hived off the possibility that the notion of the inner as that reference point—an idea that forms a crucial part of our everyday understanding of ourselves—can itself be interrogated. For all of its revealings, it leaves this central aspect of itself concealed. The public world is forgotten, and then the forgetting itself is forgotten; in short, the "outer" world is repressed.

Consider my alternatives with Cheryl. I can discuss the vagaries of her feelings toward Ron with her in great detail, drawing upon my own training and experience. We can discuss the personal history that seems to have affected her choice of husband, the way that unresolved conflicts about her father might have led her into, and kept her stuck in, this marriage. I have at my command (as she will, if she remains in therapy with me) a vocabulary and an array of techniques that are quite effective at delineating her interior landscape. We can use this armamentarium even to investigate the question of her sense of guilt and duty about her wish to leave. We can talk about the lonely child growing up and telling herself stories about the importance of being a "good girl" in order to end her isolation, the fruitless gambit of playing the dutiful daughter. I can support her in taking seriously her commitments, even remind her to consider them if I feel she has given them short shrift. And, of course, I can use the dance of transference and countertransference to show her to herself.

But what I cannot do in anything like the same sort of depth is to discuss with her the obligation to a marriage vow, *insofar as it is an obligation,* and exceeds or otherwise functions independently of her feelings about it. Therapy, at least to my knowledge, does not offer anything like the vocabulary or array of techniques available for a discussion of the inner to guide us to an understanding of questions like this one.

Of course, there is no law, or even a canon of ethics, that precludes me from taking up "external" questions. Cheryl and I might, for example, look at her problem from an explicitly political perspective, perhaps discussing the history of the marriage covenant. We could talk about its implication in the oppression of women and the state's regulation of sexual activity, how the ideology it supports and is supported by might be understood as having created a "false consciousness" in her that means her vow was made without full knowledge of its consequences. We might then understand her wish to be out of the marriage as not only a question of her individual feelings for Ron, but also as a desire for liberation in a political sense. On the other hand, I might remind Cheryl of her obligation to God and family, might direct her to one of Dan Quayle's speeches on family values and talk about the way in which the "selfishness" that threatens her family is yet another force pulling apart the tapestry of the American Dream. We could have this kind of discussion, but, it seems to me, the less we focus on the question of Cheryl's inner life, the less we are doing what we are accustomed to think of as "therapy." And as my latter example perhaps makes clear, this is not altogether a bad thing. The profession's authority may cloak ideological coercion as kindly help.

So long as the patient's inner life, and the therapist's encouragement of its presentation, must guide psychotherapy, it is difficult to know what to do with questions of obligation or duty, or other externally imposed considerations. There is little room in the therapy office for considerations of publicly shared understandings of the Good (whether those of the dominant culture or of a counterculture) qua public understanding; there is a concomitantly vast space there for the private sense of what is good. I can respond to Cheryl's anguish about her husband's feelings with compassion and support. But I cannot tell her that she ought to put her obligation to him first because that is what is universally held to be right; indeed the inverse is more correct: what we seem universally to agree upon is that only she can tell herself what she ought to do, that she ought to be her own moral source. So I can only tell her that she must judge for herself the relative merits of hurting him and taking care of herself, that, in the end, she "ought" to listen to herself. And I am likely to remind her that her husband is "responsible for himself," just as she is, that there is only a limited amount that any one person can do to relieve or prevent the suffering of another. I am likely, that is, to encourage her to pay closest attention to the interior landscape, which is, of course, the territory through which I am most suited to guide her.

This focus on the inner may well bring about a good conclusion to Cheryl's story. She may find a way to stay with her husband *and* feel good about herself; she may find a way to leave him *and* feel good about herself. Either way, obviously, what determines my ability to assess her story as a good one is the extent to which she feels good about herself. And perhaps this is not such a bad thing. But looking at her story in this fashion does give rise to some interesting questions, which can best be seen in some less innocuous examples.

A man named Mark came to see me. He was a thirty-two-year-old engineer who worked at a defense plant. His marriage was, as he put it, "in deep shit," and his wife, herself already in therapy, had insisted (on her therapist's advice) that Mark see a therapist "to straighten out my own problems." I will not go further into this very interesting case because my purpose in bringing it up has to do with what we never discussed, and what, from most clinical perspectives, we had no business discussing in any event: Mark's job. The fact that he was an engineer designing propulsion systems for nuclear weapons was an aspect of the everyday that was never raised to the level of the problematic. We, of course, discussed the way his "engineer's mentality" made it difficult for him to respond to his wife's "emotional needs," and the way that this was a burden of being a man in our culture. We talked about the discrepancy between his sense that he ought to be a good husband, and his dawning awareness that he was not. But we never talked about the possible discrepancy between how he ought to be as a citizen of the world and his involvement in the manufacture of mass-death technology.

Mark's contribution to the arms race, the fact that he engaged in work that was highly questionable from a moral point of view (or at least from *my* moral point of view), was not on the table for discussion, nor could it have been unless it somehow showed up in his exploration of his inner world. If it was not a blight on his interior landscape, if we were not guided there by considerations of his inner life, we would not (as we did not) take up this question. To the extent that it affected his feelings about himself, Mark's work seemed to function in a positive manner: he derived a measure of self-esteem from his apparent professional competence, and he found the problems to which he was asked to engineer solutions to be interesting and engaging. He certainly did not question whether, given the nature of his work, he *ought* to feel good about himself. My job as therapist was, it seemed to me, *not* to inject my own "political" opinions into our work in such a way as to make him "feel bad" about himself for doing something of which I did not approve. Even more than in the case of Cheryl, it is difficult, if not impossible, to discuss with Mark questions that go beyond his inner life, even if those questions are of global significance.[1]

It is perhaps easy to say that there is nothing wrong with focusing on Cheryl's inner life, while minimizing such abstract considerations as the sanctity of the marriage vows. We might return to Boesky's comments and bring them to bear on her dilemma: "Divorce (or staying married to a man you don't love) is all right, by the way. I want you to know that. I think divorce is healthy [at least in this case]. You can get divorced (or stay married to a man you don't love) and still feel good about yourself." But can we bring them to bear on Mark? "Building nuclear weapons is all right, by the way. . . . You can contribute to the potential destruction of all of human life, participate in the draining of the economic wealth of this country and the world and still feel good about yourself." Can we be content with this agnosticism, which maintains an enlightened indifference to the public implications of the private world of "feeling good about yourself"? If the only worthwhile distinctions we are to explore in therapy are those of the inner world, then we might have to be.

Let us take this one step further. Let us imagine a man like Mark, a well-intentioned person whose marriage is in "deep shit." And let us say that his job is designing crematoria for concentration camps, or, for that matter, shoveling corpses into one of those crematoria. His job causes him no apparent inner distress; mostly he is concerned with keeping his marriage intact, and he must provide economic security to do so. Can this aspect of his everyday life remain unquestioned in therapy? Should his hypothetical therapist be willing to say, "Genocide is all right, by the way. . . . You can shovel corpses and still feel good about yourself"? This would seem to be the implication of the therapeutic premise: that what is significant is the inner, that worthwhile distinctions are to be made by an exploration of how one "feels" about oneself and one's engagement in the world of others, and that the most important question is how one feels about what one is doing.

Clearly Cheryl, Mark, Berkeley MBA's, and my hypothetical corpse-shoveler exist on some kind of moral continuum. It seems a matter of common sense that Cheryl's hurting her husband is far less an atrocity than feeding corpses into a holocaust. I do not mean to blur the important distinctions among these possibilities. Rather, my intent is to point out that those distinctions are always already blurred in psychotherapeutic practice. The arising of the inner world as the most important source of oughts threatens to make psychotherapy an impoverished discourse, for it makes difficult, if not impossible, the raising of certain important aspects of the everyday world—what I have been calling the "external"—to the level of the problematic. The therapeutic silence about the question of Cheryl's obligation qua obligation is the same as the therapeutic silence about Boesky's greed or Mark's participation in mass death; it is based on the placing of all important distinctions into the realm of the private. For all of its power to reveal, psychotherapy can also leave hidden, and further conceal, problems that ought not to remain in the dark.

Now, we might say that there comes a point where the therapist has to speak up. There are laws, for instance, that require me to report my knowledge of child abuse to state authorities, even if this means breaking my promise of confidentiality. Our society, undoubtedly led by therapists' concerns about the sequelae of child abuse, has decided that the public interest in the protection of the child ought to take precedence over the question of the patient's inner landscape. After all, anyone who has worked with a pedophile has been struck by the intense good feeling that he experiences in his sexual contact with children. Despite this, we therapists are no longer content to remain silent about the breach of the commonweal represented by child abuse, and this is perhaps as it should be. But as soon as I enter the world of the child protection bureaucracy, I have left the world of therapy; my experience is that therapy ends, or changes dramatically, when I "turn in" my patient. I am no longer proceeding on the basis of the imperative to derive values from within the patient's experience. Instead, I have deferred to an external ought, in this case the state's saying that one ought not to abuse children.

The question that looms, of course, is where do we draw the line? At what point is my consideration of which aspect of the everyday I raise to the level of the problematic to be guided by questions other than those of the patient's feelings about him or herself? There is perhaps a calculus that can guide therapists in this regard, one that measures the question of the patient's inner life against the consequences of his or her actions for the world of others. But the current absence of such a calculus is further evidence that a problem arises in psychotherapy's substitution of the inner for the outer as a moral source.

And the idea that therapists should start considering the outer world is also highly problematic. I have all sorts of opinions on public matters; are they to guide me in my interventions with my patients whose comportment indicates that they don't agree? If I follow Dan Quayle and believe that the sanctity of "family values" should take precedence over all else, am I to urge Cheryl to turn back from her inner exploration lest she wander into a forbidden zone? More likely, if I feel this way, if I have "oughts" that go beyond Polonius's injunction "to thine own self be true," then, it seems, I am in the wrong profession. And yet if I cannot make the distinctions that allow undeniably problematic practices to be interrogated in therapy, then I might be guilty of a "repression" that aids and abets those practices.

In general, a therapist is held to be effective to the extent that he or she can help the patient make a frank and fearless exploration of his or her inner landscape. The problem here is that, in being "effective," I may simply be contributing to a practice and, by extension, to a social order that ought to be resisted. The substitution of the inner as the source of the ought imposes a certain silence that I believe must itself be questioned, particularly given the apparent fact that people can engage in all sorts of atrocity without necessarily "feeling bad" about themselves. There are many practices—more, it seems, all the time—in which we all engage in our everyday lives that would appear to be worthy of being raised to the level of the problematic. The "greenhouse effect," for instance, speaks of the problems inherent in a taken-for-granted practice like driving, a practice about which very few people seem to "feel bad." The adopting of the inner landscape as the important landscape, and of the notion of "feeling good about yourself" as the magnetic north of that landscape, leaves us bereft of a way to explore questions of the common good. Indeed, therapy may be seen as working to obscure such questions (see Hillman and Ventura, 1992).

While we worry with our patients about what is these days called "self-esteem," we may be overlooking the possibility that just beyond the closed door of the therapy office stand phenomena such as the global environmental threat and the proliferation of mass-death technologies, phenomena which might justify the claim that there is no particular reason why any of us should feel particularly "good" about ourselves. As we take up psychotherapy's recent preoccupation with the alleviation of "shame," we may forget the possibility that we perhaps ought to be ashamed of ourselves for creating, and failing to do very much about, such a world as ours. Focusing in the privacy of the clinic on the private implications of these important public matters, and doing so in a way that precludes taking the latter up as anything other than more questions about how our patients feel, therapy threatens to leave the public world increasingly to its own devices even as we therapists encourage our patients to pursue privately their own satisfactions. Psychotherapy, in this view, risks becoming a technique for making Nero a better violinist even as the firestorm rages.

SELF AND OTHER AS SOCIAL CONSTRUCTIONS

As interesting as the question of psychotherapy's implication in pernicious social practices is, my intention in this book is not to engage in a wholesale critique of psychotherapy. Such broadsides have been fired, based on reasoning something like the foregoing, by critics such as Robert Bellah et al., whose *Habits of the Heart* provides deep insight into the way that psychotherapeutic language and practice work to undermine (or at least make highly diffuse and inarticulate) communal commitments. My point here is to begin the work of interpretation by identifying a set of problems that needs to be looked at, and that we can expect to find in any therapeutic discourse. By focusing on the codependence literature, I am not suggesting that it can go proxy for the entire field of therapy. Rather, I am arguing that we can take a problem that arises in that field and trace its fate in one particular location in order better to understand that problem.

In chapter 2, I will discuss in detail my reasons for choosing this particular body of texts as the object of my interrogation. But for now, let me clarify the isomorphism that I think allows me to make the leap from the highly heterogeneous, often complicated and sophisticated realm of psychotherapy to the homogeneous, simplistic world of the codependence literature.

I do not mean to gloss over these qualities of the codependence books. As we will see, the texts engage in highly suspicious reasoning; they contain logical contradictions galore; they are a representative of a decidedly noncritical thinking. They are heavy on references to such journals as *Reader's Digest*, and the quality of the scholarship in them is perhaps best illustrated by this endnote citation from Melody Beattie's best-selling *Beyond Codependency and Getting Better All the Time*:

> I read about this concept—negotiating with people who don't play fair—in a magazine article at the doctor's office two years ago. I got the phrase from it, but I can't remember the author or article. (p. 207)

Debunking or discrediting such a literature is like shooting fish in a barrel; its excesses, as we will see, are almost self-parodying, and have been ably examined by Kaminer (1992) in her *I'm Dysfunctional, You're Dysfunctional*. But debunking is not my point. Rather, I intend to take the literature as a serious document of the self we have come to think of ourselves as, and which is the self that comes into my office for treatment: the self-contained author of its own story. We may not agree with the codependence literature's simplistic claims, with its description of a disease that is said to affect 96 percent of us, and its proposal for "recovery" from that disease. But I think that it is justified to take it as a source for understanding the idea of self that most, if not all, of us live with, which is, as we will see, the self that is amenable to the "cure" offered in psychotherapy.

Part of this claim hinges on a sort of "back-door" empiricism. First of all, millions of people have bought these books. I cannot claim that I know whether or not these consumers have read the books, let alone what sense they have made of them; this is why I equivocate about the empirical validity of my observation. But it is at least a safe bet that they have read the books and found them "helpful," that is, that the books serve to help them to clarify their psychological distress and offer some hope for overcoming it. This apparent resonance can be taken as evidence that the books have hit upon an important aspect of our everyday understanding of ourselves.

Moreover (and again I must qualify my claim, for I have no systematic "proof" for it), the literature presents an account of human suffering and its relief that is, in its broadest contours, congruent with that which is offered in many forms of psychotherapy. A person who has been in psychotherapy, or is a practicing therapist, or has some other acquaintance with the field will recognize much of the language and many of the premises of the codependence literature. The books talk about the importance of early childhood history on later life experience, of the deleterious effect that trauma can have on one's efforts to maintain "ego boundaries" in the face of demands of family, work, and society at large. They speak of the importance of the inner life, particularly of the value of emotional experience and the difficulties one encounters in understanding and finding support for that experience. They understand one's colloquy with oneself as the dialogue that gives shape to one's destiny. They do not offer a revision of mainstream psychotherapeutic discourse so much as a distillation of some of its crucial claims into an easily accessible form.

I am claiming, then, that the codependence literature, while obviously not psychotherapy as such, is a psychotherapeutic discourse, a body of thought that, broadly speaking, addresses the questions brought to the forefront by the notion of the human individual as a self that is amenable to "treatment" by means of the kind of self-understanding sought in psychotherapy. And while there are undoubtedly vast differences between the concerns of this literature and those of (at least some) other psychotherapeutic discourses, still it is fair to say that these books give us a view of that self. Without setting out intentionally to propose a definition of "self," the books, simply by offering "self-help," necessarily present a definition. And their popularity indicates that the idea of self they present is a recognizable one: those who buy and are somehow aided by the books encounter themselves in their pages.

To take this self as the subject of this kind of inquiry hinges on an understanding of the general notion of "self" that bears some discussion. It is customary for us to think of "self" as a given, that is, as an attribute of the human consisting of certain faculties that are transhistorical. We can see this assumption at work in Freud's examinations of such historical figures as Leonardo da Vinci (Freud, 1910) and Christopher Haizmann (Freud, 1923), or of literary figures like Oedipus (Freud, 1912/1950, 1897/1950); it surfaces also in his speculations on prehistory, most notably in *Totem and Taboo*. Because the self was for Freud a fixed entity, something that does not vary from time to time or place to place, he could apply the template of ego, id, superego, his notions about development, and so on, to such figures as Leonardo, or to questions such as why men (rather than women) seem to be the engineers and builders of civilization. He could do so without attention to the possibility that the self develops through history, attributing Hamlet's dilemma to an apparently transhistorical Oedipal conflict or men's ability to renounce instinct (and thus to be civilized) to their anatomical ability to urinate standing up. Freud's interpretations are notably elegant and consistent. Of course, there is no way of verifying them empirically, and we must take note of the assumption that grounds a work like *Leonardo da Vinci and a Memory of His Childhood*: Freud takes for granted that the concerns of the self in end-of-the-century Europe were the same as those in seventeenth-century Pottenbrunn or Renaissance Italy or Elizabethan England.

This claim is not problematic so long as we assume with Freud that the self is, in some way, an "organic" entity, an analogue to other aspects of the human that are governed by physical or biological laws that appear to transcend time and space. Unfortunately for this kind of theorizing, there is ample evidence to the contrary. In an early work that voiced dissent from this orthodoxy, Dodds (1951), an ancient historian, examined the question of how the irrational was understood in ancient Greece. He concentrated primarily on the Homeric epics, and concluded that the "self" of that epoch was far different from the modern "self," that, in particular, the unitary notion of a bounded identity that we take for granted is quite different from what the ancient Greeks understood themselves to be. Particularly as it is explored in the *Iliad*, the ancient Greek self is a host of forces and attributes, some of which, as in Freudian theory, are "internal" or "instinctual," but many of which are external, visitations from the gods that are not really a part of the self, at least as we think of it.

Adkins (1970) makes a similar point. In his book *From the Many to the One*, he notes that Homeric man appears in the epics to be "a being whose parts are more in evidence than the whole, and one very conscious of sudden unexpected accesses of energy" (p. 27). This self-understanding gave a far different destiny to such crucial experiences as shame, guilt, responsibility, pride, merit, and the like, locating them (at least potentially) in a realm that we would think of as "outside" the self. In his *Sources of the Self*, which itself is an epic account of the historical changes that the idea of self has undergone throughout Western history, Taylor (1989) notes that

> Agamemnon excuses his unfair and unwise treatment of Achilles by referring to the "madness" visited on him by the god. But contrary to our modern intuitions, this doesn't seem to lessen the merit or demerit attaching to the agent. A great hero remains great, though his impressive deeds are powered by the god's infusion of energy. Indeed, there is no conces-

sion here; it is not that the hero remains great *despite* the divine help. It is an inseparable part of his greatness that he is such locus of divine action. (118, emphasis in original)

We moderns might interpret these visitations as "enlargements" of the self, but that is just my point: such an interpretation hinges on a prejudice that the self is a unitary agent. But Taylor (1989) reminds us that there are other possible interpretations. If we have a notion of self that allows for "parts" rather than "wholes," then

> [w]e stress the special nature of these states by marking their lack of continuity with ordinary thought and feeling. But if, in contrast, the highest condition for us is one in which we are reflective and self-collected, then to be in a special state, discontinuous with the others, is a kind of loss of centring, a falling off, something which has to be overcome. . . . [T]he privileged condition is not a special state in the sense of being out of communication with all the others, but is on the contrary the one in which all thoughts and feelings are under purview. (pp. 119-20)

I do not wish to debate here the question of which possibility provides a "better" understanding of "who we are." Rather, I wish simply to show that the notion of self is, historically speaking, up for grabs. It is what is currently called, in some psychological circles, a social construction.

The social constructionist view, which this book adopts, is well-articulated in a definition offered by Cushman (1990). For him, "self" is

> the concept of the individual as articulated by the indigenous psychology of a particular cultural group, the shared understandings within a culture of "what it is to be human." . . . The self embodies what the culture believes is humankind's place in the cosmos: its limits, talents, expectations and prohibitions. . . . There is no universal, transhistorical self, only local selves; no universal theory about the self, only local theories. (p. 715)

The only thing we can say universally about the self, according to this analysis, is that it is culturally located and determined. What Freud came upon in his theories is thus not so much an understanding of who we are for all times and in all places. Rather, he gives us the understanding that guided people's experience of themselves in turn-of-the-century Europe (see Schorske, 1981). And, as a result, he gives us, perhaps unwittingly, a glimpse of the culture in which that self is a possibility. The problem, for instance, of the son's sexual feelings toward his mother cannot emerge as a possibility until there is a political, social, and cultural matrix in which the nuclear family is the primary unit of organization and has thus taken on a kind of psychological significance that it might not have in, say, a tribal culture. Indeed, the whole problem of infantile sexuality speaks of a culture that has become preoccupied with sexuality, which, of course, Victorian era Europe (primarily through its repressive views of sex) had become. Moreover, the very idea that the individual stands alone, can forge his or her own destiny by means of self-understanding itself, cannot arise until the universe has become "disenchanted," that is, emptied of an agreed-upon transcendent force which guides all individual destinies.

When Cheryl and I ponder the future of her marriage and her self, then, we are taking part in a cultural conversation which has already determined that she is the kind of being that can do such pondering (and that psychotherapy is a valid way for her to take up her place in that conversation). It is this very peculiar self-understanding, or, I should say, this very peculiar self-constituting cultural conversation, that I am addressing in this book. Modern discourses understand the self as a self-contained agent, but we cannot take this definition for granted as the only, or even the best, understanding of who we are. What we can do is to look at the self that most of us think we are as a window into the cultural conversation that constructs us that way.

I have already alluded to one of the major problems of this discourse: it leaves us bereft of ways to understand and take up our human agency outside of asking questions about how we feel about ourselves, about "who we are." It thus leaves open the possibility of atrocity, and it does so in a concealing way. For so long as we take this notion of self for granted, not only are we without a way to address questions of social obligation qua obligation; we are also likely not even to allow them to emerge as questions in the first place. It may not even occur to me to ask Mark about the moral implications of his work as a weapons engineer, let alone to raise the question of "family values" with Cheryl. And these silences are not accidental; to the contrary, they reflect the prejudice that is inherent in this notion of self, a prejudice that is central to the practice of the psychotherapy of that self.

The understanding of self that is my target here has a rich history in our culture. Its onset is gradual, and its roots can be traced back at least to Plato's time. But the problem I am interested in can perhaps best be seen in the Cartesian *ego cogito*, which Dallmayr (1984) has called "a metaphysical pillar of the modern era" (p. ix). For, as another contemporary philosopher has pointed out,

> with the Cartesian "I think," an egoity appeared and became the essential definition of humanity. The I provided an origin from which a certain but egocentric and dualistic universe was secured for Western experience. (Liberman, 1989, p. 127)

Descartes' formulation of "who we really are"—the doubting I cogitating its way to certainty—brings us to an important dualism. We are familiar with this dualism in at least two important manifestations: the mind/body split and the self/world split. It is the latter distinction in which I am interested. The stories I have told about Cheryl and Mark are stories about the way the "egoity" that ushers in the modern age has brought us to think of ourselves as separate individuals, able to direct ourselves through our own lives without necessary recourse to a plan or a purpose or a set of rules imposed by others.

The modern self, or at least the modern self with which I am interested here (and which I think is the dominant form of self in contemporary Western culture), is an understanding of the individual that cuts him or her loose from any necessary moorings in a social world, except insofar as this "social world" is the location of that cutting loose. And an important problem that arises from this understanding is the question of how that modern self is to find its way back into the social world, how we are to discover moorings to replace those from which we were severed when the "metaphysical pillar" of our age was erected. The codependence literature is a document of one very popular proposal for how we are to do this. Its popularity, I think, speaks not of its having hit upon "who we really are" so much as of who we think ourselves to be, and, in light of the foregoing, of the cultural conversation that gives us this thought.

The discourse that gives us the self as a self-contained master of its own house creates the opening for the question of how we are to build a neighborhood of such houses. This is a question that has been put before us in recent wrestlings over what kind of community our society is to be. And it is the question that the codependence literature, in offering a way to be in relationship without being codependent, addresses. In philosophy, this question is often referred to as the problem of the Other. It should not be surprising, given the broad remarks I have already made about the contemporary self, that "few issues have exercised as powerful a hold over the thought of this century" as that of the Other (Theunissen, 1977/1984, p. 1).

Now what does this capitalized, perhaps mystical looking word mean? Let us return for a moment to my story about Cheryl. The problem I encountered with her is, obviously, a problem of how she is to negotiate her way between her "feelings" about herself and her own unhappiness on the one hand and her "feelings" about her obligations to husband and family on the other. Of course, it is possible to say that this is really just an argument between two compelling aspects of Cheryl's "self." She might be understood as "wrestling with her conscience," or, in psychoanalytic jargon, dealing with an "introjected superego." But consider this language. In both cases, Cheryl is struggling with something "other" than herself: a "conscience" or a "superego." Her attempt to find a new path for herself must take into account her husband and her family, the "others" in her life. And it is clear that those others are not purely "out there," mere objects for the cogitations of rational reflection; nor are they purely "in here," mere simulacra of her psyche. Rather, they are entities beyond her which constitute her. They are both part of the self and not part of the self. Whether those others are her "conscience" or the people who stir her conscience, they are vitally important to her; they are others who inhabit her and demand response from her. And this is what I intend when I talk about the Other in what follows: it is that which is not self, but which still somehow demands response from and is thus also a part of the self.

The complications and paradoxes of this notion of the Other are unfortunate. They defy language in many respects, but this might be seen as more evidence that the notion of self that we take for granted is impoverished. Kovel (1981) has made this point quite well.

> If this is puzzling it is because we are deeply attached to the delusory idea that the self is a separate and detachable entity from other selves, as if it were a body in the world, with an envelope of time and space separating it from other bodies. We view the self this way for a number of interlocking reasons: because the felt experience of the "I" peremptorily excludes all others; because we look at the physical body we inhabit and observe that it is substantially different from other bodies; and because we live in a civilization organized around the meeting of discrete individuals in the marketplace, the social ideal of which is the maximization and autonomy of the individual self. For all these reasons we conclude that the self is like a discrete body. (p. 47)

We are not accustomed to considering the self as inhabited by the Other. Indeed, we sometimes characterize such an experience of self as "pathological" when it shows up in what is called "multiple personality disorder" or "schizophrenia" or "spirit-possession." Moreover, we customarily reduce all discussion of others to the "I" of the discrete body. The unfamiliarity of the Other makes it seem like an esoteric concept. But, again in Kovel's words:

> In truth, the Other is anything but esoteric; it is the mark made upon subjectivity by the real, historical conditions of living, in love and hate with other beings, the very fabric of life. Otherness is not some uniform mush within the psyche, but the specific product of specific relationships. (p. 48)

The Other is a part of our everyday life that we are often not aware of as such. This concealment, its sources and consequences, figure importantly in the problems I have alluded to above: the self understood as a discrete entity is left without a certain way to moor itself in a world of others, to bind itself to a community of other discrete individuals. Such a self does not know how to address those aspects of self which are Other, but rather can only address its own feelings about itself. And it is in this gap in our conversation about ourselves that the codependence literature finds its place. By telling its readers how they are to be with others, it offers, as we will see, an understanding of otherness as it arises in everyday life. The reader's interaction with a codependence text might be understood as one of those "specific relationships" that give shape to the experience of the Other.

These simplistic books actually address one of the most profound questions of our time: the question of the Other. What follows will ferret out the answer the books propose to that question. We will see that this answer is most unsatisfactory for a number of reasons, but for the most part because the books suggest that the good life is the one lived when the aspect of the Other that is truly "other"—that is, beyond and yet part of the self—is fully concealed, when the self determines its highest condition as that in which no Other can inhabit it. It is then, as we will see, that pronouncements such as Boesky's make sense, that the notion "you can be x or y or z and still feel good about yourself" becomes the algebra of our time. Such pronouncements can be read as a formula for obliterating the Other, and thus erasing that without which there is no hope of community.

This book, then, examines a psychological literature, but is content to leave largely unexamined the psychologistic aspects of that discourse. Instead, I will focus on what are more properly termed moral concerns by examining the way in which the codependence literature asks and answers the question of what makes for a good life. In this examination, the contours of a dominant understanding of the modern self, and the cultural conversation which constitutes that self, will come into view. This will allow us to glimpse some of the problems inherent in our everyday understanding of ourselves, in the "mark made upon subjectivity by the real, historical conditions of living, in love and hate with other beings, the very fabric of life."

2

The Cat's Grin

"All right," said the cat, and this time it vanished quite
slowly, beginning with the end of the tail, and ending with the
grin, which remained some time after the rest of it had gone.
"Well! I've often seen a cat without a grin," thought
Alice; "but a grin without a cat! It's the most curious thing."
—Lewis Carroll, *The Adventures of Alice in Wonderland*

PROLOGUE

The questions that I raised in the previous chapter might be understood as taking up Alice's curiosity about the cat's grin. My examination
of the codependence literature's cultural determinants is a search for
what "lies behind" this currently popular self-help literature. The codependence books constitute a genre that, as we will see, bears only the
vestigial traces of its culture, which seems to be a social order that erases
itself even as it shows itself. The presence of the cat, its size and shape,
must be deduced from the phantasmic grin that it has left behind in the
form of these books. To fill in the body that lies behind the grin, I will be
using an interpretive method known as ontological hermeneutics. My
method is far less mystifying than this unfortunate phrase would make it
seem. It is really only a systematic way to satisfy Alice's curiosity about
the Cheshire cat.

I have already begun to lay the groundwork for this interpretation by locating the self that is its subject, and describing some of the

problems inherent in that self. In this chapter, I will continue this foundation building. First, I will elucidate some of the claims I have already
made regarding the kinds of problems that emerge in texts such as
those of the codependence literature. Next, I will address in detail the
rationale for choosing the codependence texts in particular. Finally, I
will describe the hermeneutic method and discuss its suitability for this
inquiry.

THE PROBLEM

Self-Help Psychology

To see the problems that emerge from the codependence literature, it is
useful to turn to a wider body of texts to which it belongs, the world of
self-help psychology literature in general. In this section, I will discuss
some of these books in order to illuminate the questions that they raise,
albeit in a concealed way. I will cite studies of these books that illuminate
these questions, and other studies that leave them hidden. We will see
that those questions have largely to do with the way in which the texts
are inscriptions of certain cultural understandings, and that it is a lack of
critical thinking among those who would be critical which brings about
a failure to ask those questions. I will indicate some of the possible
implications of this failure. In the next section, I will make a similar
analysis of the codependence literature.

Throughout this discussion, I will be taking for granted a distinction made by Kaminer (1992) regarding the various kinds of self-help
books available to the American consumer. She distinguishes

> between practical (how to do your own taxes) books and personal (how to
> be happy) books. Of course, sometimes the practical and personal con-
> verge: Saving money on your taxes may make you a happy person. A diet
> book may offer helpful, practical advice on how to eat, while reinforcing
> cultural ideals of slimness and promising to boost your self-esteem. But if
> few books are purely personal or purely practical, some are clearly more
> personal. It is a strong emphasis on individual, personal, or spiritual devel-
> opment that connects the self-help ideals I'm reviewing and composes a
> tradition. (p. 5)

A visit to any American bookstore catering to a mass market will expose
the browser to a wide array of books from this "personal" self-help tradition. Their titles indicate that these books claim to provide counsel for
difficulties that might arise from the womb (*Infants and Mothers*) to the

tomb (*On Death and Dying*). People seeking help for their troubled selves, it would seem, need only find a store with a large enough selection in order to locate a book that claims to address their concerns.

Perhaps the best known exponent of American self-help, and one whose work is still popular ("Over 3 million copies in print"), is Norman Vincent Peale (1952/1956). He introduces his most famous book, *The Power of Positive Thinking*, by telling his reader

> that you do not need to be defeated by anything, that you can have peace of mind, improved health, and a never-ceasing flow of energy. In short . . . your life can be full of joy and satisfaction. (p. ix)

There is nothing that a confident, positive-thinking self cannot achieve; and there is no reason why a person should have anything less than a life full of joy and satisfaction. All that is needed is that "you believe in yourself and release your inner powers" (p. 13). The fullness once reserved for salvation in an afterlife is available without benefit of death. All that is needed is to look within, to tap the inner powers that make eschatology unnecessary.

This optimism continues to be an important part of the contemporary self-help horizon. Here is an excerpt from a recent catalog of "New England's center for the education of mind, body, and spirit" (Interface, 1991):

> ### The Empowerment Workshop
> #### Gail Straub and David Gershon
>
> The purpose of the Empowerment Workshop is to assist you in moving toward optimal wellbeing [*sic*]. This is done by providing you with greater access to your sources of power, and then specifically applying these power sources to those areas of your life most vital to full, integrative living: Relationships, Sexuality, Money, Work, The Body, Emotions and Spirituality.
>
> The Empowerment Workshop was created as an advanced training to build upon the insights you have gained from past personal development work. It offers you hands-on tools that support you in translating these insights into tangible results. In addition, the workshop explores how the sources of personal empowerment can be applied in achieving your larger purpose in the world.
>
> The methodology of the Empowerment Workshop has been created to bring fuller consciousness to the power our thoughts have in creating the reality of our lives. Initially, we examine any limiting thoughts we may hold in each of the vital areas. Then, though comprehensiveness and

> advanced work with affirmation/visualization tools, we build and mold
> powerful new thought forms that provide the impetus for manifesting
> what we want in life. (p. 13)

The language has been updated, but Dr. Peale's simple message is preserved intact: only a poor relationship of the human self to itself prevents it from getting what it wants. No necessary horizon limits the possibilities for happiness, completeness, and "empowerment." The self
here is conceived as a reserve of "power," which is waiting to be tapped
by the right "methodology." Any limitations are self-imposed and can be
removed by "molding new thought forms" that will empower us to get
"what we want." All that stands between the self and its "fulfillment" is a
lack of adequate tools for gaining access to that reservoir, which tools, of
course, this workshop will provide (for $375).

Peale, of course, is no more the originator of this catechism
than are Straub and Gershon. Indeed, Fuller (1982) notes that what
he calls "the cult of positive thinking" is the "only surviving contribution to American culture" of mesmerism, the "science of animal magnetism" founded by Franz Anton Mesmer in late eighteenth-century
Vienna. In 1779, Mesmer proclaimed his theory of animal magnetism,
and condensed it in twenty-seven logically linked principles. Principle
23 helps to give an idea of Mesmer's importance to the self-help tradition.

> One will notice by the facts, according to the practical rules which I estab-
> lish, that this principle [animal magnetism] can immediately cure illness of
> the nerves and mediately all others. (Fuller, 1982, p. 5)

Like Peale and Straub and Gershon, Mesmer is offering a pansophia that
is a panacea. Once the fundamental source of "power" is known and has
been "tapped," subjective distress can be eliminated. Human beings
need not carry the burdens often associated with original sin and the
fallen human condition. Salvation is available, not just as pie-in-the-sky
and by the grace of God, but here and now, and through a person's
proper understanding of and relation to the putative wellsprings of
human being.

In 1836, Charles Poyen brought Mesmer's theory to the United
States, lecturing and demonstrating the techniques in a tour of New
England, where he found an eager reception. The various effects of
inducing a somnambulic state, according to Fuller (1982), found a philo-
sophical home amid the utilitarianism and individualism of the United
States in the middle nineteenth century. Mesmerism was not to be taken

up simply as a parlor game. Rather, as Fuller tells us, it was understood as a kind of religion, an offering of salvation through access to the perfection within. It was a

> psychological doctrine whose chief value was that it reassured individuals that they possessed within themselves the ability to harmonize with what Buchanan [an American mesmerist] called "the modus operandi of life powers." (Fuller, 1982, p. 68)

A certain kind of personal wholeness was thus made possible. The usually doubt-filled subjective domain—the "inner life" of the individual—could become the location of certainty, if only the individual could attune himself or herself to those powers. Here, at least according to Fuller, is the birth of American popular psychology. And, he points out, its gestation took place in a culture that already valued the "power" of the individual, already held self-containment to be a worthwhile aspiration, and was already optimistic about the individual's prospects of achieving that aspiration.

In the end, Fuller (1982) argues, this inscribed individualism was the undoing of mesmerism.

> The mesmerists had ushered in a new era in the American cure of souls. They were the first to popularize psychological ideas as a resource for religious self-understanding. . . . It appears, however, that the mesmerists' psychological doctrines were in many respects solipsistic; they failed to take into account the moral values and institutional structures which alone link subjective vitality with responsible social conduct. (p. 183)

Mesemerism succumbed to what Tocqueville (1840/1990) described as the singular danger of individualist democracy: it makes

> every man forget his ancestors . . . hides his descendants and separates his contemporaries from him; it throws him back forever upon himself alone and threatens in the end to confine him entirely within the solitude of his own heart. (p. 99)

Here, Fuller "reads" mesmerism as the inscription of this kind of problem, as a grin that reveals the presence of the cat of nineteenth-century American individualism and utilitarianism. He thus opens up the possibility that both its arising and decline can be understood in terms of the culture in which they take place, rather than in the "psychological" or "scientific" claims of the doctrine. It would be possible to ask the same kinds of questions of texts like Peale's and Straub's and Gershon's, to ferret out the ways in which certain problematic aspects of culture show up "underneath" those texts.

Unfortunately, this kind of reading is not to be found in the area which would seem, at first glance, to be most suited to such an endeavor: academic psychology, whose claim to knowledge of psychological truth presumably gives it the authority to sort out the claims made by self-help authors. Consider, for example, Starker's (1988a, 1988b) studies on the "prescription of self-help books by psychologists." He claims to have found that "most psychologists consider self-help books to be generally helpful and most prescribe them to their patients" (Starker, 1988a, p. 144). He goes on to wonder what this popularity might mean:

> Does the prescription of self-help works indicate the increasing recognition of patient responsibility in the treatment process, or the progressive bankruptcy of our treatment offerings? Are the prescriptive offerings of psychologists better selected and more effective than those of naive consumers, or is this the fantasy of egotistic practitioners? Are professional psychologists being naively complacent regarding the potential harm of self-help works, prescribed or otherwise? (p. 145)

The way to determine the answers to these questions, he asserts, is "through further empirical investigation" (p. 146)—presumably by trying to assess the outcome of "bibliotherapy" according to some valid measures.

Starker's emphasis on questions of "validity" starts where most of the psychological literature regarding self-help books does: with a suspiciousness of the claims that they make. The popularity of those books, according to this literature, places a burden on psychology's shoulders, lest the discipline be accused of peddling snake oil on a mass basis. Rosen (1976) notes this danger, worrying that marketing might take precedence over good scientific work, and that, as a result, "consumers run the risk of purchasing treatment programs that may be ineffective when used on a totally non-prescription basis" (p. 140). He calls for either regulation of self-help literature, or at the very least, professional oversight of its publications. Five years later, Rosen (1981) all but abandons his hope that psychologists can get self-help literature in hand, as yet another in the panoply of psychological treatments, complaining that "the titles and claims that accompany these books have become incredible if not outrageous" (p. 189).

This shortcoming can be understood as an "ethical" problem, as Henderson (1983) points out: American Psychological Association (APA) guidelines caution authors "to be conservative in expounding methods of self-improvement and to disclose any possible limitations of such methods" (p. 169). Starker (1988b) has a suggestion for psychologists who might want to prescribe self-help books: they should prescribe without endorsing. He offers this formulation for the prescribing therapist:

> This is a book that people in your situation sometimes find interesting and useful, although it is by no means proven to have curative value. You may wish to think about its contents and discuss them with me. (p. 454)

So long as the books, and the patient's reading of them, are subjected to the psychologist's scrutiny and expertise, the APA's ethical problem, it seems, will be resolved.

This "resolution," however, is incomplete. Clearly, the occasion for the equivocation formalized by Starker is the lack of any kind of validation for the claims of the books. For him and the others I am discussing, the best solution to the "ethical" problem is to turn the light of empirical science onto the self-help genre. As Forest (1987) notes, "there is . . . some indirect evidence suggesting that self-help books influence behaviour, [but] there is little which indicates what specific changes might occur" (p. 1244). He has designed and carried out a series of studies to clarify this matter, investigating both the personality correlates of people who are interested in self-help books (Saper and Forest, 1987) and the effects of reading the texts on personality measures (Forest, 1987, 1988). His results are mixed: the Forest (1987) study on personality correlates shows a significant effect of reading self-help books on self-actualization measures (inner-directedness and time competence), while the later study shows no significant effects of self-help reading on personality characteristics as measured by the Eysenck Personality Inventory. The Saper and Forest (1987) study hypothesized that "interest" in self-help books would vary directly with "neuroticism" and "introversion," and be found more among women than men. His results indicate that only neuroticism could be correlated with interest, and tentatively at that (Saper and Forest, 1987, p. 566). What is obvious from casual observation—the popularity of the books among the general population—seems to elude the systematic explanation that would provide a scientific basis for their popularity and "effectiveness."

Starker's studies also indicate a wide gap between theory and practice, between psychologists' commitment to "base their work upon research findings and scientific principles" and the empirical finding that "[m]ost psychologists consider self-help books to be generally helpful and . . . failed to regard them as harmful . . . [or] unhelpful" (Starker, 1988b, p. 454). Psychologists, like the general populace, seem attracted to the self-help literature for reasons that remain unarticulated, awaiting only further empirical study to determine "which people and which problems benefit from reading self-help paperbacks," so that they may be prescribed confidently as "a relatively cost-effective method of solving life's problems" (Saper and Forest, 1987, p. 566).

Despite their suspiciousness, then, psychologists seem sanguine about the possibility of adding self-help books to their panoply. All that is needed is a better understanding of the value of "the technology of the self-help book" (Starker, 1988b, p. 454). Empirical studies, however, have failed to provide this understanding. I would suggest that this is because such studies repeatedly ask the wrong questions, and thus fail to render a comprehensive understanding and critique of the phenomenon. Suggestions like Starker's and studies like Forest's take so much for granted that they overlook, and fail to interrogate, the most obvious aspect of the literature: these books are already popular. They apparently res-onate deeply with some aspect of the contemporary self. People have already found and used them without benefit of empirical validation, or a psychologist's prescription. Something about the world in which we live makes them popular, and, presumably, useful. A scientific study of their effects, even if it were to find them "unhelpful," is unlikely to deter people from buying them or psychologists from writing and profiting from them.

So while empirical investigation of personality characteristics as they relate to interest in the books, or of the books' measurable impact on personality characteristics, may yield some consistent results, such studies run the risk of missing the point. They are examples of the lim-itations of empirical scientific method, limitations which have been noted by many authors, but are perhaps best summed up by Husserl's charge that they constitute the conduct of "science in the absence of the world" (cited in Theunissen, 1977/1984, p. 185). To ask only about the self that reads the books is always to fail to ask about and illuminate the world in which enormously popular self-help books are a possibility in the first place, in which the self is already conceived as distressed and "helpable" in the way the books claim.

To assess the self-help literature phenomenon by means of empir-ical investigation of its treatment effectiveness, then, is to ignore pre-cisely the kinds of questions raised by studies such as Fuller's (1982), to take for granted that there is nothing "behind" the Cheshire cat's grin. Those who would investigate the literature in this fashion cannot help but start with some definitions of the "self" that is being "helped," and of the kind of help that is being offered. Starker (1988a) unintentionally provides an example of the problems that arise as a result of this kind of practice when he offers a partial explanation for their [self-help books'] popularity and prescription. That is, the past decade has seen a marked shift away from the once dominant psychodynamic model of psychological diagnosis and treatment. Cognitive and cognitive-behavioral perspectives on the other hand, have become increasingly important . . . there has been less emphasis on hypothesized instinctual or infantile motivations and greater concern with the defensive and coping strategies of the ego. Consequently, the matter of conscious choice has resumed stage center after its long eclipse by issues of unconscious influence. Rather than the helpless victim of instinctual urges and internalized prohibitions, the individual is increasingly viewed as an active agent making important choices. This perspective has supported the reemergence of a rational/educational approach to treatment. . . . (pp. 145-46)

Even as Starker argues that a changed understanding of the self makes the self-help phenomenon possible, he does not question that understanding. Even if he is not, as I think he is, implying that this "marked shift" constitutes a *better* understanding of the self, still the kind of study he is proposing would take that understanding for granted. It would thus leave unquestioned such notions as a self that can be "treated" with rational education, a self that is perhaps best conceived as an active and conscious entrepreneur in control of its choices, or what Taylor (1989) calls "a lucid calculator of payoffs" (p. 33). If an empirical study were to demonstrate that self-help books indeed help people become better at being such selves, still it would not say much about the nature of that self. It would remain possible that the self being urged on us by the literature contains some problems that are concealed and confounded by it, and which could not be disclosed by research that took the assumptions of the literature for granted.

Indeed, the understanding of "self" that Starker (1988a, 1988b) naively refers to (and evidently approves of) has been criticized in many ways. Sampson (1981), for example, argues that "cognitivism . . . represents a set of values and interests that reaffirm the existing nature of the social order" (p. 730). By noting this concealed ideology, he makes suspect the kind of self described by that psychology as an object of legitimate inquiry. Earlier, I alluded to Bellah et al.'s (1985) contention that the idea of a self as an autonomous agent among other autonomous agents can and has led to what might be called hyperindividualism. This, in turn, they argue, contributes to a social order in which commitment to a community is tenuous, ethics inarticulate, and moral action endlessly ambiguous. Thompson (1986) has questioned the emphasis found in American psychology on the ego as a maker of defensive strategy as a fundamental misunderstanding of the "selves" that we are. Such an understanding, he argues, turns a self into an entrepreneur who views others as means to its own ends. Cushman (1990) has noted an ongoing philosophical incoherence about the modern self that confounds much of the psychological research that purports to describe and to treat its problems.

These critiques, and many others like them, would seem to indicate that before self-help literature is assessed for its efficacy in the clinic, we must ask what kind of self is being helped and what kind of help is being offered to it. To ask these questions is to examine critically the phenomenon under study so that we are sure we know what we are talking about when we investigate the effectiveness of "bibliotherapy." It is to allow us to question not only whether or not a particular set of books is "effective," but also how that "effectiveness" affects and is itself affected by culture and public life. If, to return to the hyperbolic example I used in the previous chapter, a self-help book was "effective" at helping concentration camp employees maintain their "self-esteem" even as they shoveled corpses into crematoria, it would clearly not be enough to conclude that such a book helps that person become an "active agent making important choices." We would want to know how it happens that such a possibility emerges from a text that undoubtedly did not intend to make people happier concentration camp employees, and what this means about the "rational education" that it offers. To find this out, it is necessary to stalk the cat, or, to invoke a different metaphor, to read the books as palimpsests in which the inscription of the culture lurks underneath the more readily visible text.

The Codependence Literature

Later in this chapter, we will see what the hermeneutic method is, and why it is suited for this kind of reading. For now, however, I would like to turn to the specific self-help books with which I am concerned, the codependence literature, and extend the above analysis to them.

I have already given a general sense of what is meant by codependence, and much of what follows in this study will be concerned with a further understanding of that word. In this section, however, I will limit myself to a discussion of how the books themselves define codependence, and of the way that problems like those that can be seen in the self-help literature in general arise specifically in the codependence literature's proposed understanding of the "disease."

Most authors of codependence books start with definitions. The following excerpts will give an idea of the broad contours of the concept the texts are advancing.

> Co-dependency . . . [is] a dysfunctional pattern of living and problem-solving, which is nurtured by a set of rules within the family system. (Friel and Subby, 1984, p. 32)

> Co-dependency is a primary disease and a disease within every member of an alcoholic family. (Wegscheider-Cruse, 1984, p. 2)

> Codependents [are] all persons who (1) are in a love or marriage relationship with an alcoholic, (2) have one or more alcoholic parents or grandparents, or (3) grew up in an emotionally repressive family. (Wegscheider-Cruse, in Schaef, 1986, p. 15)

> Codependence [is] ill health, or maladaptive or problematic behavior that is associated with living, working with, or otherwise being close to a person with alcoholism. (Whitfield, in Schaef, 1986, p. 17)

> Co-dependency is a pattern of learned behaviors, feelings, and beliefs that make life painful . . . [The codependent] is human-relationship-dependent and focuses her/his life around an addictive agent. (Smalley, in Schaef, 1986, p. 14)

> A codependent [is] anyone who has been *affected* by the person who has been *afflicted* by the disease of chemical dependency . . . anyone who lives in close association with anyone who has a neurotic personality. (Larsen, in Schaef, 1986, pp. 17-18)

> A codependent person is anyone who has let another person's behavior affect him or her, and who is obsessed with controlling that person's behavior. (Beattie, 1987, p. 31)

Clearly, these are highly general statements, "so vague as to be meaningless," as Krestan and Bepko (1990, p. 220) put it. But somewhat more precision can be gained by examining the accounts of how this "disease" shows up in everyday life. Schaef (1991) gives us this description of the experience of the codependent.

> Codependence is found everywhere in our society. It is characterized, in part, by a strong need to exist not for oneself but for others and to care for others at one's own expense. Codependent persons tend to lack personal boundaries, distrust their own perceptions and feel like martyrs. . . . Codependence works against healthy intimacy because intimacy involves the connections of persons with well-defined self-concepts, clear boundaries and the ability to be involved without losing themselves. (Omega Institute Catalog, 1991, p. 42)

When people "let another person's behavior affect them" they run the risk of "losing themselves," and this loss shows up in the kind of "martyrdom" Schaef describes.

Codependence, then, might be understood as a "misguided" approach to relationship; its "cure"—"recovery"—is to learn a better way. Krestan and Bepko (1990), following a list of definitions much like the one above, summarize these concerns succinctly:

> The basic message of codependency implied in these definitions is a relational one—it reflects the common struggle we all face to maintain the integrity of our separateness in the face of our need for relatedness. (p. 220)

The codependence literature is concerned to show a reader the way to carry out that struggle, or, as Beattie (1989) says, to "extricate our emotions, mind, body, and spirit from the agony of entanglement" (p. 58).

If the range of concerns addressed by the literature is wide, so too is the population for whom the "diagnosis" is relevant. It is not just the spouses and children of alcoholics who suffer, but "anyone who lives . . . with anyone who has a neurotic personality," anyone who has "let another person's behavior control him or her." And, as Kaminer (1990) says, "Who hasn't?" The codependence literature does not hesitate to affirm that its potential audience is virtually "anyone." The "96 percent" figure cited earlier is commonly found in these books (see, for example, Bradshaw, 1988a, cover; Weinhold and Weinhold, 1989, p. xvii [actually, this book claims an "infection rate" of 98 per cent]; Schaef, 1986, p. 14). The "disease" is of epidemic proportions. The vast majority of people do not know how to conduct their love lives without "losing themselves." And the codependence literature is a genre concerned to tell them how to do so.

Clearly, to take up this question is to take on an enormous task. It is to attempt to clarify what Krestan and Bepko (1990) identify as a struggle common to all of us. But the codependence literature may not offer us, as it claims to do, an "objective" understanding of this difficulty. Just as we can understand mesmerism's claim on U.S. culture in the 1840s as an inscription of that culture's concern with individualism, or the claim of Starker's "active agent making conscious choices" on contemporary culture as an inscription of certain of our own concerns, so too we might understand the claims of the codependence literature in terms of the society in which it arises.

Some critics have provided critiques based on this understanding. Van Wormer (1989), for instance, is not content to accept the idea that codependence is best understood as a quasi-medical malady. Indeed, she claims that the uncritical acceptance and proliferation of the codependence label results in a failure to "take a historical view of codependency." This lack conceals the fact that "the use of this label has sociopolitical roots in sexism and oppression of women" (p. 52). This view shows codependence to be a diagnosis that makes pathological what

> are essentially exaggerations of women's prescribed cultural role. The wider society places a premium on autonomy and independence. . . . The high frequency with which the co-dependency label is used for female clients is suggestive of an overlap between the central dynamics of co-dependency and key dimensions in the sex-role socialization of women. (p. 55)

Krestan and Bepko (1990) make much the same point. Codependence is, in their view, "the social reconstruction of female experience." By pathologizing what is actually a socially constructed understanding of women's roles, they argue,

> [t]he language of codependency blames people, women in particular, for assuming a social role that has previously been viewed as normative and functional. It takes what was once considered healthy, defining it as sick. In the process it fails to acknowledge that change needs to occur at the level of social belief, attitude and expectation. (p. 231)

Critiques like these take the codependence literature to task for forgetting that the "personal" is also the "political." Krestan and Bepko (1990), along with Gomberg (1989), suggest that this depoliticization is not only socially destructive but also naive.

> The culture's current obsession with codependency may be, on a metaphorical level, another version of the quest for painless relatedness. . . . Recovered from codependency, one could magically achieve the paradoxical feat of being perfectly fulfilled in relationship without ever focusing on the other person. (p. 220)

Haaken (1990) also criticizes the literature for its naivete.

> While this clinical concept [codependence] articulates concerns that are common to many in our society and points to the need for sociological and cultural explanations for psychopathology, it assimilates far too much in attempting to offer one simple construct to explain the multifarious existential, social and psychopathological bases of human emotional suffering. (p. 405)

Her objection, however, is not only to the oversimplification inherent in the widespread cast of the codependence net. Moreover, she argues, the codependence literature overlooks an important aspect of human psychological functioning.

> While the codependence literature does reject the repressive moral categories of the past, it provides a morally and psychologically impoverished substitute world, devoid of the tensions inherent in differentiated consciousness. (p. 404)

This "impoverishment," Haaken suggests, can be countered by ensuring that "clinicians . . . are . . . anchored in broad-based traditions backed by well-developed theories" (p. 405).

Kaminer (1990, 1992) has also attempted to situate the codependence literature in a social and political context. In her book *I'm Dysfunctional, You're Dysfunctional*, and in an article adapted from the book and given prominent display in the *New York Times Book Review*, she addresses what she feels are the salient shortcomings of the codependence literature and the self-help tradition from which it arises. While she notes and praises the former for its view of the self not "in isolation . . . [but] in the context of familial relations" (Kaminer, 1990, p. 26), she also accuses it of making "a significant contribution to the general dumbing down of books and . . . changing the relationships between writers and readers" (p. 27). By emphasizing action over reflection, prescription over self-direction, the genre becomes an appeal to authority and conformity in everyday life.

> In the self-help universe, anyone can be healthy, spiritually centered, rich and thin—with faith, self-discipline and the willingness to take direction. . . . But if the how-to phenomenon reflects a democratic belief in the power of will to overcome circumstances of nature and class, it's built on an authoritarian mystique of expertise that encourages conformity . . . self-help books collectivize the process of identity formation, exploiting readers' fears of embarking on the search for self without the aid of exercises, techniques, assurances of success, and, of course support groups. (p. 27)

The danger of such literature, she argues, is that it will encourage submission to its teachings rather than responsibility to "confront the complexities of a solitary creative effort, as well as its failures." While I agree with her argument in many respects, I will be concerned later on to show that the question of authority in these books is not so straightforward as Kaminer implies; neither, as we will see, is the romantic individualist alternative she proposes without its own substantial problems.

Another critique comes from Rapping (1990) who, like the other critics, notes that these books are intended for women, and that "few women reading these books . . . will fail to feel a shock of recognition at [their] analyses of heterosexual relationships." She goes on, however, to challenge the limitations of those analyses, arguing that the codependence literature, and particularly its emphasis on addiction models of disease and treatment, encourages a kind of submissiveness that is pernicious, particularly insofar as

> . . . these books do not show how the personal becomes the political. Instead, they present addiction as a disease from which one never really recovers, which only the most vigilant and permanent adherence to the 12-step program . . . can control. (pp. 317-18)

By seeing the individual only in the most limited social context, these books fail to uncover what she believes to be the true cause of our distress:

> Whether we are heroin addicts or credit card addicts . . . we all got that way in the process of growing up and trying to survive in a world that is based on impossible ideals and values. (p. 318)

Critiques like these succeed in raising questions about the social and cultural determinants and effects of the codependence literature. To suggest, for instance, that the books pathologize "female experience," making an intrapsychic illness out of a collective problem, is to say that we cannot take their claims to be describing a "disease" for granted, but rather must consider the possibility that they, perhaps unwittingly, comprise yet another instance of our culture's oppression of women. To assert that the texts are instrumental in a "dumbing down" of literature or a reduction of the political to the personal is to say that we cannot be sanguine about their effect on the society in which they are read. These interpretations move our understanding of this dominant form of public discourse beyond questions of psychological "effectiveness" and toward questions of the commonweal.

One way to understand the critiques I am concerned with here is to say that they are not content to take the literature as it presents itself, to assume that there is nothing behind its grin. Instead, they penetrate the literature's pretense to being an "objective" rendering of the "whole picture," which is perhaps signaled most clearly by its presentation of codependence as a "disease," as a phenomenon which can be fully accounted for in a "medical" or "scientific" discourse. Despite this pretense to being presuppositionless, the literature can be shown to embody certain problematic prejudices, which in turn can be seen as underlying certain coercive institutions and practices. Later on, I will describe what these prejudices and practices are and how the codependence literature embodies them. For now, it is sufficient to notice that it is possible to get "behind" texts that present themselves as having nothing "behind" them, to see the way the culture lies, like the Cheshire cat behind his smile, invisibly and silently in their words.

NOTES ON METHOD:
RATIONALE FOR A HERMENEUTIC ANALYSIS

Of course, we could ask many questions of a text, and each question has its own prejudices; each can thus itself be "read" as a cultural inscription. In this section, I will describe the rationale for using a ontological-hermeneutic analysis to shape the questions that comprise this inquiry. First, I will discuss ways in which the critiques I have already mentioned fall short. Then, I will turn to a somewhat abstract consideration of hermeneutics in order to show how that method addresses those shortcomings. Finally, I will describe why I think the codependence literature is suited to such an analysis, with some attention to why it is important to carry it out.

The Necessity of Entering the Circle

Consider for a moment Haaken's (1990) claim that the codependence literature "provides a morally and psychologically impoverished substitute world, devoid of the tensions inherent in differentiated consciousness" (p. 404). Here, she is certainly penetrating the pretenses of the literature, suggesting that what they offer amounts to a "cheap" way out of the otherwise unavoidable "tensions." Haaken is claiming that this "tension," and the wish to avoid it, is (unwittingly) inscribed in the texts, that the ideal world the codependence books present can be "read" as a gambit to alleviate a suffering that the books do not even know they are addressing.

But this reading, insightful as it is, raises other questions. For, we might ask, what is the status of that which Haaken claims to have found lurking behind these texts? What does it mean to say that "tensions" are "inherent in differentiated consciousness"? Is this a claim about "human nature"? Is it based on some biological notion that our consciousness is somehow inherently differentiated in such a way that we must necessarily and always experience some kind of tension? Are these to be understood as philosophical claims, an ontology of the human, or are they "scientific" claims, based on some kind of empirical studies about consciousness? What is the "consciousness" she is referring to? Haaken's own presuppositions do not come to light, although she speaks strongly for restoring to the notion of codependence certain distinctions made by what she calls "psychodynamic" theories. But what are the cultural determinants of these theories, or are we to take them as given? To the extent that her presuppositions are hidden, they become their own Cheshire cat, and such questions as these cannot be asked; the background of her interpretation of the texts remains concealed, so there appears to be nothing to question. While Haaken brings to light certain problems in the codependence literature, she does not make her own interpretive stance clear. It is not in the scope of this book to answer the questions I have raised about the notion of "differentiated consciousness," but it is clear that such an inquiry could be conducted, and a cultural inscription in her critical work could thereby be found.

The same point can be made about a study like Krestan and Bepko's (1990). They suggest the codependence literature overlooks the inescapability of the "pain of relatedness," the inherent difficulty of the "common struggle . . . to maintain the integrity of our own separateness in the face of our need for relatedness." But whence does this dialectic arise? How does its resolution come to be our "common struggle"? Just because the claims of autonomy and community are in conflict in the contemporary United States does not mean that this is as it always has been or must be. This struggle has a history, but Krestan and Bepko are content to formulate it as a conflict between two apparent "facts": our "integrity" and our "need for relatedness." Perhaps these truly are "facts"; but they are far from proven as such, even if they have a certain appeal to common sense. Such ideas as a "need for relatedness" and "integrity" may also be hidden inscriptions of a culture, which, so long as they remain in the dark, cannot be questioned.

I do not intend to accuse these writers of intellectual skulduggery or laziness. They, after all, do not claim to be intent upon illuminating the erased text of the palimpsest, and they may not intend their presuppositions to be "objective" statements about "human nature." I simply mean to point out some of the difficulties that arise when this intention is absent. Nor do I mean to say that all prejudices can (or should) be explicated in and expunged from projects of interpretation. Rather, my point is the necessity of carrying out interpretation in a way that is aware of problems like these, that takes into account the inescapability of cultural inscription in both the texts being interpreted and in the questions being asked of them; that, indeed, takes that inscription as its object. Critiques like Haaken's (1990) or Krestan and Bepko's (1990) are after an understanding of how the texts contribute to the oppression of women or blur certain important clinical distinctions. But it is also possible to pursue the "meaning" of the texts qua cultural inscription, to make the point of the interpretive work that explication.

This kind of interpretation is what I understand to be meant by hermeneutics and is what I will carry out in the following pages. To enter the hermeneutic circle is to take for granted only that nothing can be taken for granted, that all texts, including interpretive ones, must speak of a culture. So the necessary starting point for a hermeneutic inquiry is, as Packer and Addison (1989) put it, "entering the hermeneutic circle in the right way: discovering an appropriate workable perspective from which interpretation can proceed" (p. 3). Later on, I will specify my interpretive perspective. But first, I think it is appropriate to acknowledge that hermeneutics in general is a perspective, and to discuss in some more detail what that perspective is, why it is suited to the self-help texts I am concerned with here, and what the strengths and limitations of such an approach are.

Hermeneutics and Self-Help

Central to the notion of hermeneutics is the text. The word itself was originally coined to distinguish scholarly or "scientific" interpretation of Scripture from practical exegesis. It thus refers to a systematic method for interpretation, one that claims to find the "truth" of a text while still acknowledging that that "truth" is still a matter of interpretation. While the truth of biology's interpretation of human conception as the joining of sperm with egg can be verified empirically, the truth of a hermeneutic interpretation of a text can be verified only through the rigor and illuminating power of the method itself. As I noted above, my use of a hermeneutic method here draws its strength from my claim that I am after the cultural determinants of the texts under consideration: I am not so much interested in the practical exegesis proposed by the psychologists I discussed earlier as in the illumination of what is "behind" the text, what makes it arise and take hold in a particular cultural soil.

But hermeneutics does not take the text as an isolated object, as something to be parsed in a laboratory-like isolation. Rather, the text is important insofar as it can tell us about the world which both it and we occupy. Ricoeur (1971/1981) makes this clear in his claim that "the text is the medium through which we understand ourselves." Hermeneutics can be an integral part of our reading, even if we do not know it, for the text can give us the world we occupy. But for Ricoeur, this possibility of the text is always hidden, to be discovered not so much in the book itself as in the dialogue that unfolds between the reader and the text.[1]

This is true of *all* texts, but it takes on an added dimension when we turn our attention to books that intentionally offer us self-understanding, that set out to tell us who we are. For it is clear such books purport to tell us that we are certain kinds of selves with certain possibilities that we can be helped to realize. The interpretation of this kind of text is of particular interest, because the work of understanding ourselves in front of a text, at least according to Ricoeur, has as its product "an enlarged self"; "the self is constituted by the 'matter' of the text" (pp. 143-44). But self-help literature in general, and the codependence literature in particular, announces itself as offering precisely an "enlargement" of the self, or, as one self-help writer (perhaps borrowing from the U.S. Army) puts it, a way "to grow into all I am capable of being" (Norwood, 1985, p. 273). The self-help book is already telling us explicitly what constitutes that "enlargement," and it works largely by providing us with the very self-interpretation that Ricoeur understands as the work of appropriating a text. It thus draws upon a consensus and tradition about the nature of the self and the conditions for its improvement.

But this evocation, as I hope I have already made clear, is not to be found in the manifest meanings presented by these texts. Indeed, a danger arises with the explicitness of self-help texts: that precisely the work which Ricoeur understands as essential to the constitution of the self will not be done, that those questions will be concealed by the very baldness with which the subject of the self is being addressed. The books' stated objective is to tell us readers who we are, so, it seems, we need not ask who we are as we read. We need only take at face value the presentation of our selves to ourselves. This would appear to be the problem in a program like Starker's. It forgets that "we constantly mean something other than what we say" (Ricoeur, 1970, p. 15), that in meaning to tell us how we might be helped, authors of self-help texts might also be telling us something else. It forgets that the work of understanding the text is not simply some technique of reading, but also must involve the practice of interpretation.

While Starker's proposal has as its starting point the notion that human subjectivity is constituted by a self that can be meaningfully understood through empirical, experiment-based research, the method I am using takes as its starting point the "notion that human subjectivity can be fixed in writings" (Barclay, 1990, p. 65), but that inscription leaves only traces of itself in the texts. It is not implanted intentionally, as in an allegory, but rather enters as the inevitable consequence of the author's having a world that constitutes him or her, and of the world's "having" an author. Nor does the world enter the text as a faithful and intentional inscription of the author's horizons; rather, "the text's career escapes the finite horizon lived by the author" (Ricoeur, 1971/1981, p. 202). Even texts, like those of the self-help tradition, which set out "intentionally" to inscribe a possible self and world, or, as we have seen, texts which seek to criticize them, are not fully transparent. The horizon against which that inscription is made possible must be explicated in a dialogue before those texts can be understood. This dialogical process, by illuminating both the self and its world, is what Ricoeur is suggesting enlarges the reading self. An account of that illumination is the goal of a hermeneutic approach to a text.

There is, then, at least in a view like Ricoeur's, an inevitable surplus of meaning in our utterances, one which holds forth the possibility of a robust understanding of the world of the text and its reader. The "meaning" of the text lies not in its content, but elsewhere. If we take the manifest meaning of the codependence literature as a starting point, and interrogate it thoroughly, we may arrive at that elsewhere. We may find and describe the horizon against which the inscription of subjectivity lying latent in the account of codependence is made possible. To do so is to uncover the sine qua non of the the text, and thus to be hot on the trail of its fuller meaning. In this search, we may come upon an account of how we think we are supposed to be, of who we currently think we are and how we can best live. This will occur when we illuminate the cultural understandings that make it possible for the text to emerge in the first place.

To adopt a hermeneutic standpoint, however, is to take on certain burdens. After all, a proposal like Starker's "neutral" prescription of a self-help book has as its virtue a seemingly unprejudiced point of view: the value of self-help books can be assessed by discerning their treatment effects and reporting them in quantitative measures. It thus makes clear the criteria against which the self's improvement can be measured, and the value of the literature determined. An interpretive method, of course, starts with a critique of this kind of empiricism, namely, that it necessarily overlooks the world-embeddedness of the experiencing human subject and its artifacts. It sacrifices a full account of a phenomenon in favor of the precision achieved by considering it outside of its context. It thus ends up accurately describing a phenomenon that might easily be only a manifestation of empiricism.

An interpretive method makes a different sacrifice. It cannot claim to be establishing "the truth" on the basis of which predictions and prescriptions can be confidently made, and to which other experimental outcomes can be compared. Rather, it seeks, as Gadamer (1967/1981, p. 37) puts it, a "reflection on a given preunderstanding [that] brings before me something that otherwise happens behind my back." It seeks to find the obvious that is hidden, to place what is always already there in front of me as an interpretation. In taking this approach, a hermeneutic method purports to understand and articulate the phenomenon in its world.

But such an endeavor, it must be remembered, cannot claim to render fully transparent the "meaning" of the phenomenon. It is not an exhaustive description, but an illumination of the text that shows up aspects which would not otherwise appear, but which are essential to the constitution of the text. This illumination, at least in Gadamer's (1967/1981, p. 32) view, "need not always shake the dogmatism of life-praxis"; it need not be a challenge to the authority of the text, but may rather simply be the occasion for "tak[ing] possession of what [one] has obediently followed." To take what is behind our backs when we read the codependence literature and place it in front of us may simply be to affirm the tradition that was once silently constitutive of who we are. Our preunderstandings, in this view, cannot help but evoke that tradition; hermeneutic reflection brings to light the prejudices that we already have, and cannot claim to liberate us from those prejudices any more than it can claim to bring about an "objective" representation of its object of inquiry. It can only claim to illuminate the understanding of being that allows a text like a codependence book to arise and take hold in a culture in the first place.

Interpretation whose object is to disclose the tradition that gives rise to a text is not the only kind of hermeneutic method. Indeed, the hermeneutics of tradition (or, as it has been called, ontological hermeneutics or the hermeneutics of affirmation) has been challenged from within the interpretive sciences, notably by Habermas (1973/1980; see also Bleicher, 1980). It is dangerous, this argument runs, to assume that prejudice is inevitable, and that the way is always clear to dialogue, to the fusion of horizons that brings about the illumination of our pre-understandings. The danger is that a pernicious prejudice inherent in a given tradition will not be seen as such, that in not actively seeking to dissolve, as well as to disclose, prejudice, an affirmative hermeneutics may perpetuate practices that ought to be eliminated. Indeed, a program like Gadamer's offers no privileged place to stand in order to make judgments about such "oughts"; rather, it seeks to take its stand in the midst of an ongoing dialogue in an attempt to resolve misunderstanding without appeal to values that may transcend that dialogue.

Habermas argues, however, that understanding does not take place only against the backdrop of a given tradition, but in anticipation of freedom from the prejudices of that tradition. It is possible, and indeed necessary, to adopt a stance that "requires a systematic pre-understanding that extends onto language in general" (Habermas, 1973/1980, p. 201). What ontological hermeneutics discovers as a consensus might be a false consensus, a tradition that has been systematically distorted in order to further the power and interests of a particular group within a culture. The ideology and power relations of a given tradition must be examined from and compared with a perspective that seeks emancipation from all ideology and domination.

The problems that arise in the absence of this kind of analysis have been compellingly illustrated by critics like Farias (1989) and Wolin (1990), who have narrated the ugly history of Heidegger's active involvement in the Nazi party, and tied it to the decidedly "non-critical" nature of his ontological hermeneutics (see Heidegger, 1926/1962). To prevent this kind of problem, according to the critical school, any interpretation of a cultural phenomenon must hold it up against the standard of universal unforced recognition. To approach this quasi-Kantian goal, Habermas suggests that hermeneutics must begin with a suspicion that dominating interests distort our preunderstandings, and offer a critique of the ideology of the text in order to disclose the distortion that lies latently within it.

This book does not attempt to reconcile or resolve this conflict of interpretive traditions; indeed, they may be irreconcilable. Such a project is, in any event, outside the scope of my study. I recite it in order to point out that my analysis, which takes much more of an ontological than a critical perspective, is not the only possible way to interpret these texts. Here my interest is in the (concealed) understanding of being that provides the horizon against which the texts at hand emerge and take hold, rather than on the ideological determinants of those texts. I am concerned to show the problems inherent in the ontology embodied by the texts (see Stigliano, 1989, for a discussion of this method of appropriating a text and its relevance to the human sciences).

By taking this stance, I am not denying the legitimacy of a claim that certain social, political, and economic interests might benefit by, or even perpetuate, the distortions these books contain; nor am I claiming that these considerations are unimportant. We might, for instance, understand the codependence literature as a "commodity fetish," in which the "self" becomes an item to be purchased in the marketplace, and subjectivity becomes objectified. We might talk about the ideological implications of this reversal, about how it serves the interests of free-market capitalism for one's self-definition to be yet another "product" for sale. And this would be an interesting and fruitful discussion, one that would by no means be antagonistic to the purposes of the present analysis.

But an ideology-based inquiry would still leave open the ontological question: what bare understanding of being allows such an ideology even to make sense to begin with? What kind of beings do we already understand ourselves to be such that we can even come to see ourselves as that commodity purveyed in mass-market paperbacks? The "always already," I am arguing, must be seen as prior to, or at least equiprimordial with (and irreducible to), the prevailing beliefs and practices that are embodied in, and masked by, the texts. No ideology, I am arguing, is without its ontology. And it is this background of "bare understanding" that I am interested in illuminating. A critical hermeneutician might point out here that "bare understanding" is impossible, that there are always interests "behind" a given ontology. But here we are thrown back into a debate that may not admit of resolution. I am clearly taking a stand on one side of the argument, or at least toward one end of the spectrum constituted by these two schools of interpretive theory.

By taking this approach, then, I do not mean to dismiss the importance of ideological critique, or to overlook the possible shortcomings of my approach. The excesses of a Heidegger must stand as a warning to those like me who would carry out this kind of project. So while I must remain muted on the question of the specific economic, political, and social interests that are concealed by the codependence texts, I will make reference to the ways that the ontology I illuminate shows up in certain problematic aspects of everyday life within our culture. I will not remain silent about the dangers of the codependence discourse, nor claim that those dangers are somehow unique to the texts at hand. Indeed, I offer this work as an example of how a disclosure of ontology can, without specific reference to an ideology, shed light on critical problems in a culture's practices. These problems can perhaps be addressed more directly in a critique of ideology, but this analysis can still bring them to presence.

In seeking the concealed "always already," I do not intend to take an Archimedean stand, that is, to make transcendent claims about human nature from what amounts to a view from nowhere. With Gadamer, I agree that there are always more prejudices to be ferreted out. But by acknowledging and explicating my interpretive stance and its prejudices, I hope to do more than simply bring a phenomenon to light and less than fully master it; I hope to be methodical, if not, properly speaking, methodological.

Some of the prejudices that make up my interpretive stance are, in what follows, explored and substantiated (or at least critically discussed) in detail, others are only mentioned in passing. (Yet others, of course, remain unsaid; they will constitute the elsewhere of this text.) The first, and perhaps the most important of these prejudices, is the one I have just discussed: that an ontological interpretation is an important one, that a "bare understanding" of the concealed "always already" inscribed in a text is necessary, and possible, to show.

Another related prejudice has also been discussed above: that, as Ricoeur says, meanings lurk silently in the text, that a cultural inscription of human subjectivity can be found there, that in this finding is the opportunity for an "enlargement of the self." This suspicion of latent meaning is what I am arguing makes a hermeneutic method both necessary and possible. It corresponds to a prejudice that I will explicate more fully regarding the nature of subjectivity: that, like the texts in which it is inscribed, it cannot be rendered fully transparent. Neither, as Foucault (1983, pp. 211-16) points out, would this necessarily be desirable, leading as it might to a totalizing of power over the human subject. Human being is constituted by a conversation that goes on because it has to, because there is always something more to say. This is not an epistemological point so much as an ontological one. It is not simply that our ways of knowing are imperfect (for that opens the possibility of a technique by which we might achieve a full knowing). Our immersion in a world that always eludes our grasp is not a matter of contingency, a problem awaiting the negotiations and calculations of empiricism. Rather, we are human precisely because, and to the extent that, we cannot know the truth, but must try find it. If one were to achieve a "total" knowing, a "final" truth, the conversation would end, and we would become something other than human. Claims to such absolutes have always been shown to mask power or interest or desire (see Sloterdijk, 1983/1987). Indeed, they can be seen as standing behind such unmitigated disasters as the Nazi holocaust, an event in which an entire nation hid its atrocities behind a "knowing" that legitimized them.

A related prejudice, which will be explicated in what follows, is that much of modern technological culture has as its elsewhere precisely that kind of totalized truth which I am calling other than human, that it is a nihilistic culture insofar as it aspires to that totalization. By "nihilism" I mean the loss of seriousness that accompanies the leveling of all meaningful distinctions. This nihilism, I will argue, can be found particularly in the denial or concealing in that culture of a fundamental entanglement of one person with another, and shows up as the basis of the good life called "recovery" in the codependence texts. That entanglement is also not to be understood as contingent or negotiable, but as ontological, namely, *Dasein* is always already *mitsein* (Heidegger, 1962, pp. 154ff.). The "self," as I will argue in chapter 4, operates necessarily in a moral space; morality is always already a matter of entanglement with others. And it is as a precipitate of a nihilistic culture—that is, one which forgets or otherwise obscures this entanglement, with vast and dangerous implications for our understanding of the good life—that I will be looking at the codependence literature. Indeed, this focus helps to explain my use of the ontological-hermeneutic method: I am interested in nihilism as an ontology with certain implications for our moral lives, so I will be primarily concerned with the moral and ontological dimensions of the self which are presented to us in the codependence texts.

Another prejudice that I am assuming, but whose validity I will not be at great pains to demonstrate, is that there is a psychological realm which it is valuable to investigate, and which can give rise to techniques of psychotherapy that are also valuable. While I will be critical of a psychology that forgets, leaves silent, or otherwise conceals its own ontological and moral claims, I by no means intend to throw the baby out with the bathwater. I believe there is individual, psychologically comprehensible suffering, some of which is disclosed by the codependence texts, and that it cries out to be ameliorated. I am suspicious, however, of attempts at that amelioration that take place without due regard given to the explication of the horizon against which both the suffering and the healing can take place. With Habermas, I am aware of the possibility that such attempts might unwittingly reproduce and strengthen an ideology which contains domination of one set of interests over and against another. The point, then, is not to accuse the writers of self-help books of confusing us about our identities so much as it is to look at the suffering they seek to ameliorate, and to interrogate both the problem and the proposed solutions from a point of view that is psychological without being psychologistic.

This prejudice also implies a limitation of this book. I do not claim to be discussing the lived experience of those whose distress is described in the codependence texts and who turn to these books for help. This means that, for instance, my critique of the literature's presentation of the Twelve-Step program cannot be read as a wholesale critique of that therapeutic milieu. By concentrating on texts alone, I necessarily remain muted about what is actually happening in the world of a particular codependent person, or how the experience of participation in a Twelve-Step group is actually taken up in the lives of individuals. Such questions as these, as I will discuss further in my concluding chapter, are important to raise. I intend this study, however, to give a shape to research into those questions which sidesteps the pitfalls of traditional psychological research.

Why the Codependence Literature?

I have already indicated that I think the codependence literature offers a unique kind of text for hermeneutic explication. As a genre concerned to tell us who we are, and how we can be better at being what it says we are, it announces itself openly as providing what Ricoeur claims is only present latently in a text.

This "openness" raises some important questions. Some texts, it can be argued, leave little room for the "self-enlarging" dialogue that Ricoeur identifies as the work of appropriation. We can glimpse this problem in the ongoing debate among feminists, civil libertarians, and social commentators (and others) on "pornographic" works such as those of various rap groups. Some understand the texts as leaving no room for interpretation, offering only what amounts to a prescriptive account of prejudice, cruelty, and violence. Seen in this light, the texts are alarming, and censorship or some other public sanction becomes a possibility for the commonweal. Others argue that the texts offer an opportunity to glimpse practices that might otherwise be concealed, to understand them as the cruelties of a culture, and thus to engender criticism and amelioration of those cruelties in the society at large. The debate, then, hinges on the question of the texts' openness to interpretation and criticism.

I noted above that this question takes on an interesting dimension as the text more baldly purports to tell us who we are, as the codependence books do. A danger arises here: the texts might put the possibility of enlargement through dialogue with them out of play completely. As I will argue in detail later, this possibility is crucial in an age in which, as Nietzsche proclaimed, God is dead. Taylor (1989) points out that this proclamation, which he understands as the breakdown of metadiscourse, leaves us to invent our own moral orientation through narrative. My "sense of the good has to be woven into my understanding of my life as an unfolding story . . . we grasp ourselves in narrative" (p. 48). This essential work of being human in an inhuman age, then, encompasses both recollection and anticipation: the narrative gives us a sense of ourselves in the present only by a particular understanding of where we have been and where we are going. Following MacIntyre (1984), both Taylor and Bellah et al. (1985) argue that a central problem of modern culture is in the inarticulacy of these narratives. But self-help literature in general, and the codependence genre in particular, would appear to represent an articulation of at least one narrative. In MacIntyre's reading it is a narrative given to us, which itself purports to shape the "quest" that constitutes modern life. It is thus capable of determining the direction and structure, as well as the content, of the narratives by which we understand the good and strive to achieve it. And it is capable of doing this not by inviting a self-enlarging dialogue, but rather by invoking an authority that explicitly leaves no room for interpretation, as if the Cheshire cat appeared to Alice as only a grin, and insisted that there was no body attached to that smile.

A text such as "Nasty as They Wanna Be" (an album by the rap group 2 Live Crew which led to their arrest) at least leaves open the possibility of a critical and ironic self-understanding (Hitchens, 1990). It does not announce itself as telling the listener who he or she ought to be; it is ambiguous as to whether it is presenting a situation that is, and that should be, criticized, or one that is already acceptable, whether it is social satire or social prescription. But the codependence text, as I will argue in detail later, does not even contain that ambiguity, and, in important ways, explicitly conceals it. It announces itself to the reader as an articulation of an ideal identity, provided by an "expert." It strengthens its claim to that authority by presenting an account of the distress the reader is suffering, an account which is, to judge by the reception of these books, compelling. To present a text about self-understanding to a self that understands itself in front of a text thus threatens to short-circuit that understanding in a way other kinds of texts might not. Self-help books, as Kaminer (1992) observes, contribute to the "dumbing down of general interest books" (p. 8); they invite the reader to engage in reading as a technique for gathering information rather than as an occasion for practicing interpretation or for otherwise being critical. The work that Ricoeur suggests is crucial to reading is put out of play by these texts; this is a part of their latent meaning. That work has already been done by the authority. All the self must do to be enlarged is to take in the material presented.

The retrieval made possible by a hermeneutic analysis of the codependence books, then, has a twofold aspect. First, it might, like any such analysis, ferret out the cultural inscriptions lying beneath the texts. Second, it might open up a space that is specifically foreclosed in the text, a space whose eclipse is really the eclipse of the texts' cultural world; it might bring the cat out of its hiding place. In what follows, this concealment will itself be seen as an inscription of the culture, perhaps as its characteristic way of inscribing itself: the books will show up as a sort of anticulture, and this erasure will show up as a major constituent of the horizons within which we live. A hermeneutic analysis of the codependence literature will thus allow us to glimpse the nihilism of our culture at work.

Another reason for pursuing this particular literature is its enormous success in the marketplace. We will see nihilism at work not in obscure philosophical argumentation, but rather in a mass phenomenon. Indeed, as Kaminer (1992) notes, "this amorphous disease [codependence] is a business, generating millions of book sales, countless support groups, and . . . the First National Conference on Co-dependency . . ." (p. 9). As of 25 November 1990, *Codependent No More* (Beattie, 1987) had been on *The New York Times Book Review*'s "Advice, How to and miscellaneous" best-seller list for 116 weeks. As of February 1994, it had sold over three million copies. Some publishers, for example, HarperColliins and Dell, have created special lines of "recovery" books; and one publisher—Health Communications, Inc.—claims sales of 1.5 million for its top-selling book, *Adult Children of Alcoholics* (Woititz, 1983). These figures, while falling short of proving the claim that codependence affects 96 percent of us, lend prima facie support to the notion that these books strike a chord in the consciousnesses of many Americans. If discovering ourselves in front of texts and understanding our lives in narratives are central themes of the modern age and if people are buying narratives by the millions in which to discover themselves in a particular way, then an examination of the meanings of those texts promises to provide a glimpse into the understanding of the modern self and its vicissitudes.

Nor is this popularity limited to the world of mass-market paperback readers. Indeed, the language and concepts of the codependence literature pervades the current clinical climate. "Recovery" has come to dominate the offerings of seminars and workshops offered to professionals. Peele (1989) has noted this trend with dismay, referring to it as "the diseasing of America," accusing this kind of treatment of being "out of control." My observations as a therapist lead me to believe that this understanding of the self and its relationships is emerging as a paradigm for psychopathology and psychotherapy among both practitioners and their clients. I have heard many therapists express a concern regarding the pervasiveness of this literature, a vague discomfort with its popularity and its teachings. Such discontent, however, remains largely unarticulated, and can easily be dismissed as the grumblings of disaffected, and possibly envious, psychologists. An interpretive study can provide an understanding of, and a way to evaluate, this clinical dimension of the literature.

Finally, I would note that the philosophical dimensions of the psychological self have come into question in the last decade. Works such as

Hales's (1986) exposition of the "inadvertent rediscovery of the self" in social psychological research, Bellah et al.'s (1985) indictment of the inarticulacy of the therapeutic, Cushman's (1990) account of psychology's "empty self," and Hillman's (1992) recent charge that "we've had a hundred years of psychotherapy and the world's getting worse" all issue a challenge to psychology to clarify the self that it purports to study and treat. These challenges call into question the social, political, and moral dimensions of a widespread contemporary self-understanding, and particularly psychology's complicity in the inarticulacy of those dimensions. And the codependence literature is, I think, particularly well-suited to shed light on those aspects. For it is an account of modern selfhood which, as I have already noted, turns on a particular understanding of human relatedness. The distress we suffer comes about, according to these texts, primarily because of a misguided approach to relationships, which itself is the legacy of other troubled relationships, and which is ameliorated by a better understanding and practice of interpersonal relationships. I have suggested above, and I will be at great pains to detail below, that the modern construal of relationships is a key to understanding the nihilism of our times.

The codependence literature, then, by inscribing, albeit unwittingly, a moral world, offers a document of that construal. That inscription remains to be illuminated. A hermeneutic interpretation of these texts will offer a way to get at how we understand ourselves and our entanglement in a world of others. Moreover, it might begin to answer the challenge posed by critics like those mentioned above. It can do this by asking a question that many psychologists, in their pursuit of "science in the absence of the world," have failed to ask: what kind of self is being sold in these books, and what are the implications of such a self?

3

The Contours of the Codependence Genre

The growing importance of the publishing business is not merely based on the fact that publishers (perhaps through the process of marketing their books) come to have the best ear for the needs of the public or that they are better businessmen than are authors. Rather their peculiar work takes the form of a procedure that plans and that establishes itself with a view to the way in which, through the prearranged and limited publication of books and periodicals, they are to bring the world into the picture for the public and confirm it publicly.

—Heidegger, *The Age of the World Picture*, Appendix 3

INTRODUCTION

What "world" does the collection of books that comprise the code-pendence literature bring into focus for the public? This is one of the guiding questions of the work at hand. To answer it, we must first delineate the field of our investigation, mark its boundaries, and describe its contours. Once we know which books we are reading and what they have to say to us, we can begin to bring into focus the world picture that they offer.

This chapter will attempt to provide this focus, first by examining the larger body of literature in which the codependence books find their place. A look at these books will give us an idea of both the history of the wider popular psychology discourse that takes up the concerns addressed by the codependence literature and the nature and breadth of those concerns. Next, I will argue that while these issues are salient in a large number of books, only certain texts announce themselves as codependence texts; these books can thus be said to comprise the codependence literature. Finally, I will address the question of which of these books ought to be examined in order to make good a claim to be offering an interpretation of the literature as a whole. I will argue that the literature is largely homogeneous. This homogeneity will show up both in the uniformity of the texts' accounts of codependence and "recovery," and in their suppression of any differences which do emerge. The books that comprise the literature will thus be seen as virtually interchangeable units. At the same time, there are significant differences within the literature, which are openly acknowledged, usually on the covers of the books. These have to do with their popularity, measured in sales volume. So, I will argue, it makes sense to look to the four best-selling books, which have collectively sold more than three million copies, to be our exemplary texts.

THE ALGEBRA OF "RECOVERY":
ACOA + WWLTM = ACDF

Bookstores and publishers have provided an environment so favorable to the "recovery" meme that it is possible to speak of a "recovery" genre. This category of literature has not been constituted by agreement among scholars, but instead democratically, at least to the extent that the marketplace is democratic. According to store owners and publishing company spokespersons, at some point in the late 1980s, many people began to ask for books about "recovery," and the industry responded by creating a category and shelf space to hold the books that already addressed this issue, but had previously been called "self-help" or "psychology" books. Subsequent books were included under the new rubric from the time they were published.

I visited a random sample of 17 bookstores in urban, suburban, and rural areas in southern New England, and found that this distinction has been widely adopted. All but three of these stores have a shelf area devoted either to "recovery" or "self-help." In two of the exceptions, the titles found in the other stores under "recovery" are found in shelves labeled "psychology." The third exception is a store called "The Quest" which advertises itself as "your one-stop recovery shop," and offers a wide range of books (approximately 225) on the subject of addiction and recovery. One publisher—Health Communications, Inc.—publishes a sixty-three-page consumer catalog, titled *Discover Recovery* (HCI, 1990), offering approximately 300 books, pamphlets, and audio- and video-tapes related to "recovery," most of which it publishes. In addition, the "recovery" shelves often contain periodicals such as *Changes: For and About Adult children* (a monthly magazine), the *U.S. Journal* (a trade news-paper for the "recovery" field), and various local newsletters (e.g., *Northeast Recovery Network*).

The books on these shelves concern themselves with a vision of psychological suffering and healing based on an addiction model. Addiction, according to this vision, is not limited to chemical dependency (see Peele and Brodsky, 1975), but is a concept used to describe "any process over which we are powerless" (Schaef, 1987, p. 18). Addictions to drugs and alcohol are considered to be a subset of addictions in general, what Schaef (1987, p. 20) calls "ingestive addictions." But because addiction is powerlessness in the face of a dependence on a "process that relieves intolerable reality" (Mellody, Miller, and Miller, 1989, p. 52), it is possible to be "addicted" to such everyday experiences as "accumulating money," "gambling," "sex," "work," "religion," or "worry" (Schaef, 1987, pp. 22-24). This is by no means an exhaustive list; as Schaef points out "almost anything, substance or process, *can* become addictive" (p. 24, emphasis in original).

Indeed, the addiction model is held not only to explain most psychological dysfunctions; it also describes the existential condition of most people: "96 percent of us" need to be "in recovery." Schaef (1987) argues that "the system in which we live is an addictive system" (p. 4), that society has itself become an addict: our social institutions themselves function like addicted individuals. And addiction, in turn, is best understood as a disease.

> It fits the disease concept in that it has an *onset* (a point at which the person's life is just not working, usually as the result of an addiction), a *definable* course (the person continues to deteriorate mentally, physically, psychologically and spiritually), and, untreated, has a *predictable outcome* (death). (Schaef, 1986, p. 6)

This understanding of psychological suffering caught on. Aided perhaps by the "war on drugs" declared in the early 1980s, the American public, by decade's end, had become preoccupied by the apparent existence of widespread addiction.

The "recovery" referred to by the name of this genre is thus a recovery from addiction, an end to the dependence held to be common to most of our psychological distress. And it has a universal cure: participation in a so-called Twelve-Step group, modeled on the principles of Alcoholics Anonymous. (See Appendix A for a list of the Twelve Steps for codependents.) Beattie (1990b, pp. 231-40) lists thirty different Twelve-Step groups "for codependency and related issues." This list shows the wide range in focus of the recovery model, listing along with the well-known Alcoholics Anonymous groups like "Emotions Anonymous," whose goal is "to help people recover from a variety of emotional difficulties, from severe, chronic mental illness to anger, guilt depression grief, anxiety and phobias" (p. 234); "Fundamentalists Anonymous," which assists "people recovering from an experience with a fundamentalist religious group" (p. 235); and "Recovering Couples Anonymous," intended "for couples in recovery together" (p. 237). There is a Twelve-Step group, it would seem, to help bring about "recovery" from any problem. And, it seems, there is at least one book to describe that problem as an addiction and to urge its readers to seek the support and healing fellowship of such a group.

The codependence literature occupies the area within this genre that concerns itself with "recovery" from an "addiction" to debilitating relationships. In this concern, the literature can be seen as the intersection of two separate but related streams of self-help discourse. The first of these streams is a literature that originated in the late 1970s and early 1980s, and by 1989 had developed into what Peele (1989) has described as

> the single hottest theme on the alcoholism and addiction-conference circuits . . . spread[ing] well beyond professionals to reach the general public as the result of best-sellers, television specials, and magazine stories. (p. 123)[1]

This stream of literature is concerned with a population known as Adult Children of Alcoholics (ACOA's); it offers an account of the "disease" thought to plague such people, and a program (almost always based on the Twelve Steps) for recovery.

The notion that alcoholism is a "family disease" is not new to the ACOA literature. Indeed, the "co-alcoholic"—usually the wife of an alcoholic, and later to be known as the codependent—was identified as a clinically relevant entity as early as the 1950s, when Al-Anon (the Twelve-Step group for families of alcoholics) was formed (Cermak, 1986, p. 15). By its own account, Al-Anon "began with the wives of early AA members who realized their own need to change" (Al-Anon, 1981, p. xi). These wives had come to think of themselves as "enabling" the drinking, contributing by force of their own personalities to the other person's addiction. This idea found theoretical support in the family systems theories that began to emerge in the 1950s (see, e.g., Bowen, 1978, or Bateson, 1972, pp. 309-37, for accounts of the interplay between these two fields). Alcoholism was, according to these theories, best understood as a "family disease" insofar as the drinker was a part of a system that required all of its members to act in certain ways in order to ensure the homeostasis of the system. Each person, caught up in a system that determined his or her role in it, had no choice but to participate. The alcoholic had to drink, according to this theory, and the co-alcoholic had to enable the drinking, and neither would change until and unless the whole system had changed. Family therapy became important in alcoholism treatment, because it could focus "attention on each family member's contribution to the family's dysfunction" (Cermak, 1986, p. 15).

If the co-alcoholic is to be understood as suffering from her own disease, which requires its own treatment, then what of the children in the alcoholic's family? This question is addressed by the ACOA literature, which is perhaps best represented by two of its most popular books: Woititz's *Adult Children of Alcoholics* (1983), whose publisher claims sales of 1.5 million copies (HCI catalog, 1990), and Black's *It Will Never Happen to Me* (1981), whose cover proclaims it to be a "million copy best-seller." ACOA's, of course, cannot be said to come into the family with their disease already in place, as the co-alcoholic does. Rather, as Black (1981) tells us,

> For children in the family, the combination of alcoholism and co-alcoholism results in neither parent being responsive and available on a consistent, predictable basis. Children are affected not only by the alcoholic parent, but also by the nonalcoholic parent (if there is one), and by the abnormal family dynamics created as a consequence of alcoholism. (p. xv)

If the parents are "victims" of a disease of uncertain etiology, the children's difficulties have a clear provenance: the unavailability of their parents deprives them of the care they need to flourish. They are forced to find ways to cope with this deprivation, and the "development of [such] coping behavior often results in emotional and psychological deficits" (Black, 1981, pp. 9-10). These deficits, in turn, become hindrances in their adult lives, and ACOA's are, as a population, according to Black, "drawn into problem drinking, marrying someone who becomes alcoholic, or having an unusual number of problems in their adult years" (p. 10). This fate is all but inescapable. In capital letters,

Black announces that "the bottom line is: ALL CHILDREN RAISED IN ALCOHOLIC HOMES NEED TO BE ADDRESSED. ALL CHILDREN ARE AFFECTED" (p. 23).

Although there is some disagreement within the alcoholism treatment field about the homogeneity of the population constituted by children of alcoholics (see, e.g., Gierymski and Williams, 1986), the sales numbers indicate that the marketplace has heartily endorsed these books' characterization of ACOA's. The message that is so popular and lucrative is also relatively simple. People reading an ACOA book would find that they belong to a population whose members, because of their history of childhood "deprivation," have come to lack "self-esteem" and "self-definition." This, in Black's (1981) words, brings the person to

> have difficulties identifying and expressing feelings. They become very rigid and controlling. Some find themselves overly dependent on others; they feel no sense of power of choice in the way they live. A pervasive sense of fear and guilt often exists in their lives. Many experience depression and frequently do not have the ability to feel close or to be intimate with another human being. (p. xvi)

Woititz's (1983) list of ACOA characteristics, while longer and more comprehensive, is clearly similar to Black's.

> Adult children of alcoholics guess at what normal behavior is . . . have difficulty following a project from beginning to end . . . lie when it would be just as easy to tell the truth . . . judge themselves without mercy . . . have difficulty having fun . . . take themselves very seriously . . . have difficulty with intimate relationships . . . overreact to changes over which they have no control . . . constantly seek approval and affirmation . . . usually feel that they are different from other people . . . are super responsible or super irresponsible . . . are extremely loyal even in the face of evidence that their loyalty is undeserved . . . are impulsive. . . . (pp. 4-5)

Both of these accounts hold that a lack of identity and of feelings of well-being characterize ACOA's. As a result of these deficiencies, these people cannot engage in successful relationships. They are too reactive and dependent to do so, and will either drive the other away with their relentless need to control him or her; or, more likely, they will find themselves loyal beyond reason to someone who is undeserving of it, and thus without the choice to leave such a person. Because their parents failed to provide them with a sense of security about themselves, ACOA's do not have the sense of autonomy that would allow them to "continue into adulthood with a greater sense of self, well-being, and a growing ability to have their needs met—and most importantly to live a satisfying life" (Black, 1981, p. xvii). Woititz (1983) explains the problem this way:

> As a result of the fear of abandonment, you don't feel confident about yourself. You don't feel good about yourself, or believe that you are lovable. So you look to others for what it is that you cannot give yourself in order to feel O.K. You feel O.K. if someone else tells you that you are O.K. Needless to say, you give away a great deal of power. In a relationship you give the other person the power to lift you up or knock you down. You feel wonderful if they treat you well and tell you that you are wonderful, but when they don't these feelings no longer belong to you. (p. 44)

The "disease" proposed by this literature, then, is largely characterized by the failure to be able to function ("feel O.K.") independent of the assessment or actions of another, and thus to be a self who is "powerful" and "self-contained." A person is "sick" to the extent that he or she cannot attain this hermetic autonomy.

If the loss of this kind of self is a disease, then it stands to reason that "recovery" consists of an an "empowering" of this self, and a concomitant attaining of hermetic autonomy. In Woititz's (1983) rendering of this "recovery," the ACOA moves from being someone who is not "O.K." to someone who is "no longer a victim" (p. 106). She describes the outcome of "recovery" (and the role of her book in it) in this way.

> You are in the center of your own universe. What a special place to be.
>
> When you start to feel pulled, or driven, explore those feelings, don't judge them, and then let go of them in order to maintain your serenity and stay in the flow of your life.
>
> The process of life is an adventure. Twisting, turning, going where it needs to go and you with it right in the center but letting it take its course. This is a peaceful and serene attitude, like that of Alcoholics Anonymous. . . .
>
> Life is an ongoing process. If you are centered, if you are in control of your feelings, thoughts and desires, you journey through life taking many little roads along the way and experience each phase fully and completely. If you are in the center of your life and not being pulled and swayed by your own impulses and by the desires of others you will have a sense of serenity, a sense of real comfort within yourself.
>
> That's what this book is all about. It offers the knowledge of where you were, and where you are. It puts today and tomorrow firmly in your hands. The choices are yours, whatever they may be. You are in charge of you and that's all that really matters. (p. 106)

Woititz's description of the recovered self discloses the background against which the ACOA's condition shows up as a disease: a "healthy" self is one that has "recovered" the qualities of being centered, in control, and firmly in possession of its destiny. A "de-centered" self, on the other hand, is the legacy of a childhood in an alcoholic family, and is what must be "recovered" from.

The ACOA literature, then, introduces the idea that the "loss of self," while not itself an addictive disease, is nonetheless a symptom of one's having such a disease. The "recovery" of a "centered" self, one which knows independently of others that it is "O.K.," is the only way out of the addictive system, and constitutes "health." This notion of sickness and cure, as we will see, is figural in the codependence literature. But our examination of that literature awaits another development in the recovery genre, one that focuses some of the issues raised in the ACOA literature, while at the same time broadening its claims.

This literature is best represented by a series of books that appeared in the middle 1980s. With titles like *Smart Women, Foolish Choices* (Cowan and Kinder, 1985) and *Men Who Hate Women and the Women Who Love Them* (Forward and Torres, 1987), these books take up a problem perhaps best summarized by the title of one of them: *Do I Have to Give up Me to Be Loved by You?* (Paul and Paul, 1983). Of course, Black (1981) and Woititz (1983) both sound this theme: a de-centered self is "overly dependent on others" (Black) and is "extremely loyal," even beyond reason (Woititz). But this second stream is primarily interested in the tendency of many women (not only ACOA's) to sacrifice themselves in order to keep a relationship, to "lose themselves" in love. These "women who love too much" suffer from a condition discussed in a book by that name (Norwood, 1985), whose cover claims sales of over two million copies.

While there are, of course, some differences among these books (e.g., Forward and Torres [1987] concentrate more on the psychology of the "men who hate women" than does Norwood [1985]; Paul and Paul [1983] do not explicitly limit the problem to women), there is no conflict in their claims about what the problem is, and how it arises. Some women, they argue, repeatedly find themselves in relationships with men who cannot satisfy their "needs." But instead of reacting to this situation by becoming dissatisfied and ending the relationship, these women go on to try to change themselves and, as a result, the man's reaction to them, so that the relationship will become sufficient to meet their needs. Although this project is like getting blood out of a turnip, the woman knows no other means of pursuing and securing love relationships; moreover, she is "searching for a relationship to give her a sense of self-worth" (Norwood, 1985, p. 272), so she ends up narrowing the focus of her life to repeated, but futile, self-sacrificial efforts to improve the relationship. The relationship becomes an obsession.

> Loving too much . . . means . . . obsessing about a man and calling that obsession love, allowing it to control your emotions and much of your behavior, realizing that it negatively influences your health and well-being, and yet finding yourself unable to let go. It means measuring the degree of your love by the degree of your torment. (p. 5)

This kind of "obsession" had perhaps its most vivid portrayal in the 1987 film, *Fatal Attraction*, which played to large audiences nationwide, and engendered a number of articles in the popular media about women who love too much.

But while "obsession" may be a good description of this manner of being in a relationship, it is not the most favored by authors of the woman-who-loves-too-much (WWLTM) books. Rather, they argue, the intense focus is better understood as a "disease process, [an] addiction to doomed relationships with emotionally unavailable men" (Norwood, 1985, p. 13; see also Cowan and Kinder, 1985, pp. 120-37, and Cassell, 1984, for accounts of "love addiction"). Norwood describes the experience of one of her clients in this fashion:

> The addictive aspect of Jill's behavior in her relationship parallels the addictive use of a drug. Early in each of her relationships there was an initial "high", a feeling of euphoria and excitement while she believed that finally her deepest needs for love, attention, and emotional security might be met. Believing this, Jill became more and more dependent on the man and the relationship in order to feel good. Then, like an addict who must use a drug more as it produces less effect, she was driven to pursue the relationship harder as it gave her less satisfaction and fulfillment. Trying to sustain what had once felt so wonderful, so promising, Jill slavishly dogged her man, needing more contact, more reassurance, more love as she received less and less. The worse the situation became, the harder it was to let go because of the depth of her need. She could not quit. (Norwood, 1985, p. 13)

If being an ACOA can be understood as a malady that is a consequence of living with someone who has an addictive disease, loving too much can be understood as, in itself, constituting a full-fledged addictive syndrome.

The WWLTM genre can be understood as offering an expanded exposition of the interpersonal consequences of the kind of deprivation described by the ACOA. Because she does not have a strongly defined self, the WWLTM, like the ACOA, becomes susceptible to addiction, which in turn can be understood as an excessive dependence on something outside oneself. But where Black (1981) is vague about this "something"—noting that women who do not become or marry alcoholics face the prospect of "having an unusual number of problems in their adult years" (p. 10)—Norwood is clear: a person with a de-centered self is excessively dependent on, and thus easily addicted to, other people. She has to give herself up in order to be loved.

But if this description focuses the issues of relationship raised by the ACOA literature, it also broadens its target: Norwood introduces her book by claiming that "most of us have loved too much at least once and for many of us it has been a recurrent theme in our lives" (p. xiii). While she is aware that "all the characteristics of women who love too much are usually present in the daughters and wives of alcoholics and other addicts" (p. 48), she claims that such a background is not necessary for a woman to suffer from excessive loving. And, judging again from the popularity of the literature, its claim of a wide applicability is not misplaced. Indeed, the accuracy of its portrayal of relationships has been acknowledged even by the critics of these books: even a critical article like Rapping's (1990) notes that books like Norwood's "lay out, in plain English, and with extensive examples, what is clearly a serious problem for many women and some men" (p. 316). The idea that women become enslaved to the men they love, and that this suffering is best understood as a disease, was apparently one whose time had come in the middle 1980s.

If it is not only ACOA's who can become WWLTM's, what is the etiology of the latter malady? Why do so many women—even those whose parents were not alcoholics—suffer from "low self-esteem, a need to be needed, a strong urge to change and control others, and a willingness to suffer" (Norwood, 1985, p. 48)? Norwood's account overlaps with that of the ACOA literature, suggesting that the WWLTM failed to receive the love and nurturing to which she was apparently entitled as a child. But this kind of deprivation does not necessarily have alcoholism at its root. Norwood (pp. 7-9) lists the fifteen characteristics common to WWLTM's, the first of which is, "Typically, you came from a dysfunctional home in which your emotional needs were not met" (p. 7). The WWLTM then goes on to "try to fill this unmet need vicariously by becoming a care-giver, especially to men who appear in some way needy" (p. 17). This explanation of relationship addiction clearly is indebted to Freud's (1920/1961) description of the repetition compulsion, in which, it is thought, the neurotic person continues to put him or herself into the traumatic situation in order to "resolve" it. The etiology of the disease of excessive loving is to be found in the family impoverished in loving. And this poverty can be found not just in families beset by addiction, but in any "dysfunctional home."

But how are we to understand this apparently pervasive dysfunction? What is "dysfunctional" about a family that produces someone who loves excessively? Norwood's (1985) account suggests an answer: if you come from such a family, then chances are "your emotional needs were not met" by it. Norwood explains:

> "Emotional needs" does not refer only to your needs for love and affection . . . even more critical is the fact that your perceptions and feelings were largely ignored or denied rather than accepted and validated. And example: Parents are fighting. Child feels afraid. Child asks mother, "Why are you mad at Daddy?" Mother answers, "I'm not mad," while looking angry and troubled. Child now feels confused, more afraid and says, "I heard you shouting." Mother replies angrily, "I told you I'm not mad but I'm going to be if you keep this up!" Child now feels fear, confusion, anger and guilt. Her parent has implied that her perceptions are incorrect, but if that is true, where are these feelings of fear coming from? The child must now choose between knowing that she is right and that her parent has deliberately lied to her, or thinking that she is wrong in what she hears, sees, and feels. . . . This impairs a child's ability to trust herself and her perceptions, both in childhood and later in adulthood, especially in close relationships. (pp. 14-15)

The "dysfunctional" family is one that fails to give the child an adequate sense of competence and validity about herself. Such a child is not one who "cherishes every aspect of herself: her personality, her appearance, her beliefs and values, her body, her interests and accomplishments" (p. 272). Instead, she places herself in relationships with people and substances which she loves too much, which in turn reflects her inability to love herself enough. Such people are common because such families are common: Norwood claims that "dysfunctional homes are those in which one or more of the following occur"

- abuse of alcohol and/or other drugs (prescribed or illicit)
- compulsive behavior such as compulsive eating, working, cleaning, gambling, spending, dieting, exercising and so on . . .
- battering of spouse and/or children
- inappropriate sexual behavior on the part of a parent toward a child, ranging from seductiveness to incest
- constant arguing and tension

- extended periods of time in which parents refuse to speak to each other
- parents who have conflicting attitudes or values or display contradictory behaviors that compete for their children's allegiance
- parents who are competitive with each other or with their children
- a parent who cannot relate to others in the family and thus actively avoids them, while blaming them for this avoidance
- extreme rigidity about money, religion, work, use of them, displays of affection, sex, television, housework, sports, politics, and so on. . . . (pp. 15-16)

This list of characteristics might apply, as a whole or in part, to many households. By focusing on a population of excessively loving women, Norwood casts a wide net.

To understand better the breadth of the notion of the "dysfunctional family," and as a final prelude to taking up the codependence literature itself, we must turn to one more source of self-help. John Bradshaw is a best-selling author (Bradshaw, 1988a, 1988b), and was the host of the popular public television show "Bradshaw On: The Family." He is described by his publisher as "an internationally recognized marriage and family counselor, alcohol and drug abuse counselor, management consultant, and public speaker" (Health Communications, Inc., 1990, p. 20). A theologian by training, he is a "recovering" alcoholic with a charismatic style, and his message is one that does not fit neatly into the ACOA or WWLTM category, for his target population is neither ACOA's or women, but rather the children of the "96 percent of all families that are to some degree emotionally impaired" (Health Communications, Inc., 1990, p. 20). If we were to name this population, it would perhaps best be called "Adult Children of Dysfunctional Families" (ACDF's), borrowing from the ACOA literature the notion that the presence of a particular pathology in a household's functioning gives rise to a congruent pathology in its children, and from the WWLTM literature the notion that many nonalcoholic families bear the same pathology.

Bradshaw's 96 percent figure reflects his sense that the "dysfunctional family" is the predominant kind of household in this country: "There is a crisis in the family today. It has to do with our parenting rules and the multigenerational process by which families perpetuate these rules" (Bradshaw, 1988a, p. 2). Because these "rules" are the predominant parenting rules in our culture, they are handed down from generation to generation; "emotionally impaired" families give rise to emotionally impaired children, who in turn "create new dysfunctional families" (Bradshaw, 1988a, p. 62). ACOA's and WWLTM's are only subpopulations within the larger group of ACDF's, and the latter group can be thought of as comprising virtually all of us.

Like writers such as Norwood (1985) and Black (1981), Bradshaw (1988a, 1988b) places his notion of dysfunction against a normative idea of a functioning family. And, like them, he contends that it is the work of families to produce children who love themselves.

> There are healthy and fully functioning families. To say that something is functional is to say that everything works. My car, for example, may have rust spots on the trunk, but if it drives well, then it is fully functional. It works. (Bradshaw, 1988a, pp. 41-42)

When the family "works," then all of its "running parts," including its children, also "work"; and for children this means they can attain "maturity." According to Bradshaw (1988a):

> A mature person is one who has differentiated himself from all others and established clearly marked ego boundaries. A mature person has a good identity. Such a person is able to relate to his family system in meaningful ways without being fused or joined to them. This means that one is emotionally free and can choose to move near without anger or absorption and move away without guilt. (p. 42)

The sickness common to ACDF's is that their families have failed to provide the "soil for mature peoplemaking" (Bradshaw, 1988a, p. 42), that is, for making them autonomous people, mature in their ability to have and maintain a "good identity"—one held independently of others. As parents, then, this 96 percent go on to inflict what Miller (1979/1981) has called "the poisonous pedagogy" on their own children. In this view, a child is held to be "the most available object of gratification for narcissistically deprived parents . . . [and] thus becomes reduced to being an instrument of the parent's will" (Bradshaw, 1988a, p. 69). The child's need for others to affirm him or her is exploited in such a way that the child becomes a slave and the parent a master. The family is then not at all "the soil which provides the emotional needs of the various members . . . provid[ing] the growth and development of each member" (p. 42); rather, it becomes a polluted environment, one in which the "deep inner unity" that is held to constitute a healthy person is irrevocably contaminated.

> Born in the soil of their parents' alienated split selves, there is no way for the children to get what they absolutely need for healthy growth. More

than anything else they actually need models of good self-love and social interest. Since their parents are split and non-self-accepting, they cannot model good self-nurturing love. There is *no way for the children to learn self-love and social interest.*" (p. 67, emphasis in original)

The ACDF's loss, then, is of both self and the possibility of "healthy" relationships. As in the other books discussed here, the guiding notion of Bradshaw's work is that without a "good identity," relationship is impossible. The self that has been nurtured to maturity can "choose to move near . . . and move away," can engage in relationships without being either too distant or too close. This golden mean is attained by exercising the power of choice, and it is precisely this "power" that the ACDF lacks. The "dysfunctional" family fails to honor and encourage the child to explore his or her feelings, thoughts, and perceptions of the world, which thus impairs his or her sense of self. Such a family discourages the development of the self by means of shame, which Bradshaw defines as "total non-self acceptance" (1988a, p. 2). Shaming the child for his or her authentic expression of self, this family encourages the child to develop "a false self in order to survive" (p. 3). Bradshaw goes on:

> The false self forms a defensive mask which distracts from the pain and the inner loneliness of the true self. After years of acting, performing and pretending—one loses contact with who one really is. One's true self is numbed out. (pp. 3-4)

Insensitive to his or her own real self, ashamed of the vagaries of his or her emotional life, the ACDF suffers what Bradshaw calls "the blocking of choice" (p. 72): he or she is unable to know what he or she really wants, and is generally too ashamed to act on it even if it is known. The loss of the "true self" is really a loss of freedom, and specifically of freedom of choice. The nature of the child's contamination by the toxic family, then, is that he or she no longer has the full freedom which, in Bradshaw's view, "amounts to full functionality" (p. 49).

Bradshaw turns to Satir (1974) to flesh out his account of freedom. According to her, freedom is a natural endowment, and it comprises five entitlements.

1. The freedom to see and hear (perceive) what is here and now, rather than what was, will be or should be.
2. The freedom to think what one thinks, rather than what one should think.
3. The freedom to feel what one feels, rather than what one should feel.

4. The freedom to want (desire) and to choose what one wants, rather than what one should want.
5. And the freedom to imagine one's own self-actualization, rather than playing a rigid role or always playing it safe. (cited in Bradshaw, 1988a, p. 17)

The disastrous life choices taken up in the ACOA and WWLTM literature are here understood as the inescapable legacy of the "dysfunctional" family, which, by shaming the "real self," destroys the child's ability to make free choices. Unable to establish a strong "good identity," the ACDF has weak "ego boundaries" and, as Bradshaw says, "people with ego boundary problems contaminate their thinking with unresolved feelings, which cause the blocking of choice through the contamination of one's mind" (p. 72).

Bradshaw makes clear what the earlier literature mentioned here only implies: that the "dysfunctional family"—*any* dysfunctional family—is dysfunctional insofar as it robs the child of his or her capacity (and entitlement) to love him or herself sufficiently to make good choices without resorting to standards he or she does not constitute. One need not be the child of alcoholics to make bad choices, nor is the lack of freedom only to be found in a woman's tendency to enslave herself to a man. Rather, a person has "full functionality" only when "all the person's energy is free to flow outward in order to cope with the world in getting one's needs met. This allows one full freedom" (Bradshaw, 1988a, p. 49). And this is made possible only by a "healthy and fully functioning famil[y]" (p. 41), that is, a family that helps the child to be free to be him or herself. Then the adult child is free to engage in the relationships of his or her choice, knowing that the important questions to be asked of a prospective partner are, as Norwood (1985) puts it, "Is this relationship good for me? Does it enable me to grow into all I am capable of being?" (pp. 272-73).

A person who is not free to be him or herself is constrained in his choices: addiction might be considered a paradigm case of this constraint. A person who is addicted, whether to a substance or a person, lives without the freedom to leave behind and move close to what is outside of him or herself, according to the dictates of his or her "real self." So "recovery" becomes the re-acquisition of that "real self," who makes "good choices" and thus has the "freedom" that is his or her "birthright." This freedom might be understood as the ability to cope in a way that meet one's "needs," without taking into account other considerations, particularly those that are not derived from one's colloquy with oneself. To ask "Is this relationship good for *me*?" is clearly *not* to ask about some "good" which might come from outside the "real self."

These strains of recovery literature, then, view the ideal person as one who is autonomous in the sense that he or she is "centered" and in control of his or her life, and exercises that control by making "free choices." Those choices are, in turn, more or less successful or disastrous depending on the extent to which they reflect the person's "real self," and are independent of external constraint. The relative success of the choices can be seen in the degree of self-determination that they reflect and bring about in a person's life. And, of course, making such choices is not even possible until a person redeems the choice-making capacity that was lost to the "dysfunctional family." Prior to this redemption, such a person places him or herself in relationships and situations that are devoid of choice, namely, addictions. "Recovery," then, is the recapturing of the Satirean "freedom" taken away in the crucible of a family that enslaved the child, which led the child to become an adult who enslaves him or herself. It is important to point out that there can be no specific content to this "freedom," nothing which one ought to do or not to do. The only significant and valid distinction is not right/wrong, but rather choice/constraint. The "freedom" that one "recovers" is an emancipation of oneself from one's history so that one can go on to live a life unconstrained by forces outside the self.

The ACOA literature establishes that the destabilizing presence of an alcoholic in a family brings about a predictable "loss of self" in the children of that family. The WWLTM literature establishes that this loss shows up in daughters even of nonalcoholic families as the disease of "relationship addiction." Work like Bradshaw's (1988a, 1988b) extends those difficulties to all children of all "dysfunctional families." And the "disease" that best describes this constellation of difficulties is codependence. As Bradshaw says, "Co-dependence is the most common family illness because it is what happens to anyone in any kind of a dysfunctional family" (1988a, p. 164). The codependence literature is thus in many ways the culmination of these earlier "recovery" books. It focuses on the failure of people—men and women, children of alcoholics and nonalcoholics alike—to be free to engage in relationships that allow them "to be all that they can be." When a person finds his or her "choicemaking" (Wegscheider-Cruse, 1988) unduly constrained by the presence of another person in his or her life, then that person is said to be codependent. Beattie's (1987) definition of the disease, cited in chapter 2, is instructive here: "A codependent person is anyone who has let another person's behavior affect him or her, and who is obsessed with controlling that person's behavior" (p. 31). The codependent, because he or she has been robbed of his or her birthright of self-love and self-sufficiency, seeks peace and happiness through relationships. And, as Beattie says, "These behaviors can prevent us from finding peace and happiness with the most important person in our lives—ourselves" (p. 34). The codependence literature is an attempt to give the 96 percent of us who have forgotten this fact—that *we* are the most "important" person in our lives—a way to remember it (to "recover") and to have relationships based on this recovered self.

THE CONSTITUENT TEXTS OF THE CODEPENDENCE LITERATURE

Before turning to a closer analysis of this literature, it is necessary to describe its scope and to discuss the rationale for the sample of texts on which I will concentrate. I have been referring thus far to the codependence literature as if it were an established genre. But, as Bradshaw's assertion cited above makes clear, the "disease" is held to be widespread and cannot help but be at least implicit in any text taking up the problems of "dysfunctional families." The problem arises of how to narrow the field to allow for both a coherent focus for this study and a manageable sample of books for it to examine.

The virtual omnipresence of the codependence concept may be confirmed empirically by examining a paradox: despite their prevalence (and that of the "disease"), there is within the "recovery" literature no "official" distinction between codependence texts and other "recovery" books. The subject heading given on the back of the books for the use of bookstores is generally "wellness and recovery" or "psychology and self-help." But clearly (and not surprisingly, given Bradshaw's assertion), the subject is taken up by many, if not all, of these books.

It is quite possible that the absence of an industry distinction bears witness to the widespread diffusion of the concept across a number of texts. The index of the HCI catalog gives some confirmation to this explanation. It does list a number of texts under a "co-dependency" heading, but many of these turn up in other categories, such as "adult children," "relationships," and "shame and self-esteem" (Health Communications, Inc., 1991, pp. 55-60). Reading through the books on a bookstore's "recovery" shelves gives further confirmation: many "recovery" books discuss codependence. Bradshaw, for example, devotes a chapter of his book on the family (Bradshaw, 1988a, pp. 163-88) to a discussion of codependence as "the most common family illness," and mentions it in his book on "healing the shame that binds you" as one of the consequences of shame (Bradshaw, 1988b, p. 14). Other books, for example, Potter-Efron and Potter-Efron's *Letting Go of Shame* (1989) and Friel and Friel's *Adult Child's Guide to What's "Normal"* (1990), refer to a view of relationships that is congruent with Beattie's definition of code-pendence, but do not refer to it by name. Books like Norwood's (1985) and Black's (1981) predate the emergence of the notion of codepen-dence, and by limiting the population to women or ACOA's, are evi-dently discussing a smaller group of people than Beattie is. It would appear that codependence is truly so ubiquitous it does not need its own category within the self-help discourse any more than binocularity would within those concerned with human vision. We all (except for obvious cases) have two eyes, and we all have codependence; any text that discusses our vision takes for granted two-eyedness, and any text that discusses "recovery" takes for granted that we are codependent.

But the breadth of the literature's claims and the resulting ubiquity of its concerns in the "recovery" books must not deter us from pinning the genre down sufficiently to examine it. And it is important to remem-ber that my concern here is not so much with a concept or a mechanism that is discussed in a number of different books as with the presence of those books in the first place. I am interested in this literature as a pub-lic phenomenon, as a dominant form of popular culture, which, as I noted in the first chapter, announces itself as a "mirror" before which readers might stand in order to discover themselves. My interest is thus in what people who are reading about codependence are being told about who they are. It is, I think, safe to assume that the people buying these books are already interested in the notion of codependence, that they already think it is relevant to their lives in some way, when they go to the store. They have perhaps read or heard John Bradshaw tell them that the malaise they feel is the result of their history in a "dysfunc-tional family," and that that history makes them codependent. Or they may have seen the topic discussed on a popular television show like Oprah Winfrey's. Or their therapist has told them that they are code-pendent and ought to pick up a book or two on the subject. Or they are merely curious about this cultural phenomenon, perhaps even writing books about it. And it does not strain credulity to think that those books which announce themselves as codependence texts are those most likely to be purchased by people who, for whatever reason, want to read about codependence.

I think it is fair, therefore, to start with a definition of the bound-aries of the codependence literature that makes these assumptions, and then to say that a codependence book is any book that announces in its title that it takes that subject up, that the codependence literature is the group of books which do so. The titles thus excluded may still address the subject, but they are not as likely to be those purchased with an eye toward understanding the "disease." Moreover, as will become clear shortly, the literature is highly homogeneous; there is little disagreement within the genre about the nature of the "disease" or its cure. Very little in terms of understanding the concept of codependence will thus be lost by excluding those books that do not announce themselves as codependence texts. But we will gain a certainty that the books we are discussing are those read by people concerned with codependence.

This definition narrows the field substantially. While R.R. Bowker's August 1991 CD-ROM version of *Books in Print* lists 722 titles under the subject of "recovery" (most of which conceivably cover subjects closely related to codependence), it lists only 57 books with the "codepen . . ." root in their titles or subtitles. But this listing is not complete. Most of the books, for example, listed in the HCI catalog are *not* included in this database, and neither are those of CompCare, another press dedicated to books on addictions and related topics. Moreover, Bowker's June 1991 CD-ROM listing showed only 48 titles with the "codepen . . ." root; this 20 percent increase from June to August indicates that the books proliferate rapidly. A visit to The Quest (the "one-stop recovery shop") reveals books and pamphlets listed in neither *Books in Print* nor the private catalogs; rather, they are sent directly to the stores by small presses. It is impossible, then, to determine the exact contours of the genre even when it is narrowed to those books which announce themselves as codependence texts. But it is clear there is a substantial, if somewhat unaccountable, body of texts whose titles would appeal to a consumer in search of information about and help with his or her codependence.

THE HOMOGENEITY OF THE CODEPENDENCE LITERATURE

If the field is narrowed to the books with "codepen . . ." in their titles, this still leaves a large number of books, perhaps too large to allow for a concise description and analysis. To sharpen the focus further, I must take account of the risk that excluding some books that announce themselves as codependence texts would weaken my claim to be interpreting the genre as a whole.

But I think this risk is minimal because the literature, as we will soon see, is highly homogeneous. Clearly, with such a large number of texts, there is variety within the genre. But this variety has primarily to do with focus, with the particular aspect of codependence that is dis-

cussed, rather than with substantive alterations in or contention about
the claims made by other texts. Some books, for instance, focus on the
implications of codependence for parenting (Becnell, 1991), or even
grandparenting (Smith, 1988); others on the committed, adult, dyadic
relationship (Kritsberg, 1990; Ricketson, 1989); still others on love relationships in general (Cruse, 1989; Meier, Minirth, Hemfelt, and
Hawkins, 1989; Schaeffer, 1991). Some are explicitly Christian in their
orientation (Meier et al., 1989), although most adopt the nondenomi-
national spiritual focus of Alcoholics Anonymous (see, e.g., Bundesen,
1991). Some books are primarily theoretical (although still written for
the general reader), concerned with the etiology and development of the
"illness" (for instance, Schaef, 1986; Subby, 1987), and others are practical, offering workbooks for recovery (Mellody and Miller, 1989; Des
Roches, 1990; Weinhold and Weinhold, 1989). Yet others, notably
Beattie's *Codependent No More* (1987) and *Beyond Codependency* (1989),
have no particular focus but are concerned with a general description of
the condition that is the legacy of our "diseased" families.

But if focus is the variable, the notion of codependence is the constant. To make a preliminary review, I chose the twenty-seven books
that were available in one three-day period in three different types of
bookstore: a store in a national chain (Waldenbooks), a local independent bookstore, and the Twelve-Step specialty store called The Quest.
(See Appendix B for the list of these titles.) My reading of these books
indicates that they take up essentially the same concerns and treat them
in essentially the same way. This should not be surprising, given the literature's conceit that it is addressing a problem that "we" all have; in this
respect, it is possible to understand the codependence literature as an
intentional attempt to render a homogeneous picture of "the pain of
relatedness" and its palliation.

But clearly, I cannot sufficiently prove my claim that the codependence literature is homogeneous by reporting that I have read a number
of books and find them to be monolithic in their concerns, or by pointing out that this sameness fits one of the central tenets of the literature. One way to demonstrate this contention more conclusively would
be to place their claims side by side and show that they provide the
same understanding of the "disease" and its "cure." This approach, however, would be cumbersome and tedious; moreover, the homogeneity
can be shown in other ways, by appeal both to sources outside the genre
and to the texts themselves.

Even in outside sources, there is, as van Wormer (1989) has
pointed out, "a paucity of criticism . . . regarding the concept of co-
dependency" (p. 51). But even this small body of literature notices the

interchangeability of the texts. Krestan and Bepko (1990), for instance, refer to the "familiar language of codependency" (p. 216), and suggest that this language comprises a "myth" within the culture (p. 231). Descriptions such as this seem to assume the unified nature of the field; nowhere in the critical articles is there mention of controversy or disagreements among the codependence authors. Kaminer (1990) makes the point explicitly.

> What's striking about all the codependency books on the market (I've read 21) is their sameness. They may differ in levels of literacy and how they balance the discussion of codependency theory with recovery techniques. But they describe the same syndromes in the same jargon and prescribe the same cure—enlistment in a support group that follows an overtly religious recovery program . . . borrowed from Alcoholics Anonymous. Codependency books line the shelves in bookstores like different brands of aspirin in a drugstore. (p. 26)

Of course, I have no way of knowing what Kaminer's definition of "codependency books" is, or which twenty-one books she read, but her observation is consonant with my own reading of the twenty-seven books listed in Appendix B: these books all seem cut from the same cloth. They may be like aspirin, but another apt analogy (and one more suited to the analysis I will offer of the codependence literature as a narrative space) is to the Gothic romance novel: both genres comprise texts that tell the same story in different ways.

Still, however, this is only indirect and anecdotal evidence. The absence, observed by critics, of reference to conflict within the texts may only indicate the critics' overlooking controversy in order to make their arguments more convincing. The word of two outside observers, the construction of two analogies, is not sufficient to establish that the genre is monolithic. More proof is needed, and we can find it in the books themselves—not by turning to a comparison of their claims, but by examining their treatment of the few differences discernible among them.

The codependence writers are, of course, aware of one another, and, as Beattie (1989) points out ". . . many people in the recovery field say many of the same things" (p. xii). They freely quote one another. But they do disagree, and it is in their disagreements that the homogeneous nature of the genre can best be seen. For these conflicts are presented in such a way as to be suppressed: they disappear in the monolithic claims of the literature. It is not only that the texts "describe the same syndromes in the same jargon and prescribe the same cure"; moreover, the conflicts and controversies that do arise out of this sameness are treated in a way that makes them disappear *qua* difference.

The first "controversy" in which we might glimpse the suppression of difference is over the question of whether codependence is a "disease." Without referring to any text in particular, Weinhold and Weinhold (1989) assert that "co-dependency has been defined by an overwhelming majority of the medical and therapeutic community as a primary disease that has an onset, a definable course and a predictable outcome" (p. 18). This, they suggest, is misguided, as it encourages codependents to think of themselves as victims of an incurable disease. The disease model places codependents in the hands of the medical profession, which

> rather than searching for the roots of addiction in the family system or by examining the culture . . . frequently zeroes in on the most obvious symptoms, trying to eliminate them with drugs and their traditional tools. (p. 25)

According to Weinhold and Weinhold (1989), this approach hinders, rather than facilitates, "recovery," as it encourages the codependent to continue to be dependent on external forces—in this case, on the array of techniques offered by medicine, which they, following Peele (1989), understand to be inextricably linked with Alcoholics Anonymous. A better recovery, they argue, will come about when codependents realize that, far from being the victims of a lifelong disease, they suffer from a "learned disorder that results from arrested development . . . that can be remedied" (p. xviii). This remedy, in turn, is dependent on realizing that it is possible "to exercise free will over co-dependency" (p. xx).

But this disagreement turns out to be insubstantial; the conflict disappears quickly. It is discussed in the introduction and seems of little ultimate consequence in the body of the text. Weinhold and Weinhold (1989), although abandoning the medical model, still propose that codependence results from failures of the family to provide a healthy environment for the development of an adult who is free to choose the best life for him or herself, and still consists of a lack of freedom and control in interpersonal relationships. The departure from the medical model is in service of emphasizing what, it should by now be clear, is already important in the "disease-model" "recovery" discourse: that freedom is a matter of making the self a master of its own affairs, a "choicemaker":

> We believe true freedom comes from within and not from without. True freedom cannot be achieved by focusing on the social "evils" outside your-

self. To be free you must also focus on the psychological evils that exist inside you. By becoming more aware of your inner self and the reasons why you react the way you do in certain situation, you can begin to develop a sense of mastery over the forces that seem to control you and keep you from feeling free. The more you become aware of all your internal psychological parts and can orchestrate or direct them consciously, the more freedom you will experience in your life. (p. xx)

Weinhold and Weinhold (1989) are still describing a self impaired by its being held "hostage" by others, and which must master itself in order to break free from this captivity.

The difference between codependence understood as a disease and codependence understood as a "developmental arrest" is of little consequence to the description of the problem or of recovery from it. Moreover, Weinhold and Weinhold's sense that we must understand codependence as "a cultural phenomenon that grows out of the evolution of our species" is hardly distinguishable from Schaef's (1986) contention that in examining codependence "we are dealing with an underlying, generic disease syndrome that has various manifestations and is inherent in the basic culture as we now know it and as it now functions" (p. 39; see also Schaef's [1987] description of "when society becomes an addict" for an understanding of our "culture" as "diseased"). The major discrepancy between the disease accounts and Weinhold and Weinhold's accounts is the degree to which the self can be "free": for the former, one is always capable of slipping back into "bondage," while for the latter "freedom," once attained, is permanent. It might even be said that the nondisease account is only an intensification of the notion of self-mastery that is at the heart of the concept of "recovery," that it removes any vestige of constraint on the self's ability to attain absolute "freedom."

But it is not just that this "radical difference" is elucidated in such a way as to make this book indistinguishable from the others. Moreover, any possible controversy that might arise out of this claim is, as it were, whitewashed over, concealed behind an overt claim to homogeneity. We can see this concealing in the failure of a debate to emerge between the Weinholds and a major exponent of the disease model, John Bradshaw. In keeping with a practice whereby the various codependence and "recovery" authors quote from and promote each other's books, Bradshaw (1989a) writes the foreword to Weinhold and Weinhold's (1989) book. It must be noted that writing an introduction or providing a cover blurb does not necessarily mean agreeing with the substance of a book; and neither medium is the usual one for a trenchant critique of another author. But we might expect, at the very least, a friendly but critical commentary, or some other acknowledgment of the disagreement, when an author introduces a book that proclaims on its cover to propose a "radically different framework" from his own. Instead, however, Bradshaw hails the Weinholds' book as advancing "hope and promise for all of us" (p. xiii), and ends his foreword in a most laudatory fashion:

> This book is far too rich to highlight in a foreword. I am amazed at the thoroughness of this treatment. . . . My heartfelt advice is for you to read and study this book carefully and then read it again. BRAVO!!! Barry and Janae!!! This book is a gift!!! (p. xiv)

Bradshaw has not changed his view that codependence is a "disease," and his adulation of the Weinholds thus eliminates the "debate" without resolving or even acknowledging it. It is as if there is no debate to be had. Differences among these authors are suppressed in favor of a monolithic presentation that makes any conflict seem insignificant or, even, nonexistent.

Another "debate" is sidestepped in another Bradshaw (1989b) foreword. In their book, Weiss and Weiss (1989) present an understanding of codependence and recovery that incorporates the language of Transactional Analysis (TA). This represents a departure from other codependence texts, but it is not one which the authors hold to put them at odds with other codependence writers. And Bradshaw's introduction demonstrates that any possible differences implied by Weiss and Weiss's focus are unimportant.

> The Weisses bring their rich array of TA tools in offering resources for each level of developmental need. While TA has not used the terminology of the Adult Child movement, it is a therapy model with enormous resources for Adult Children. We owe the Weisses a debt of gratitude for bringing us these powerful resources. (Bradshaw, 1989b, p. xii)

The difference introduced by the Weisses' use of TA "terminology" is held by Bradshaw to be only a small technical matter. These differences—between TA and ACDF verbiage, or between the disease model and the mastery model—are clearly not to be understood as substantial. The possibility that Bradshaw is wrong not to use TA language, or that the Weisses are wrong to use it, or indeed that it makes any substantial difference at all to introduce a different body of theory into the codependence discourse, cannot emerge out of this kind of concealment.

The difference between TA and the "Adult Child movement" is only a difference between "tools" of equal "effectiveness," which are better understood as "resources" than as competing explanations of a phenomenon. The notion of codependence, and the normative understanding of human being against which it emerges as a problem (disease or not), remains the same. More important, the very possibility of conflict is removed by this apparent "ecumenicism."

Another "controversy" that emerges and disappears can be found in Schaef's (1986) presentation of the definitions of five "pioneers in the field" (pp. 14-18), which can be found in the second section of chapter 2 above. After giving these accounts, Schaef details some of the discrepancies among these accounts: Wegscheider-Cruse, Smalley, and Whitfield refer to alcoholism or addiction in their definitions, while Subby and Larsen do not; Smalley "appears to reject the disease concept" (p. 15), while the others do not; Whitfield extends the diagnosis to corporate and government institutions, while the others limit it to individuals and families. She also quarrels with them: Smalley's view that codependence is a personality disorder tries to

> fit our perceptions of addictions and codependence—experientially gathered data—into typical DSM-III-R categories, which depend on objective, linear, rational forms of data. The two are being conceptualized from very different systems and perspectives. (p. 15)

Subby defines the "family as the primary system out of which personal behaviors evolve. I think the family is an *important* system, but I don't believe it is the *primary* system" (p. 16). Whitfield offers "a broader perspective within a constricted context," and fails to see that "the disease of codependence was present before alcoholism emerged, and when it is untreated and triggered it emerges" (p. 17). Larsen is guilty of exaggeration when he says

> that there are fifteen million alcoholics in this country and that each one directly and adversely affects between twenty and thirty persons. Using his figures, and not accounting for any overlap, we see that the number of codependents in the United States exceeds the total population. Interesting and impressive! (p. 18)

But, in the end, these criticisms and areas of conflict do not make the field less unified. Schaef may worry that Larsen's definition is statistically impossible, but she is quite clear that "the addictive process"—of which codependence is a primary manifestation—is a "basic, 'generic' disease" (p. 1) that is widely prevalent, affecting, for instance, "80 percent of all helping professionals" (p. 30). Although she points out that some do not agree with the disease model, she does not speculate on the importance or meaning of this conflict. There appear to be two reasons for this minimizing of conflict, even when it is unmistakably present. The first is that the differences are inconsequential to the overall synthesis she is offering.

> I think that what many of the definitions described here touch on is a conceptualization that there is a disease process that underlies both alcoholism and codependence. This basic disease process is what I would call the *addictive process*. (p. 20)

In other words, everyone is right; all differences are purely semiotic, and the reason so many say the same thing is that there is only one thing to say. All these theorists, their differences notwithstanding, are "contributing greatly to our understanding of this disease" (p. 13). There is no need for disagreement within the field, because "we" are all talking about the same thing.

Schaef's (1986) second reason for sidestepping the conflicts she has drawn out helps to clarify further the kind of homogeneity found in this literature.

> I . . . believe that trying to generate definitions from a rational, logical premise is actually a manifestation of the disease process. I want to avoid that sort of analysis. I will attempt to describe, discuss, and list the characteristics of codependence while also examining this sub-disease within the larger context of the addictive process in our culture. (pp. 21-22)

Schaef "wants to avoid" the clarity and precision that are achieved when conflicting accounts are placed into debate with one another. Conflicts, she seems to be saying, are not to be resolved through a careful juxtaposition of difference; rather, their possible significance is to be intentionally suppressed in favor of a move away from "rational and logical" premises and procedures. To highlight differences in a way that allows for genuine debate, according to this analysis, is only to act out a "manifestation of the disease process." Conversely, to eschew the "diseased" thinking by minimizing difference is an important part of "recovery."

Beattie (1987, 1989) also helps us to see how the "ecumenicism" of these texts, while not denying the presence of differences among them, minimizes their significance. In what she calls a "brief history" of the concept (Beattie, 1987, pp. 27-31), she gives a list of "definitions" that is substantially the same as Schaef's (1986, pp. 14-18). She then poses the question, "which definition of codependency is accurate?" and answers it in the following fashion.

> They all are. Some describe the cause, some the effects, some the overall condition, some the symptoms, some the patterns, and some the pain. Codependency has either meant, or has come to mean, all the definitions listed earlier. (p. 31)

Like Schaef, Beattie is not claiming that there are no differences, but rather that what differences there are, are insignificant and thus do not need to be clarified or resolved. Codependence "has a fuzzy definition because it is a gray, fuzzy condition. It is complex, theoretical and difficult to completely define in one or two sentences" (p. 31). So long as an author claims to be writing about codependence, it seems, he or she can be counted on to be as "accurate" as all the other authors. Even if his or her book makes a different (and divergent) claim from others', still "codependence," it seems, can "come to mean" that claim as well.

    If the concept's inherent "fuzziness" makes differences insignificant, so too does the apparent "effectiveness" of the texts in explaining and palliating a widespread form of human suffering.

> In spite of the emergence of the word codependency, and so many people recovering from it, it is still jargon. No standard definition exists. We haven't agreed on whether codependency is a sickness, a condition, or a normal response to abnormal people. We still haven't agreed on whether it's hyphenated: *codependency* or *co-dependency?*
>   What most people have decided is this: whatever codependency is, it's a problem, and recovering from it feels better than not. (Beattie, 1989, p. 11)

So long as the text gets the "job" done, it offers a "right" understanding of codependence, and its possible difference from other codependence texts is unimportant. Pia Mellody (Mellody, Miller, and Miller, 1989) makes a similar point when she anticipates the objection of the "sophisticated student of psychology" to the broad claims of her book with this disclaimer.

> I am not entering a debate, but merely presenting a clinically based description of the illness and insights that have already helped hundreds of people begin the journey to recovery. (p. xxii)

Here Mellody is arguing that by offering a "clinically based description," she remains outside any possible debate. It is as if to be "clinically based" is to be in possession of some bedrock foundation of knowledge that is beyond contention. There may be a "debate" somewhere, some attempt to highlight, account for, and resolve differences among claims about codependence. But that "debate" is outside the concerns of the codependence texts, perhaps even a "manifestation of the disease"; so the differences are to be disregarded in favor of a monolithic presentation, in which all definitions of codependence are acceptable so long as they are "effective." To select a codependence book from the marketplace is to enter a discourse in which discrepancies among authors' claims can safely be disregarded as insignificant cavils. In this respect, the codependence literature is like a totalitarian discourse: disagreement is not simply frowned upon or otherwise openly suppressed; instead, it is declared impossible.

Another way to understand this suppression of difference is as a concealment of authority, which is also suggestive of totalitarianism. A literature in which everyone is right cannot have the structure of authority that would allow for dialectical conflict. There is no Freud with whom to argue or to agree, no population that might have some other disease, no need for "differential diagnosis" to be made through debate among clinicians. If everyone is right, then no one author is saying any one thing; there is no talk of "Bradshaw's account of codependence" or "Beattie's description of the dysfunctional family."

I will have more to say about this concealment in later chapters. For now, it is sufficient to notice that the authority of these texts is remarkably diffuse. Many of them (see, e.g., Beattie, 1987, 1989) are written in the first person plural, addressing some homogeneous "we," presumably the 96 percent of us who are diseased, which generally includes the authors themselves; most of these authors describe themselves as "recovering codependents." There is no "they" who is not codependent, or who could challenge the homogeneity of the literature. This "we" is maintained, even when it requires a torturing of language or logic. Schaef (1986), for instance, dedicates her book "to all of *us* who seek recovery and are joyfully recovering" (emphasis mine). She, as author, is not to be distinguished from the reader, so she takes her place among those for whom she has written the book; she is "in recovery," so her authorial voice disappears with this dedication.

Similarly, and perhaps more obviously, Beattie (1987, 1989) continually obscures the possible difference between herself and her readers, and thus her status as an authority, in passages such as this one:

Omit the shoulds. We have enough shoulds controlling our lives. Make it a goal to get rid of 75 percent of our shoulds. Don't limit ourselves. (Beattie, 1987, p. 158)

Clearly, Beattie intends these statements as imperatives: (I am telling you to) omit the shoulds; (I am telling you to) make it a goal; (I am telling you) don't limit (yourself). But the "I" and the "you," and the difference between them, are hidden behind a "we"; given this concealment of authority it may easily escape the reader's notice that she is being told that she *should* omit the shoulds. Just as there is no space in this discourse for debate among the "experts" (indeed, they tell the reader again and again that they are not experts, just fellow sufferers), or for differences among the "96 percent" of "us" who are "diseased," so too there is no opening for debate between reader and author. This is the case not because the authors forbid contention, but because "we" is held to be everyone and anyone; so no one is being told what to do by anyone else. There can, therefore, be no debate because there is apparently nothing to argue about, no differences to resolve, and thus no possibility of heterogeneity. The literature remains seamless, and it seems that the authors *intend* the reader to understand the literature as homogeneous.

If the codependence literature presents itself as monolithic, if this unity is congruent with certain aspects of the concept itself, if the literature suppresses differences that might make it less homogeneous, and if this seamlessness has been observed by critics from outside the discourse, then I think it is safe to say that the field is homogeneous. Book consumers are being told that they are codependent, and that they ought to read a book about it; and the genre openly presents itself to them as offering the same wisdom in any number of packages. To return to Kaminer's (1990) aspirin analogy, some people buy Anacin, some buy Bayer, and while the manufacturers will urge us to buy their product, none will claim that they differ in any way other than packaging and inert ingredients, and in the way that they are advertised. Either product will affect your headache; indeed, we might say that the fact that so many companies manufacture the same product only helps to lend credence to the authority of all of the aspirin companies' claims to relieve headaches. Similarly, any codependence book will address your codependence (from which you undoubtedly suffer), and the various vendors do not try to distinguish their product on the basis of their offering a different or better understanding of the concept. Everyone is right; the proliferation of codependence books is only the marketplace's response to consumer demand for more of the same, effective product. The field declares itself unified; this is a part of the message it presents to its consumers. And since this is a study of what is being presented to the readers of a mass paperback genre, I will be taking the literature at its own word, as a homogeneous discourse. Further narrowing of the field, beyond the title restriction, then, need not risk excluding aspects of the codependence phenomenon.

To say that the literature is homogeneous in the same way as the aspirin market or the Gothic romance genre is to say that the books are largely interchangeable units, and that we might glean as good an understanding of the codependence literature from one of its books as from another. Then we might legitimately narrow the field by a procedure like random sampling. But again I return to the point that I am examining a consumer phenomenon, and differences show up from this perspective, notably in sales figures. These differences are not paved over, but rather proclaimed loudly on the covers of these books. Although precise sales figures are a closely guarded secret in the publishing industry, a HarperCollins associate publisher claims the following for its codependence book sales as of February 1994 (Ani Chamichian, personal communication):

> *Codependent No More* (Beattie, 1987): Over 3,000,000 copies
> *Beyond Codependence* (Beattie, 1989): Over 1,000,000 copies
> *Co-Dependence* (Schaef, 1986): Over 600,000 copies
> *Facing Codependence* (Mellody, Miller, and Miller, 1989): Over 285,000 copies

Health Communications, Inc. (HCI) declares two of its books with the "codepen . . ." root in them to be best-sellers: Subby's *Lost in the Shuffle: The Co-Dependent Reality* (Subby, 1989), with "over 150,000 copies sold, and *Choice-Making for Co-Dependents, Adult Children and Spirituality Seekers* (Wegscheider-Cruse, 1988), which has sold "over 180,000 copies" (Terry Miller, personal communication). From the publisher's point of view, these figures can only be interpreted as signifying the books's success: Chamichian told me that any sales of a given title in excess of 20,000 copies are considered "quite satisfactory." It is clear, in addition, that HarperCollins produces more "best-selling" books than does HCI, and that the former's best-sellers are better sellers than the latter's. This undoubtedly has to do with the greater resources of the larger company, its advertising and public relations budget, and so on. It may also reflect the fact that Beattie's first book (1987) was a relatively early entry in the field, and its success may have bred further success for her publisher. But, given the analysis offered above of the homogeneity of the literature, it is unlikely that HarperCollins's codependence books are more successful because they say something different from HCI's, or from any of the other smaller publishers' entries in the market.

My method, then, for narrowing the field beyond the title restriction is to use these alleged sales figures. After all, if we are after the world that is brought into focus by the "recovery" book publishing industry, then it is reasonable to take that industry's assessment of which of its "pictures" has the most widespread display, and to turn our attention to those exemplary texts. Even if the publishers' sales figures are inflated or otherwise inaccurate, we can safely assume they are all distorted in the same way, and so provide a reliable index of the extent to which particular books are making their way to the public, if not an accurate assessment of their actual sales. Therefore, in my analysis of the codependence literature, I will use the above-mentioned "bestsellers" (Beattie, 1987, 1989; Schaef, 1986; Mellody, Miller, and Miller, 1989) as the exemplary texts.[2] My use of examples from each book will, to some extent, reflect the relative popularity of the texts as indicated by their publicized sales figures. So the preponderance of my examples will come from Beattie's two books, which, it should be noted, have sold 4 million copies, or four times the figures for Schaef's and Mellody's books combined. This indicates that it is Beattie's version of codependence that is making its way into the marketplace most consistently, and hers on which we should concentrate. It is not necessarily the case that these books will give us a better view of the concept of codependence than some other group of books, but it will allow us to make a reasonable claim that we are reading the texts that exemplify a dominant form of public discourse.

4

The Codependence
Literature as a
Moral Discourse

Ethical thought consists of the systematic examination of the
relations of human beings to each other, the conceptions,
interests and ideals from which human ways of treating one
another spring, and the systems of value on which such ends
of life are based.

—Isaiah Berlin, *The Crooked Timber of Humanity*, pp. 1-2

So far, I have attempted to provide a rationale for the selection of certain texts of the codependence literature as being exemplary for the
purposes of this study. I would now like to examine certain crucial
themes that emerge from these texts and to develop a thesis that will
open the way to a hermeneutic analysis of them. In general, I will be concerned in this chapter to show that the codependence literature can be
understood as a moral discourse, that, despite their insistence that they
take up only matters of "illness" and "health," the texts actually present
their readers with a particular understanding of the good by telling
them what a good life consists of. This aspect of the literature, I will
argue, is best seen when we consider what kind of "ought" a reader is
given when she is told that she is "codependent" and "ought" to

"recover." That "ought," it will turn out, can be understood as what Taylor (1989) calls a "strong evaluation," or an evaluation of my desires that refers to a "standard, independent of my own tastes and judgments" (p. 4). That the codependence literature contains such oughts gives the lie to its claims to be making "scientific" or "medical" or otherwise neutral claims, and opens the way to a critical interpretation of their moral claims. This interpretation, I will argue, can best be carried out if we understand the texts as comprising a narrative space in which a reader is oriented by the understanding of the good life—the life to which one ought to aspire—which lurks in the texts.

CODEPENDENCE AS A STRONG EVALUATION

At first glance, the codependence literature does not appear to be a moral theory, at least not in the way that "morality" is generally understood. In a remark whose importance to this study will become clear later in this chapter, Taylor (1989) notes that contemporary moral philosophy

> has tended to focus on what it is right to do rather than on what it is good to be, on defining the content of obligation rather than the nature of the good life. (p. 3)

We can see how far outside this kind of focus the literature falls if we return to Beattie's advice to the reader to "omit the shoulds. We have enough shoulds controlling our lives" (CNM, p. 158). The goal of "recovery," after all, is to be a freely choosing, autonomous person, and authoritarian formulas of what it is right to do can only be seen as obstacles to this kind of self-determination. This does not mean that there are no rules, but rather that they are to be found in the increasing self-understanding and self-reliance achieved in "recovery." As Beattie puts it, "if we're working at recovery, we have an internal moral code that will send us signals when it's violated" (BC, p. 107). Similarly, Schaef asserts that "dishonesty" is a sign of codependence, and that "recovery" can be understood as a restoration of honesty, in one's dealings both with oneself and with others (CD, pp. 59-60). To use Taylor's language, these authors are arguing that right action will follow upon a good self-understanding; considerations of the good life are precisely what will tell us what it is right to do.

But, as I noted before, there is clearly an "ought" in Beattie's exhortation, even if it is the absurdity, "We (or you) ought not to have shoulds." To understand that "ought" is to see in what way the codependence literature is a moral discourse. To make this analysis, it will be helpful to consider the following passages from our exemplary texts.

> When children are born, they have five natural characteristics that make them authentic human beings: children are valuable, vulnerable, imperfect, dependent, and immature. All children are born with these attributes. Functional parents help their children develop each separate characteristic properly, so that they arrive in adulthood as mature, functional adults who feel good about themselves. (FC, p. 61)

> I believe God has exciting, interesting things in store for each of us. I believe there is an enjoyable, worthwhile purpose—besides taking care of people and being an appendage to someone—for each of us. I believe we tap into this attitude by taking care of ourselves. We begin to cooperate. We open ourselves up to the goodness and richness available in us and to us. (CNM, p. 104)

> All of me, every aspect of my being, is important. I count for something. I matter. My feelings can be trusted. My thinking is appropriate. I value my wants and needs. I do not deserve and will not tolerate abuse or constant mistreatment. I have rights, and it is my responsibility to assert these rights. The decisions I make and the way I conduct myself will reflect my high self-esteem. My decisions will take into account my responsibilities to myself. (CNM, p. 105)

> The dishonesty of codependents is not to know what they need, to be externally referenced, to be looking outside themselves for their value. (CD, p. 80)

> . . . recovery begins to have less to do with coping with the "other person." It becomes more of a personal affair—a private journey of finding and building a "self" and a life. We may start to dream and hope again, but our hopes usually center on our own dreams, not someone else's. We may get protective of the new life and self we're building. (BC, p. 27)

The content of these statements, and the others like them that are pervasive in the literature, bears extensive interpretation, and chapters 5 and 6 will provide that. But for now, I want to try to understand them not so much for their "meaning" as for the kind of statements that they are, the kind of "oughts" they offer. We will see that these statements are actually declarations about the kind life that is worth living.

Initially, the "ought" can be understood as an exhortation to follow a particular kind of advice: you, the reader, ought to adopt a certain manner of parenting, or to "take into account [your] responsibility to [yourself]," or to stop looking outside yourself for value. And these pieces of advice stand against a background of counterclaims: one ought to pay attention to one's "self" more than to the other; one ought to help one's children "feel good about themselves" rather than shaming them; one ought to be "honest" and internally referented rather than practicing the dishonesty of other-reference, and so on. But what is the basis of these exhortations? What makes this advice sound advice? Why ought we to do any of these things, particularly if above all else we ought not to have "oughts"? To answer this question it is crucial to examine the notion of codependence as a disease, because all of this advice is in service of helping the reader recover from the "disease" that has presumably brought him or her to read the book in the first place.

One ought, then, to follow this advice out of considerations of "good health," just as one ought to listen to the various suggestions made by the American Heart Association to reduce the risk of heart disease. And we have become accustomed to thinking of such claims as constituting a non-ideological, noncontroversial realm of "objective truth": perhaps oat bran will reduce our cholesterol levels, perhaps not; perhaps reduced cholesterol levels will decrease our chances of heart disease and stroke, perhaps not; but undoubtedly the "health" we might attain by following the advice of the moment is not in question. We all know, or think we know, why we are eating oat bran or exercising three times a week: it is a matter of prudence, something we "ought" to do in order to be "healthy." And it is against this standard, against its ability to bring about this "health," that a piece of advice can be measured and tested empirically. The only relevant question is, will eating oat bran reduce my cholesterol and in turn increase my health? If it proves to do so, and if am concerned with my health, then I ought to partake, as a matter of prudence; and, for the same reasons, if the "experts" tell me it is bad for me, then I ought not to eat it.

It is possible, of course, to penetrate even such apparently noncontroversial standards as "health-promoting" and reveal their ideology. This is much of the thrust of Foucault's (1954/1987, 1980, 1984/1986) work: his point is not to deny the existence of various diseases (including those we call "psychological"), but rather to show that the clinical construction of those maladies can be seen as gathering and revealing the power relations that determine the everyday practices and beliefs that hold sway in a given culture. And indeed, one of the questions I will be addressing here is Foucauldian: what historical background has led to, and can be glimpsed in, the emergence of a "disease" such as codependence?

But first I want to raise an issue that arises not from Foucault's analysis of the clinic, but rather from Taylor's (1985, pp. 16-27; 1989, pp. 4-5) analysis of the considerations that might underlie our decision to follow any advice in the first place. He suggests that the basis of the "ought" implicit in the codependence author's advice to the reader is an evaluation that is either "strong" or "weak." The understanding I have suggested so far for following the advice of the codependence authors involves "weak evaluation," which Taylor (1985) illustrates with an example about his finding it "hard to resist treating myself to rich desserts" (p. 21). Speaking of this difficulty, he says,

> I might be induced to see it as a question of quantity of satisfaction. Eating too much cake increases the cholesterol in my blood, makes me fat, ruins my health, prevents me from enjoying all sorts of other desired consummations, so it isn't worth it. (p. 22)

Considerations such as these refer to primarily utilitarian concerns. They are matters of prudence, or practical judgment, in this case based on quantitative measures of health. He is motivated to give up desserts in order to attain a level of health, just as it might appear that the codependence authors would have us give up "external referentedness" in order to free ourselves from a disease that, as Schaef puts it, is "progressively death-oriented" (CD, p. 21).

Weakly evaluative "oughts," of course, are not limited to what we ought to do out of concern for health. To say I ought to change the oil in my car every 3,000 miles, or to save a certain percentage of my paycheck, is to make practical judgments regarding automobile maintenance or thriftiness. What these evaluations have in common is that they do not necessarily refer to any particular shared understanding of the Good; they do not need to rely for their recommendations on a publicly held hierarchy of values which makes it clear that one action is "better" than another, except insofar as good health is a valued goal. Nor is a person who obeys these "oughts" necessarily entering a moral space, that is, acting in accordance with a shared understanding of what the Good is, or with some aspiration toward that Good. The object of being thrifty is to save money, perhaps for a vacation or retirement or a new home; the purpose of changing the oil is to preserve the car; the intention of losing weight is to prevent a heart attack. But one could have many reasons for saving money or maintaining a car or staying healthy. Clearly, to say one ought to do these things, one need not necessarily refer to a public shared understanding of what the Good is.

When considerations of the good life enter the picture, however, the nature of the ought changes. One might evaluate rich desserts as something to be eschewed out of prudence. Or one might make a different kind of evaluation.

> As I struggle with this issue [of whether to eat eclairs], in the reflection in which I determine that moderation is better, I can be looking at the alternatives in a language of qualitative contrast. I can be reflecting that someone who has so little control over his appetites that he would let his health go to pot over cream-cake is not an admirable person. I yearn to be free of this addiction, to be the kind of person whose mere bodily appetites respond to his higher aspirations, and don't carry on remorselessly and irresistibly dragging him to incapacity and degradation. (pp. 21-22)

Here the desire to give up eclairs reflects not only the quantitative, prudential question of levels of health, but also the qualitative question of what constitutes a noble life. "Strong evaluation," he says, "is concerned with the qualitative worth of different desires" (p. 16). To the extent that it serves the "higher aspiration" (which, of course, is "higher" only in relation to some understanding of the Good) to control one's bodily appetites, the desire to give up eclairs is more valuable than the desire to eat them. The advice to eschew rich desserts is thus sound advice not only because it promotes health but also because it promotes a desire that is strongly valued. To say we ought to want to diet is to invoke a strong evaluation, and the basis of that "ought" is to be found in whatever hierarchy of values holds the aspiration to control bodily appetites in high esteem.

The aspiration to follow the advice of the codependence authors can be understood at this second level. Certainly, the desire to live by others' dreams, or to bring a child to feel something other than good about herself, or to be "externally referented" can be weighed against a consideration of the quantity of "health" that is brought about by acting on that desire. This is consistent with our first level of analysis: one ought, as a matter of prudence, to be internally referented in order to be free of a "disease." But the language of the texts makes it clear that a deeper claim is being made here, that the kind of "illness" they are discussing is not merely a matter of weak evaluation. Codependence is not just a matter of "health"; it is a matter of "maturity," of "rights and responsibility," of "goodness and richness," of "dishonesty," of "hopes and dreams." The language of strong evaluation creeps into the codependence authors' invocation of standards of sickness and health; those claims must then be understood as an invocation of a quality of life to which we ought to aspire. If "recovery" is a matter of "maturity" or "responsibility," then to be told that I ought to live *this* way ("in recovery") and not *that* way (codependent) is to be told about more than a matter of prudence. It is to invoke a "standard independent of my own tastes and judgments, which I ought to acknowledge" (Taylor, 1989, p. 4). This "ought," in turn, necessarily refers to an understanding of the

Good, which, far from being a simple matter of prudence, is a matter of some hierarchy of values. And this means that these "oughts" must be understood as strong evaluations, that is, as inscriptions of a particular understanding of the good life.

Of course, the strong evaluation implicit in the notion of codependence is concealed by its rhetoric of "disease," and by its explicit rejection of any standards imposed upon the person from without. This makes the strongly evaluative dimensions of the literature somewhat elusive, and sometimes tortuous to tease out. For example, when Beattie tells us to "omit the shoulds," the fact that she is telling us this is itself concealed. She does not hold herself out as making an authoritative statement about what *she* thinks one ought to do in order to live the good life. Rather, cloaked in the nonauthority of the "we," and in the weakly evaluative language of sickness and health, she is just reporting to us that this is the way "our" lives are "supposed to" work: shoulds control us, we are not "meant" to be controlled, therefore we should get rid of them (or at least "75 percent" of them). It is important to see that as a result of this kind of concealment, Beattie's claim that oughts shouldn't be desired is not placed into contention, any more than General Motors' claim that oil ought to be changed at certain intervals is. Rather, she presents it in a way that denies that this kind of claim is being made in the first place. But this concealment does not change the strongly evaluative nature, and thus the contestability, of the claim that we ought not to desire oughts. It just makes that claim harder to ferret out.

The reason that it is sound advice to "value my wants and needs" or to have "high self-esteem" is not just that it makes me "healthy" (i.e., disease-free), but also that it helps to make my life worthwhile. There is more to this advice than a regimen that will bring about relief from a disease (although it may accomplish this, if we go along with the contention that codependence is indeed a "disease"). And this "more" is to be found in the strong evaluation by which the desire to have high self-esteem or to be internally referented or to raise children to feel good about themselves itself becomes desirable. We "ought" not to have the desire to act and feel in ways that make us codependent; "recovery" can be understood as a reorientation of our desires such that we come to want to act in ways that enhance self-esteem, develop autonomy, etc.

What at first glance might appear to be an "ought" in the same sense that one "ought" to take an antibiotic to fight an infection becomes an "ought" in a much different sense. To say that I ought to live a meaningful and fulfilled life, that I ought to "tap into" [my] worthwhile purpose," is not just to help me to be healthy, but is also to tell me that my health consists of a certain kind of life toward which I ought to aspire. To propose this kind of standard is to propose a strong evaluation by which I might articulate the extent to which my life is meaningful or fulfilling, and thus to give me the basis for explaining any sense I might have that it is not.

That codependence is offered in this literature as this kind of "ought", as the standard by which we can evaluate our lives, is made clear in anecdotes like this one from Beattie:

> "I can't figure out what's wrong," Jane said. "I feel disconnected from people and God. I'm worried and frightened. I'm having trouble sleeping. And I feel so helpless. What's going on?"
>
> I told her it sounded like codependency, and asked if she was going to her Al-Anon meetings.
>
> "No," she said. "Why should I? I'm not living with an alcoholic anymore."
>
> "I'm not living with an alcoholic anymore either," I said. "But I'm still living with myself, so I still go to meetings." (BC, p. 233)

According to Beattie, Jane suffers not from major depression or generalized anxiety disorder or schizotypal personality disorder, as a clinician using the DSM-III-R might be inclined to suspect on the basis of her enumeration of symptoms. Rather, her problem is to be found in her "codependency": this inchoate set of complaints is to be understood, by Jane and by the reader, as pointing to the "disease." Of course, we might understand codependence as just another diagnosis like major depression, one that reduces an experiential, existential malady to a quasi-medical complaint. Certainly the literature's use of the disease model invites this understanding. But even if this is what Beattie has in mind, her language betrays her: Jane's symptoms, after all, quite clearly concern the quality of her life: she is alienated and anxious, preoccupied and helpless. The "diagnosis" here is not of an illness but of what we might call an existential condition, one from which, apparently, most of us suffer.

The word "codependence" names and explains our pain: it tells us *why* we are suffering from such maladies as alienation from God and anxiety. We desire to be the wrong kinds of selves—the codependent kind—and we ought to desire to be a different kind of self—the kind who knows that the business of living with oneself is best conducted by going to meetings. And if codependence names our pain, "recovery" names its "cure"; in light of the above, this means that "recovery" names the good life.

Taylor makes it clear that the kind of articulation implicit in what I have just called naming the pain lies at the heart of the notion of strong evaluation. "[S]trong evaluation is a condition of articulacy, and to acquire a strongly evaluative language is to become (more) articulate about one's preferences" (p. 24). Simply to introduce this language—to tell Jane from what she suffers and how she ought to go about getting better—is, perhaps unintentionally, to invoke strong evaluations, and the advice in which this language is embedded is made sound by its ability to bring about a consonance with those evaluations. So this articulacy also gives me the standard by which I will judge my life: "strong evaluation is not just a condition of articulacy about preferences, but also about the quality of life, the kind of beings we want to be" (p. 26). To read that I am important and ought therefore to pursue my own dreams is not only to gain a language for understanding what criteria underlie my preferences, it is also to gain an understanding of what constitutes the best way to live a human life. It is in this sense that we "ought" to find ourselves important, or to raise our children to feel good about themselves, or to "get rid of 75 percent of our shoulds": not that we should live in accordance with an a priori code of action, but that we should aspire to a particular way of being, or quality of life, which is the best way for a human being to be. If there is an a priori, it is to be found in this understanding of what aspirations are the "healthiest" for us to pursue, what selfhood is the "best" for us to achieve.

Strong evaluation, then, undergirds the codependence literature. Even if they are presented as a simple matter of sickness and health, the notions of codependence and recovery also function as criteria by which, readers are told, they ought to evaluate their desires. These criteria in turn point to a particular understanding of what the self is and how it ought to conduct its affairs, an understanding I will turn to in the next chapter. The literature introduces concerns regarding fulfillment, maturity, purpose, and happiness; and it claims to have found, in the notion of codependence, a way to help us evaluate the extent to which our decisions move us toward those ends. When Mellody tells us about what is "natural" for a child and "mature" for an adult; when Beattie speaks of what is fulfilling; when Schaef writes of codependents as "unhappy, destructive, and destroyed persons" (CD, p. 67); and when all of these authors discuss codependence as way of conducting one's affairs that is counter to these standards, they are referring to an implicit understanding of what the good life, and the good person, consists of. They may only intend to tell readers how they may be healthier people, but they introduce a distinction by which readers can evaluate and "improve" the overall quality of their lives. They tell people why they feel bad, where they have fallen away from the path toward the good life, and how they can find redemption from this error. They tell their readers what they ought to want their lives to be.

STRONG EVALUATION SHAPES MORAL SPACE

I spoke at the outset of this chapter of my intent to show that the code-pendence literature constitutes a moral discourse. Thus far, however, I have shown only that it invokes and develops a strong evaluation about the reader's life: codependence is a condition whose sufferers fail to achieve "good," "rich," "honest," "mature," etc., lives because they do not know how properly to evaluate their desires. It remains to be seen how this makes the codependence literature a moral discourse, and of what consequence such an understanding is to an interpretation of the texts. Two more steps are necessary to complete this argument, and the first takes us back to Taylor's (1989) claim that our everyday under-standing of what moral thought encompasses is an illegitimately nar-row one. This kind of philosophizing is, he claims, inadequate to the task of describing our moral world or helping us find our way through moral dilemmas (pp. 3-24). Furthermore, it serves "a deeply wrong model of practical reasoning, one based on an illegitimate extrapolation from reasoning in natural science" (p. 7). It excludes from consideration pre-cisely those strong evaluations which anchor our moral judgments, ignoring the questions of what makes life worth living in favor of ques-tions more amenable to "empiricist or rationalist theories of knowl-edge" (p. 5).

Taylor makes it clear that lost in employing this model is an oppor-tunity to glimpse the ontology that gives rise to the particular obligation or action that is understood as moral. If moral inquiry is not to include questions about what makes life worth living, then it becomes an impov-erished discourse, because it cannot tell us what kind of people we are or what kind of world we inhabit that we find certain obligations or actions to be good ones. It cannot tell us what shared understanding of the Good "lies behind" our strong evaluations. To follow the empiricist or naturalist line of argument is to deny precisely what gives rise to moral thought in the first place, and so is always at least to fall short of a full understanding of the moral realm, if not to obscure it entirely. Conversely, to go beyond "naturalist" thinking and to question the ontol-ogy of a given moral claim is to pursue a comprehensive, "better" under-standing of the moral world. So, Taylor suggests, we must embark on a project of retrieval, one that restores what he calls "spiritual" issues to the domain of the moral, and begin to ask what kinds of considerations about the good life make us value certain actions.

Taylor's point about the way a reliance upon empiricist and/or naturalist epistemologies impoverishes moral discourse helps to shed light on the elusiveness of the moral nature of the claims made by the codependence literature. When Mellody writes of the "natural characteristics" of children, and their development into the characteristics of "mature, functional adults who feel good about themselves," she appears to be talking about what is "natural," that is, what is universally "true" about human beings, and not about what is a matter of strong evaluation. She speaks of "function" and "dysfunction" rather than of "good" and "bad," cloaking her strong evaluations in an empiricist's neutral language. Schaef goes so far as to suggest that the "mechanisms" of codependence and recovery can be understood in terms of an alleged "right-brain/left-brain function" (CD, p. 96; see also Schaef [1987] pp. 28-29): codependence is a "biological" problem, and not a moral one. We can see the same presentation of "facts" in the following passage:

> Healthy self-esteem is the internal experience of one's own preciousness and value as a person. It comes from inside a person and moves outward into relationship. Healthy people know that they are valuable and precious even when they make a mistake. . . . The sense of worth can be felt even when their hair has been cut too short by a barber and even if they are overweight, experience bankruptcy, lose a tennis game, or realize that they have been insulted or gossiped about. Healthy individuals may feel other emotions, such as guilt, fear, anger, and pain in these circumstances, but the sense of self-esteem remains intact. (FC, p. 7)

Couched in the rhetoric of sickness and health, of what is "natural" and "functional," these claims do not appear to have a history, or to be based on a theory that is in contention. They are not capable of making distinctions between, for instance, the homeless addict and the middle-class victim of a bad haircut: both suffer the same lack of their "natural" portion of "self-esteem." Neither can this language distinguish among historical epochs. Indeed, according to Beattie,

> I am certain we could go back to the beginning of time and human relationships and find glimmers of codependent behavior. . . . People have likely been caught up with the problems of others since relationships began. Codependency probably trailed man as he struggled through the remaining B. C. years [*sic*], right up to "these generally wretched times of the twentieth century," as Morley Safer of *Sixty Minutes* says. Ever since people first existed, they have been doing all the things we label "codependent." (CNM, pp. 32-33)

By appearing to rely on a naturalist epistemology the codependence literature strengthens its previously mentioned tendency to put contention out of play.

This kind of ahistorical presentation of "truth" is a crucial aspect of the discourse from which I will later argue the codependence literature itself emerges. For now it is important to note that claims such as those about "one's preciousness and value as a person" are presented as incontestable fact: we have these qualities in the same way that we have binocular vision; and we lose them in codependence in the same way that we lose our binocular vision if we are blinded in one eye. Claims like these foreclose the possibility of interpretation by making it appear that there is nothing to interpret. But, if Taylor is right (and I think he is), claims like the one that "self-esteem" is crucial to our "health" are actually ontological claims which must be retrieved from their hiding place in a naturalist epistemology if we are to understand fully what they mean.

This project of retrieval thus follows Taylor's (1989) call to expand the moral domain beyond the naturalist epistemology so that it can include questions of the good life, and put back into contention that which has been suppressed. Certainly, such questions are related to those that dominate what we usually think of as moral discourse. Taylor (1989) points out that

> while it may not be judged a moral lapse that I am living a life that is not really worthwhile or fulfilling, to describe me in these terms is nevertheless to condemn me in the name of a standard, independent of my own tastes and desires, which I ought to acknowledge. (p. 4)

We can see just this sort of condemnation in Mellody, Miller, and Miller's reference to a codependent as a person who has failed to achieve what they understand to be a particular level of "maturity" or "fulfillment," or in Schaef's characterization of being "externally referented" as "dishonest." These are not moral lapses in the sense that one might go to Hell or to prison for being immature; but they are certainly evaluations of a person's life, and thus bear the significance of what we usually think of as moral judgments.

To claim that a healthy self is a self-esteeming entity, or that a functional self is a fulfilled entity is thus to claim something about selfhood and something about morality. Each of these claims speaks of identity, and each speaks of the Good: a particular kind of identity is a good one for us to have, spells a good life for those who adopt it. As Taylor (1989) notes, "selfhood and morality turn out to be inextricably linked" (p. 3); it is impossible for these authors to tell us what kind of self is the happiest or healthiest without telling us what kind of self we ought to want to be. So it is impossible for them not to be speaking of what Taylor calls an "affirmation of a given ontology of the human" (p. 6).

If moral discourses are understood as those which tell us about that ontology, particularly by means of explicit or implicit strong evaluations, then the codependence literature, despite its suppression of "oughts", is a moral discourse. Our ideas about selfhood can give us a glimpse of what the moral foundations of our culture are. And our culture has produced a very popular set of texts that are concerned with a particular understanding of selfhood. Those texts can thus be read as artifacts of the ontology which lies underneath that culture, as inscriptions of the understanding of the Good that is shared by the people who find these books relevant and useful. This is why I think it makes sense to look at the codependence literature as a moral discourse: the object is to unearth the understanding of the good life implicit in the texts so that we can see in what world its injunctions make sense.

THE CODEPENDENCE LITERATURE AS A NARRATIVE SPACE

That a group of mass-market paperback books takes up the serious questions of what makes life worth living, and what kind of selves we ought to be, is in itself an interesting comment on our world. Before we even know what these books are telling us about those questions, we know that there is a space for them in the late twentieth-century U.S. popular culture. I am not claiming, of course, that people who buy *Codependent No More* are trying to discover the strong evaluations that underlie their moral judgments or the ontology that gives those evaluations their credence; indeed, I suspect that I am among the very few who have bought them for this reason. But those other consumers can plausibly be said to be interested in "improving" their lives, and to find the "help" offered by these books to be credible. Why this particular rhetoric is so popular will become clear in what follows. But what I want to address here is the fact that any self-help genre is popular, and to comment on what that tells us, for I believe some understanding of this aspect of the phenomenon is necessary to my argument.

It is not enough to say that the codependence literature contains strong evaluations and thus constitutes a moral theory capable of revealing an ontology of the human. Are we then to compare this moral theory with that of a moral philosopher like Kant or Rawls? Clearly, these thinkers act intentionally to articulate a moral discourse, and the codependence writers do not. Indeed, the latter appear to suppress the aspects of their work which could most easily be seen as providing that articulation. But in their presentation of a proposed manner of everyday living, these authors willy-nilly give us a moral theory. In part, this occurs because, as Taylor (1989) says, strong evaluation is an inescapable aspect of human agency and the codependence texts are concerned to show the reader a way to go about the business of being a human agent.

But it also occurs because the question of who we are supposed to be is before us in the first place. A "self," however it is defined in a particular discourse, necessarily exists in what Taylor (1989) calls a moral space, and our strong evaluations are thus frameworks whose construction is inescapable. We must have a moral orientation, an understanding of being by which certain actions, experiences, etc., are held to be more valuable than certain others. And the presence of a literature like the codependence texts bears witness to an important feature of contemporary life: those frameworks are up for grabs. As Taylor says, "It is now a commonplace about the modern world that it has made these frameworks problematic" (p. 16). Traditional and universally binding articulations of the moral space that we necessarily inhabit, such as religion or allegiance to a monarchy or Platonic forms, have become fragmented or have disappeared entirely from public discourse. There is no agreed-upon framework, no universal strong evaluation that gives sense to our moral lives, at least for those of us who live in the Western world. This is another way of saying that there is no shared ontology which provides a common horizon against which all of us can orient ourselves, and the implications of this breakdown will become crucial in chapter 7. For now, it is important to note that the loss of horizon makes our inescapable endeavor to construct those frameworks problematic.

This problem, in turn, creates a privileged place for the project of articulating strong evaluations. That project is the way we moderns go about constructing the frameworks we cannot escape constructing, and thus open up the space in which we live our moral lives. To have strong evaluations is to gain a horizon that orients us, tells us both where we are going, and where we stand in relation to that goal (see Taylor, 1989, pp. 41-52, for a discussion of moral orientation). And this project of articulation can be understood, as MacIntyre (1984) tells us, as a quest that is lived in narrative (pp. 204-25). Because there is no commonly held metanarrative, we are left to our own devices, and as Taylor (1989) says, "[f]inding a sense to life depends on framing meaningful expression which are adequate" (p. 18). We have come to think of ourselves as what MacIntyre (1984) calls selves "whose unity resides in the unity of a narrative which links birth to life to death as narrative beginning to middle to end" (p. 205).

We are, in this view, on a quest for a narrative that gives our lives the coherence they lose when the horizon is, in Nietzsche's words, "wiped away." The moral space in which Taylor is arguing we must live our lives as human agents is not a space of unassailable assertions and beliefs and facts about what is important, but rather a "space of questions" (p. 29). Our narratives provide the provisional answers: if the space of questions is understood as a clearing in the woods, the stories that give sense to our lives can be understood as providing the features of that clearing which make it recognizable as our own.

The temptation, of course, is to think of ourselves as the sole authors of our stories, creating them de novo, as if the clearing weren't already there posing the questions that we are answering with our narratives. And, as MacIntyre points out, this is a false notion: "we are never more (and sometimes less) than the co-authors of our own narratives" (p. 213). We are inescapably in conversation with others and with a culture at large. Even the lack of horizon constitutes a horizon of sorts, and, despite its emphasis on autonomy and self-sufficiency, the codependence literature functions as one of those inescapable conversants. A literature with these concerns can only arise because the question of what makes for a good life is already up for grabs. This is true even if the texts deny that there is any question at all about what the good is, or that they are advocating a particular answer to that question. The texts comprise a narrative space, a framework for the construction of the individual stories of their readers.

We have already seen an example of this function of the literature, and the concealed way in which it is carried out, in Beattie's (1989) advice to the anxious, alienated Jane. When Beattie helps Jane to name her pain, she is giving her a way to weave those troublesome "symptoms" into her story without telling her that she is, at the same time, inviting her into a particular narrative, or giving her an orientation in moral space. Nonetheless, we must imagine that this is what happens to Jane if she listens to Beattie. Speaking with the authority of the therapist, Beattie can persuade Jane to listen to her without even claiming to be engaged in an act of persuasion. She simply claims to know Jane better than Jane herself does; but what she "knows" about Jane is only that Jane has failed to know herself adequately. She doesn't claim to know any particular "facts" about Jane's life that are unknown to Jane, as a psychoanalyst or a fortune-teller might. Instead, she tells Jane that only Jane can know best who she "really is," only she can tell her own story; and to achieve this authorship is tantamount to "recovery." With this noncoercive persuasion, Jane's narrative becomes that of the codependent; her quest finds its end in Beattie's book, where she comes upon a particular story about the good life.

The codependence literature, then, serves as a road map to the holy grail of the narrative quest by helping its readers find an orientation to the Good. It does this by providing a framework within which the reader might construct a story about herself, largely without telling him or her that that is what the texts are doing. But this function is not entirely concealed. *Facing Codependence*, for example, begins this way:

> An increasing number of people have recognized themselves in the symptoms described in the following pages. They have begun to desire to change, to clear up the distortions, and to be healed from the painful aftermath of experiencing childhood in a dysfunctional family. (FC, p. 3)

Later on, we read:

> In the following pages, you can begin to survey your own childhood experiences, looking for the incidents that led you to develop into a codependent rather than into a mature adult. (FC, p. 57)

Clearly, the reader is being told that the text intends to give him or her a way to evaluate and change his or her desires. The "recognition" Mellody speaks of (and implicitly encourages the reader to look for) is a kind of orientation: readers are told to expect to find a way to understand the disparate "symptoms" they might have as indications of their codependence. But the texts do not tell their readers what kind of orientation they are presenting, what claims are being made about the Good. Instead, they rely on a quasi-medical or naturalist rhetoric to make it appear the advice comes from no particular point of view, so that the narrative space people might enter upon reading these books will appear to come only from themselves. The story we are to come up with is really about a "disease" with an objective reality being discussed by "experts" committed only to "healing." It is not a matter of opinion, or of theory, that "childhood experiences" can lead to a certain lack of "maturity"; it is a fact. So in the end, the story does not need a specific orientation. This is the message of Beattie's assurance that

> where we [recovering codependents] are today is where we're meant to be. It's where we need to be to get to where we are going tomorrow. And that place we're going tomorrow will be better than any place we've been before. (BC, p. 40)

Coauthoring the reader's narrative means helping him or her to articulate the strong evaluations by which she will never be lost, never feel the angst or ennui or aimlessness of Jane. And it means doing this in a way that makes it appear that there is no coauthor.

I must at this point remind the reader that this interpretation of the codependence literature is deeply antagonistic to the explicit claims of the text. I have already argued that the "naturalist" claims of the genre can be seen as an attempt to place the ontological dimensions of codependence out of play, and that the homogeneity of the literature can be understood as an attempt to suppress questions about the authority of the texts. Here I am proposing another dimension of this suppression: the texts claim to be empowering their readers to tell their own stories, but in doing so they inescapably give shape to those stories. Even when, as in the excerpt from *Facing Codependence* above, there is recognition that the books are shaping the story, this shaping is not announced as the thought of one person or another about how stories are constructed, the precipitate of a particular philosophy or the tenet of an ideology. Rather, it is simply the way things are, or, at any rate, ought to be. The books do not claim to be imposing a viewpoint on anyone, but rather to be telling people to adopt their own. This can perhaps best be seen in Beattie's suggestion about how to understand her list of the "symptoms" of codependence:

> There are [*sic*] not a certain number of traits that guarantees whether a person is or isn't codependent. Each person is different; each person has his or her way of doing things. I'm just trying to paint a picture. The interpretation, or decision, is up to you. What's most important is that you first identify behaviors or areas that cause you problems, and then decide what you want to do. (CNM, p. 45)

But clearly, in even telling people to tell their own stories, the literature invokes a strong evaluation, an orientation in which "each person has his or her way of doing things." To be told that there is no necessary framework, and that one has been unnecessarily oppressed by "oughts," is still to give one a framework. This kind of suppression has a rich history, one that will continue to figure in my interpretation of the codependence literature. But for now my point is to recognize that my attempt to find the strong evaluations implicit in this genre, and to elucidate the ontology to which they point, fails to take the books at their word, and instead relies upon Taylor's (1989) dictum that frameworks are inescapable, that anyone who is telling us about how our lives ought to be is giving us strong evaluations. They are inviting us into a moral space, even if they deny that they are doing so.

But what kind of strong evaluations are being offered here? In what kind of moral space can we always be oriented, always be certain that we are where we are "meant" to be and are heading for an even "better" place—one in which we are not to be under the sway of anyone else, including the authors who told us to go there in the first place? If selfhood and the Good cannot be disentangled; if the nature of their entanglement in the modern age is that the self is constructed through narratives that disclose the Good even as they articulate the self; if the codependence literature can be understood as providing a framework for the construction of those narratives despite its claims to be setting people free from frameworks; and if that framework serves to satisfy the questing of many people, then it should be possible to gain an understanding of the ontology that underlies the modern self (or at least those modern selves who find the codependence literature attractive, and are affluent enough to buy them and find the time to read them) by investigating codependence as a strong evaluation. This is my intention in investigating the literature as a moral theory. To find out what kind of selves we are urged to be is to find out what kind of world we already live in. To read the codependence literature in this manner is to open the way to an understanding of the moral space which (at least some of) the millions of people who buy these books must already occupy in order for their advice to make sense.

5

The Reader's Coloquy
with Herself

> When we enter human life, it is as if we walk on stage
> into a play whose enactment is already in progress—a
> play whose somewhat open plot determines what parts
> we may play and toward what denouements we may be
> heading.
>
> —J. S. Bruner, *Acts of Meaning*, p. 34

> The storyteller makes no choice.
> Soon you will not hear his voice.
> His job is to shed light and not to master.
>
> —R. Hunter, "Lady with a Fan"

INTRODUCTION

It should be clear by now that the good life proposed by these texts has
largely to do with the reader's relationships. While concerns like prosperity and career success are, as we shall see, indirectly addressed by

117

these books, it is the reader's involvements with other people, with a community, and with a "God" that are crucial to both codependence and "recovery." The word "codependence" itself refers, however vaguely, to a way of being related that the literature indicates is undesirable: it is "unhealthy" for a person to "let another person's behavior affect him or her" or to be "obsessed with controlling [their] behavior" (CNM, p. 31). And "recovery is learning to function in relationships" (BC, p. 141). The texts may espouse self-sufficiency and self-reliance, but only insofar as the development of those qualities will help bring about "healthy" or "functional" relationships. The question, posed by Beattie, of "how . . . we extricate our emotions, mind, body, and spirit from the agony of entanglement" (CNM, p. 58) captures this concern succinctly. To enter the narrative space of the codependence literature is to come upon an answer to that question, to find a story about a way of being with others that is devoid of the "agony" of codependence. To live in this story is to achieve the good life.

To look at the moral claims of the literature, then, is largely to examine the kind of relatedness that they propose to replace the "agony of entanglement." If she is not to bind herself to others in a way that brings her pain, and if she still must "learn to function in relationships" in order to "recover," then how is the reader to comport herself with those others? Another way to pose this question is to ask how the texts urge the reader to understand the place of others in her narrative, or what understanding of what we might call "otherness" is implicit in the texts' rendering of the good life. To answer the question of otherness is to illuminate the nature of the good life proposed in these texts, which will be the primary concern of this chapter.

In addressing this concern, it is helpful to return to Taylor's (1989) account of what he calls "moral thought." In laying the groundwork for his examination of the moral space which the modern self inhabits, he suggests there are

> three axes of what can be called . . . moral thinking . . . our sense of respect for and obligations to others . . . our understanding of what makes a full life . . . [and] the range of notions concerned with dignity. (p. 15)

Clearly, these are general, and perhaps vague, categories. By adopting them here, I do not mean to say that there are not other possible ways to sketch the architecture of a moral space, nor to deny that they contain their own prejudices. At the same time, Taylor's proposed axes do have a certain commonsense appeal. It is hard to gainsay the claim that our moral thinking has to take into account our sense of our own dignity, our sense of respect for others, and what makes our lives worth living (and thus makes questions about dignity and respect important in the first place). I think the power of this articulation of moral space will become clear, and these dimensions elucidated, even as I use them to provide a general framework for the next part of my argument.

With this contention, Taylor (1989) is claiming that there is a moral space articulated by, and which further articulates, our strong evaluations, and that this space is constituted by these three axes. And I am suggesting that this literature proposes a moral space whose strong evaluations have primarily to do with a kind of relatedness, an understanding of otherness, toward which the reader is urged to aspire. In this and the next chapter, then, I will examine the major themes of the codependence literature as they align themselves along these axes. How is the narrative space of the codependence literature articulated, particularly with respect to questions of relatedness? What understanding of dignity, of obligation, and of what makes a full life is the reader urged to aspire toward in order to achieve a life devoid of the "agony of entanglement"?

These chapters will provide some answers to these questions and develop a thesis about those answers. This thesis has two parts. First, I will be concerned to show that the literature proposes to the reader that she ought to aspire to be the sole author of her own life's story, and to understand herself as "diseased"—that is, not living the good life—to the extent that she is not that sole author. Second, this understanding points to an ontology in which the "otherness" of beings other than that sole author is concealed. Not only should I be the only author of my story; moreover, my story ought to be one in which you are significant only insofar as you fit into that story, as an instrument or object of my narrative authority. Our stories are not bound to one another in any substantial way, in any way that takes me out of the center of my own narrative, or requires you to leave the center of yours. You are not to exceed my author-ity, and in this sense your otherness—the possibility that you are unalterably beyond me in a way that can demand response from me—is concealed.

It is important to point out that "others" refers not only to the people with whom the reader might have intimate relationships, but rather to any Other that is not the reader herself. Indeed, we have already seen what I am calling the concealing of otherness at work in the suppression of the authority of the texts themselves. This denial occurs when the books hide the contestability of their claims, or the fact that they are making contestable claims at all, when the "I" of the author and the "you" of the reader collapse into an undifferentiated "we." The books thus conceal the fact that they function as coauthors, as others who command the reader to take up a particular understanding of herself; indeed, as we will see, they offer an understanding in which there is no legitimate place for her being commanded in this fashion. The reader is told that she is telling her own story, but not told that she is being told how to do this, or that this is a claim made about her by putatively authoritative people who are situated in a particular practice with a particular theoretical stance. She is thus summoned into a narrative that starts *after* her being summoned, and thus excludes the possibility that her being called forth by others will show up in her story.

As we explore the narrative space of the codependence literature we will see other ways in which the reader is summoned into a story that conceals the very fact of being summoned. I will argue that the reader who is told to understand herself as a sole author must see herself as the only legitimate constituent of the moral space she occupies. This understanding spells the eclipse of any possible realm of the purely Other, whether that other is understood as a text, another person, or a culture in general. I will argue that this concealment shows up both in the ideas set forth in the texts and in the rhetoric used to express those ideas.

But the eclipse of otherness is not to be understood as the end of commerce with others. Rather, we will see, to be a sole author is to have a certain kind of engagement with them; but this commerce also depends on their being sole authors of their own stories, and thus never exceeding the reader herself. I will argue that each sole author is to be maximally free from the influence of others, and maximally free to engage with others without becoming unduly entangled with, or bound to, them. The codependent's story will thus turn out to be one in which she is to aspire to a particular kind of autonomy, what we might call a hermetic autonomy. This is to be understood as a condition whereby the individual is not threatened or compromised by the introduction of other characters because those characters are firmly under the sway of the author. In chapter 7 I will try to place this kind of narrative in its philosophical context.

A WALK IN THE WOODS: A DIGRESSION
ON THE "SPACE OF QUESTIONS"

In this interpretation of the codependence literature, I will be, as it were, looking over the shoulder of the person who is reading this text for "self-improvement." (See Cushman, 1990, for a description of hermeneutics as this kind of reading.) I am suggesting that we can understand this "reading" as an entrance into a moral space. This is a "space of questions," as Taylor (1989) says. But in a discourse whose authority is as suppressed as it is in the codependence literature, an important problem arises with respect to that term, a problem I will address with a brief digression that I hope will help to make my interpretation of the reader's reading intelligible.

One way to understand the concealment I am talking about here is to see that the codependence authors do not present themselves as providing answers to what Taylor (1989) claims are life's inescapable questions; indeed they tell the reader that only she can do this. Schaef makes it clear that it is important not to give "answers."

> Codependents feel that part of their role in life is to find answers and explain things for others. Interpretation is the practice of the disease of codependence. To recover, they need to do the hard work of finding their own answers. . . . Interpretation and believing you should have answers for others *is* the disease itself. (CD, p. 90)

Under the guise of steering clear of the "disease," then, no strongly evaluative assertions are openly made; and this, of course, serves to conceal further the voice of authority.

Another way to say this is that instead of offering "answers" about what makes for the good life, the literature poses the questions, which, when asked, will give the reader an orientation in moral space. She is encouraged to ask a certain set of questions about her life, and to generate her own answers in order to determine if that life is a "good" one. That these are the proper questions to be asking is never demonstrated; indeed, she is not told that she is being given any particular orientation, but rather that these questions make sense because they concern her "health." All she must do to inquire about this health is to ask to what extent she has this orientation (which of course has as a primary constituent that there is to be no one providing an orientation other than the reader herself). The strong evaluations that shape the narrative space of the reader, then, are not to be found only in the answers she finds in the texts, but also, and perhaps more fundamentally, in the questions she is urged to ask. As I noted in chapter 2, Ricoeur (1973/1981) tells us that we discover ourselves in front of the text; and in these texts, I am arguing, that discovery takes place as the result of certain questions being put into play, questions that always already exclude certain other questions.

Perhaps an example from outside the codependence discourse will help to clarify this point. There is a large tract of land near my house, an old farm donated to the state by its former owners. The state calls it a "wildlife management area." It is a heavily wooded, second-growth forest, visited only occasionally, and primarily by hunters and hikers. Recently the state's foresters began marking trees there for cutting. It seemed to me that the proposed cutting would adversely affect my enjoyment of my frequent walks in those woods, so I called the man in charge of such operations, who is a neighbor. I asked him what the state's plan and intention were. He explained that the trees were being cut in the interests of widening the road to facilitate a "timber harvest" further into the woods. He described the benefits this would bring to the forest, that it would encourage certain species of flora, increase habitat for certain fauna, and improve the accessibility for fire equipment in the event of a forest fire. He summed up his explanation with the remark, intended, I believe, to reassure me, that the project would "enhance the resource."

Clearly, the most effective challenge to the authority of this account would have to be in the form of questions about whether indeed those effects would be brought about by the proposed operation. And it is most likely that those questions have already been asked and answered in a plausible way; certainly the "scientific" calculations that can answer them are beyond my ken, and therefore immune to my "uninformed" objections. Other questions, however, are concealed by this account. What is the best understanding of a forest? Can it be apprehended in a way other than as a "resource" to be "managed" or "enhanced"? What are the various benefits of those possible other apprehensions? The "operations director," however, is under no obligation to answer such questions. By taking up the set of questions that he does, he necessarily shapes the discourse about the forest, and, therefore, the forest itself. He recognizes only a certain kind of forest, and therefore only certain questions about it. Questions like those above are excluded when the forest is already a space of questions about timber harvest and wildlife management.

By the same token, certain questions are raised and others excluded when human being becomes a space of questions about codependence. And just as it might be helpful, in a comprehensive critique of the state's stewardship of the forest, to find out what questions are giving shape to the forest so too we must seek the questions that shape the mirror in which the reader of the codependence text might "recognize" herself.

In looking over her shoulder as she looks into that mirror, then, I am trying to see both what questions the reader is being told to ask and what the apparent relevance of those questions might tell us about the world she already occupies. And the first question, perhaps the most basic one, is "Am I codependent?" This question serves as the invitation into the narrative space of the codependent, and, in the next section, I will argue that this question is held by the texts to be appropriate to a wide range of everyday actions, so that any reader could conceivably find it relevant to her own life.

THE NARRATIVE INDUCTION: AM I A CODEPENDENT?

The Cast of the Net

Beattie's way of posing the question of the reader's possible codependence is to suggest that the "disease" is characterized by certain "symptoms" which show up in the reader's everyday life. Her account of these symptoms is a nine-page list of 234 items, describing what codependents "may" do, "tend to" do, and "frequently" do (CNM, pp. 37-45). Many of these behaviors are quite commonplace. It is difficult to imagine a person who is *not* troubled by the difficulties she describes as evidence of the "disease." Take, for example, this brief excerpt:

> codependents may . . . feel anxiety, pity and guilt when other people have a problem . . . try to please others instead of themselves . . . [and] abandon their routine to respond to or do something for somebody else. (CNM, p. 37)

A person who feels that these or any of the other 234 items is present in her life is encouraged to think of them as "symptoms." We might think of the invitation issued in lists of symptoms such as these in this way: if your present life is characterized by feelings of anxiety, pity, and guilt, or the other "symptoms," then it is a sign that you should at least be asking the question of whether or not you are codependent; further reading will help you answer that question. Clearly, however, the question itself, given the analysis above, already shapes the space the reader occupies.

There is, of course, a rationale for linking these disparate "symptoms" in one narrative: they are all understood as pointing to the self's being excessively affected by the other. I will turn to the implications of this notion for the narrative of the codependent later in this discussion. But first let us look at the "symptomatology" suggested by the other authors in my sample, and the way in which their accounts invite the reader to ask the questions that usher her into the narrative space of the codependent.

Mellody suggests that the reader can understand her discomforts as manifestations of five "core symptoms."

Codependents have difficulty:

1. Experiencing appropriate levels of self-esteem
2. Setting functional boundaries
3. Owning and expressing their own reality
4. Taking care of their adult needs and wants
5. Experiencing and expressing their reality moderately. (FC, p. 4)

But the relative modesty of this list does not narrow the cast of her diagnostic net. (And it must be noted that each of these "symptoms" begs any number of crucial questions, e.g., why should we have any "self-esteem"? and in what way is "reality" something to "own"?) Mellody's explication of these symptoms makes the breadth of her intentions clear. In her discussion of the "symptom" of "inappropriate levels of self-esteem," we find that a codependent could be someone whose present is characterized by a sense that "you are worth less than others . . . [or] you are set apart and superior to other people" (FC, p. 7). A mother "who esteems herself according to what her children do" and feels "'worth less'" when her son is arrested for selling drugs is an example of someone who suffers this symptom.

Mellody describes a set of scenarios illustrating "how difficulty setting functional boundaries looks in action" (FC, pp. 18-21). "Frank" is invited to two parties for the same time (one invitation comes from his wife, the other from his mother), and finds himself "unable to take responsibility for what he himself would prefer to do," and taking "responsibility for the supposed pain and anger he could have 'made' his wife or mother feel if he had stated to each of them what he wanted to do" (FC, pp. 18-19). "Don" often "insists on having sex even after [his wife] has declined. He continues to hug, snuggle and give her intimate caresses, ignoring her protests . . ." (FC, p. 19). "Jill" goes on dates she doesn't want to go on, and "Maureen" doesn't go out at all. "Kitty" is "extremely nervous and shy," and worries about how she comes across when she goes out with her women friends. These people are all held to suffer from the inability to maintain the kind of "boundaries" that would allow them to manage the demands of the other in a more "functional" fashion.

As examples of "how difficulty owning our own reality looks in action" Mellody gives us stories like that of Sylvia and Jerry, and Jerry's friend John, who go out one night to the movies.

John's strong body odor fills the car with a nauseating stench, but Jerry and Sylvia politely converse with John as they drive. When they get into the theater, John goes to the men's room. While he is gone, Jerry asks

Sylvia, "So how do you like my ol' buddy John?" Sylvia thinks, "I don't like him—he stinks. I wish we didn't have to spend this evening with him, and I'll be glad when it's over." But knowing that John and Jerry are old friends, she can't tell her true thinking for fear of hurting Jerry. Instead she says, "Oh, he's great. I'm glad he could come out with us tonight." (FC, p. 26)

This "difficulty" also turns up in people's inability to know if they are too thin or too fat (p. 25), or to know when they are feeling angry, or to have a clear sense of "what we've done or not done" (p. 29).

People who have "difficulty acknowledging and meeting [their] own needs and wants" can be people who are "too dependent," that is, who "expect other people to take care of them [needs and wants] for me"; or "antidependent," that is, who "try to meet" their needs and wants themselves; or "needless and wantless," that is, who are not "aware of them"; or "get . . . wants and needs confused," that is, who don't know the difference between wanting and needing (FC, p. 29). And people who have "difficulty experiencing and expressing [their] reality moderately" are people who dress either immodestly or overly modestly, who are either too fat or too thin, who feel "little or no emotions or have explosive or agonizing ones," who in general do "not [know] how to be moderate" (FC, pp. 35-36).

This lack of moderation is not to be understood as a failure to conform to "normal standards." As Mellody explains,

> In my opinion using the word "normal" to describe recovery is inaccurate. Normal means "what most people do," and many people do engage in thinking, feeling, and behavior that is not healthy. . . . So instead of "normal behavior versus abnormal behavior," I use "functional behavior versus dysfunctional behavior." Functional behavior is healthy. (FC, p. 42)

Again, I must defer further interpretation of statements like this for the present, in favor of using them to indicate just how wide the door into this narrative space is. If she has a sense that her life is not "functional"—or as the Twelve Steps put it, her life has "become unmanageable" (see Appendix A)—and if she has experienced the everyday confusions and conflicts about herself and others that Mellody explains in terms of the "core symptoms," then the reader might indeed come to see these experiences as "symptoms." She might start to ask herself whether or not she is codependent, and, simply by asking after these behaviors as "symptoms," enter the narrative space proposed by these texts.

Our last exemplary text is, as I have noted, openly ambitious in its scope. In it, and in conjunction with a later book (Schaef, 1987), its author announces her intention to describe a "disease process [which] is systemic to our society [*sic*]" (CD, p. 22). Along the way, she also, not surprisingly, casts a wide net, inviting even therapists into the codependence narrative. This problem hearkens back to the beginnings of psychotherapy: Freud, Schaef argues,

> was probably an untreated drug addict, which means that his theories evolved at least partially out of the kind of thinking, perceptions, and assumptions found in the chemically dependent . . . which differ from normal thinking patterns. (CD, p. 91)

And the legacy of the founding codependent can be seen in his professional descendants:

> I firmly believe . . . that most mental health professionals are untreated codependents who are actively practicing their disease in their work in a way that helps neither them nor their clients. (CD, p. 4)

Later on, she suggests that

> [t]here are many, many codependents in this society. The disease has no respect for age, color, social standing, or sex; it touches everyone in the society in one way or another. (CD, p. 43)

Schaef backs up this contention with a list of "characteristics of codependence" (CD, pp. 44-65) that is, like Beattie's and Mellody's, extensive and comprehensive. For example, Schaef tells us that codependents are so "externally referented" that they "will do almost anything to be in a relationship, regardless of how awful the relationships is" (CD, p. 44). Their lack of boundaries leads them to get "confused when others are confused," and to do things for others that reflect their failure to know "where they end and others begin" (CD, p. 45). Schaef tells the following story as a "good example of fused boundaries in a codependent relationship":

> The husband of one of my clients felt that two of their friends didn't like him. . . . He dispatched his wife . . . to find out if his interpretation was correct, and amazingly she was willing to perform the task! This is indeed double codependence. Although my client did not think the other couple disliked her spouse, she was willing to address the issue with them because her spouse was uncomfortable bringing the subject up. (CD, p. 46)

A reader who feels this kind of confusion is invited to enter the narrative space of these texts by asking questions about the strength of her "boundaries."

This kind of question, Schaef argues, can be asked even of our most everyday transactions. She is out to "demonstrate . . . how commonplace the disease of codependence is and how we practice it in everyday events that are taken for granted in our addictive society" (CD, p. 50). More explicitly than the others, she is concerned to present codependence as a concept that can be used to shape the questions we might ask about our everyday lives. As she says,

> [f]or me, one of the most challenging aspects of the disease . . . is that it is so common and so ordinary. Of course, this is also one of the aspects that makes it so insidious. We know how to operate in it better than we know how not to. Ordinary as it is, codependence is unhealthy, however, and it will kill us, so we had better learn to recognize it and heal ourselves from it. (CD, p. 60)

Again, we can see here the narrative induction: your daily life is so dominated by this "disease" that you can't even see it; but the text will show it to you, and will, in so doing, explain for you why you suffer the way you do. (It is interesting to note that Schaef seems to anticipate the spatial metaphor I am using here, when she says that "we know how to operate in it [codependence]." "We" are "in" codependence, and she is describing to "us" what it is like in here.)

Like the other writers, Schaef relies heavily on quotidian anecdotes to shape her description and analysis of that space.

> After our meal, the waiter came by and asked if we wanted anything more. I ordered a ginger ale, and she asked if he could bring her an iced tea. When he brought her tea, he realized he had forgotten to bring my ginger ale and had to go back for it. My friend's first response was, "I'm sorry." I could not imagine what she was sorry about and asked her. She explained that I had ordered first and she had tagged her order onto mine, so she was sorry that her drink had come first, a reaction that demonstrates how far she was into her disease of codependence. She could not control the waiter, nor could she control my potential anger (I had none!). . . . Her entire response was externally referented and guided by a need to manage impressions. (CD, p. 49)

Schaef is suggesting, then, that what the reader might understand as everyday etiquette, the guiding assumptions that lubricate her quotidian social interactions, must be questioned in terms of the extent to which they show her source of "reference." Perhaps she acts in ways that "manage impressions" of herself, or that "take care of each other's impression management" (CD, p. 50). Perhaps she tries "to live up to another's expectations" (CD, p. 50). Or maybe she "dismiss[es her] own perceptions of situations unless and until they are verified externally by others" (which she illustrates with a story about going to a concert with three friends, one of whom wasn't sure whether her negative "perception" was trustworthy until it was "validated" by the other two) (CD, p. 52). In all these cases, what the reader needs to wonder is whether her actions are those of the codependent, that is, if they are characterized by an undue emphasis on being bound to others.

According to Schaef, this question can also be asked of people who are "caretakers." Since codependents "really doubt that anyone would want to have them around for their intrinsic worth . . . they have to make themselves indispensable" (CD, p. 53). So, if they find themselves doing things for others, they need to wonder if they are only facilitating another's dependence on them. They must wonder if, in acting so "selflessly," they are not actually being "self-centered," in the indirect way of the codependent. The person who, through acts of apparent selflessness, "attempts to control the uncontrollable" (CD, p. 57), who is "out of touch with [her] feelings and unable to articulate what you feel and think" (CD, p. 59) or "distorts feelings . . . to maintain the impression that codependents want to have of themselves" (CD, p. 58) or is "fearful, rigid and judgmental" (CD, p. 63), must ask if he or she has the "disease." Even "physical illness" is susceptible to this questioning:

> Codependents work hard. They are so intent on taking care of others, keeping things going and surviving that they often develop stress-related functional or psychosomatic diseases. They develop headaches; backaches; respiratory, heart, and gastrointestinal problems; and hypertension. Even cancer has been linked to the disease. (CD, p. 54)

Based on these unsubstantiated assertions, the reader is told, she ought to question her everyday aches and complaints and confusions as possible indicators of codependence.

In each of our exemplary texts, then, the invitation to ask the question "Am I codependent?" is widely issued. The breadth of "symptoms," the quotidian anecdotes, the range of concerns that are taken up, all mean that almost anyone who lives in the society in which these books are sold will find their questions relevant. *All* relationships are suspect, and should be questioned in this fashion. The texts, of course, explain this breadth of applicability of the codependence rubric as a manifestation of the universality of the "disease": 96 percent of us should find the question of codependence to be worth asking.

But I think that it is possible that the breadth of the doorway into the space proposed by this literature discloses not so much an epidemic as a vast confusion about the world we inhabit. The literature proposes that "each person who is affected by another person's problems" is codependent (BC, p. 37); evidently many people "recognize" themselves as the kind of person who cannot be sufficiently detached from others to remain "unaffected." For a reader to ask after her codependence is thus always already to understand the possibility of her being bound to another in such a way as to be "affected" as a "symptom." The problematic nature of another's effect on her, it seems, is what makes the texts a "mirror" in which the reader can easily "recognize" herself. But that this "problem" shows up across a wide spectrum of everyday activities, that the "recognition" is apparently so widespread, is perhaps not evidence of a "disease" so much as testimony to a crucial problem in the understanding of being in the culture in which these books arise and take hold: perhaps we do not know what role others are to have in our own stories, or, to put this in more abstract terms, how we are to reconcile the autonomy that is central to contemporary American culture with the possibility of being bound to a community of others.

An Interpretive Framework

The narrative induction indicates the way in which the codependence literature would address this problem. By speaking in terms of "disease," it not only further suppresses the authority of the texts, thus concealing them as others; moreover, it locates the "problem" in the "psyche" of each individual person: the "disease" may be pandemic, but it is something that each person "has." To be invited into this narrative space is already to be told that the problem and its solution lie within the individual; a technique of self-improvement will rectify the confusion about the competing claims of individuality and community. Codependence is to be found in each reader's own life story, to be read about in the privacy of her own home (where only she can assess the extent to which she "has" it), and to be rectified by her own personal "recovery."

The narrative induction, then, serves to conceal not only the authority of the texts, but also the possibility that the problem lies outside the individual's psyche. I have suggested that we cannot accept at face value the literature's claim that the breadth of this induction merely reflects the universality of the "disease." The question arises of how we might best understand the concealment disclosed by the claim to universality.

It must be noted that these concealments might be very helpful to the codependence authors. After all, as I argued in chapter 3, if "we" all have a disease, and the voice of authority comes from nowhere but within us, and if there is no basis for contention about or criticism of the claims of this nonauthority, then there would appear to be no opportunity for one author or another, or the entire discourse, to be challenged and/or discredited. To enter into the narrative space is simply to go where it "makes sense" for a "healthy" person to go. To be given the questions by which to deduce one's codependence and thus one's need for "recovery" is not really to be told what one ought to do if one subscribes to a certain philosophy of life. Rather it is to find out what any "healthy" person would do, a matter of which the codependence authors, both as "experts" of a quasi-medical discourse and as "recovering codependents," have privileged knowledge. Furthermore, if the "disease" resides in the individual, then each person has an invitation, if not an obligation, to buy a book in order to achieve this "health."

One way, then, to interpret the sweeping nature of the narrative induction is as a technique used by the codependence authors to sell as many books to as many people as possible, and thus to secure themselves a good living. Schaef's description of how she "began to write this book" gives some support to the notion that the authors' intentions are self-serving.

> I had seen this concept [codependence] as one of the most exciting ideas to evolve recently, and since so little had been written about it, I wanted to get in on the ground floor with my ideas and my experience. (CD, p. 1)

Of course, the literature urges its readers to take pride in themselves, so we should not be surprised at Schaef's unabashedness. This open self-glorification can be seen in the dedication of *Codependent No More.*

> For helping make this book possible, I thank:
> God, my mother, David, my children, Scott Egleston, Sharon George, Joanne Marcuson, and all the codependent people who have learned from me and allowed me to learn from them.
> This book is dedicated to me.

If an author simply wants to "get in on the ground floor," and sell as many books as possible, then it certainly behooves her to try to include as many people as possible in its potential audience. The texts' failure to leave space for contention or disagreement, their description of the "disease" in terms that are relevant to virtually every potential reader, and their insistence that each reader must find her own path to "recovery" are certainly viable techniques for serving the self-interest of authors; and that kind of self-interest is held to be so much a virtue in these books that at least one author feels free to dedicate her book to herself. So we might, with some justification, simply understand the suppression of disagreement and the breadth of the narrative induction as good sales techniques.

But it is not enough to accuse these authors of what amounts to a conspiracy, to allow innuendos of the advertising executive's manipulativeness to explain the popularity of these books. This may be a plausible explanation, one that would find support in works such as *The Managed Heart* (Hochschild, 1983). Moreover, Cushman (1990) has argued that therapeutic discourses and advertising are, in some important respects, indistinguishable, and MacIntyre (1984) singles out the therapist as a person who engages in (and helps others to engage in) just such manipulation. But even an advertisement needs a market, and a manipulator needs a mark. Indeed, the codependence literature itself tells us this when Beattie (1987) remarks, "we allow people to victimize us, and we participate in our own victimization" (p. 81). Something makes it possible for these techniques of authorial self-aggrandizement—if indeed that is what they are—to succeed. Of course, we might give a battery of psychological tests to readers of the codependence texts, to try to find out who is susceptible to these techniques, and then to conclude that people with certain "personality traits" are likely to "recognize" themselves in these books. But, as I have already suggested, the "susceptible" are in search of a narrative, so it is more appropriate for us to look to that narrative for some understanding of the apparent plausibility of these books.

A narrative must have some thematic unity in order for its space to be a plausible one for the reader. Lists of symptoms are coherent only to the extent that they are held together by the prevalent themes of the literature, just as the various twists of a novel's plot must have some theme which unites them. An interpretation of this literature must, therefore, look to the thematic unity of the texts in order to understand the invitation they offer. The conceit of looking over the reader's shoulder is that we are watching the reader finding her world, and herself, revealed to her in the text. It is through the themes of the literature, as much as through the "symptoms" they enumerate, that that world is evoked. To put it another way, the question of "Am I codependent?" is really a set of questions, which, taken together, point to an understanding of being that already holds sway, and which is therefore compelling to the reader. Those other questions can help us understand that ontology, to know why it makes sense to ask, "Am I codependent?" in the first place.

In keeping with Taylor's (1989) analysis, one way to elucidate the themes of a moral discourse is to look at them along three axes, which he describes as the dignity of the person, respect for and obligation to others, and the fulfillment of a life. The rest of this chapter will explore the first of these axes, and the next will take up the remaining two. My overall concern is to offer an elucidation of each dimension of the moral space that I have already argued the books constitute.

THE DIMENSION OF DIGNITY:
THE "CENTER" CANNOT HOLD

Dignity as a Private Affair

Some definition of "dignity" is in order here. Taylor (1989) defines it as "our sense of ourselves as commanding . . . respect" (p. 15). He argues that this dignity is

> woven into our very comportment. The very way we walk, move, gesture, speak, is shaped from the earliest moments by our awareness that we appear before others, that we stand in public space, and that this space is potentially one of respect or contempt, of pride or shame. (p. 15)

Although it has to do with "our sense of ourselves," then, dignity is still an intersubjective matter, having also to do with how "we stand in public space." But, as we will see, the codependence literature proposes a kind of dignity that conceals public concerns, that is derived largely by eschewing questions of how others feel about the reader in favor of questions of how she feels about herself. This dignity is not given to the reader by a community which considers certain attributes to be constitutive of that quality. Rather, in keeping with the literature's suppression of the realm of the Other, dignity is entirely the possession of the individual; indeed, it largely consists in the individual's *not* seeking her dignity through her comportment in a public space.

To see how this is the case, it is helpful to turn to the *Oxford English Dictionary*, which defines dignity as "the quality of being worthy or honourable; worthiness, worth, nobleness excellence" (p. 356). Clearly, this definition can be understood as making reference to a public bestowal of such qualities as "worth," but in the codependence literature these concerns are addressed by questions about the reader's *own* experience of her "worthiness," expressed in the texts as "self-esteem." All the authors, as should be clear by now, understand "self-esteem" as a sense of "worth" whose lack dominates the life of a codependent. Mellody identifies the "difficulty experiencing" it as a "core symptom" (FC, p. 7). The subtitle of *Codependent No More* is "How to Stop Controlling Others and Start Caring for Yourself." Schaef explains that the "external refer-entedness" central to codependence occurs because "codependents . . . have such low self-esteem that they must depend on others to prove their worth" (CD, p. 48). This lack of self-worth, as we will see, gives a thematic unity to all the disparate symptoms that comprise what I have called the narrative induction. The reader is urged to question not only whether she engages in certain behaviors or is plagued by certain con-fusions; also, and more importantly, she is to look to those "symptoms" as the indication of whether or not she values herself sufficiently.

But what is that quality whose lack marks the presence of the "dis-ease"? What understanding of "worth" is the reader being told to inquire after, and to aspire toward, as she constructs a narrative of her own life? Mellody defines "self-esteem" as the "internal experience of one's own preciousness and value as a person" (FC, p. 7). To ask if she has this experience is for the reader to wonder if she is "externally referented," instead of having her "own internal supply of peace, well being, and self-esteem" (CNM, p. 98). If she does not, then she is undignified; she experiences herself as fundamentally deficient instead of fundamentally filled with a sense of her own "preciousness and value." People whose "supply" of self-esteem is not in place "don't believe it is okay to be who [they] are" (CNM, p. 165). Instead, they look to others to provide them what they do not already possess. The reader finds, then, that she "rec-ognizes" herself in these texts because she is, in this respect, an impov-erished person; the dignity of being human, and therefore aware of her inherent "preciousness," has eluded her, and her efforts to overcome this poverty by turning to others can only deepen her poverty.

It is possible to understand this notion of dignity in at least two separate, but related, ways. First, when the reader is directed to inquire whether she "believes it is okay to be who she is," she is being told that her dignity resides in her ability to experience this inherent value, and that her "symptoms" come about because her supply of that sense of worth has been depleted. In the language of strong evaluation, she ought to aspire to the state of feeling "okay"; this is a major constituent of the good life. But second, and perhaps more important, questions about her sense of her preciousness make it clear that *she* is the person who ought to confer that sense of value. She ought not to be looking outward for it, but ought instead to aspire to be the source of her own "belief" in her "okay"-ness. Dignity is not to be found in a public space, in a story told by others about her, but in the privacy of her "own internal supply," in the story that is hers and hers alone. Her indignity is that she is not the sole author of her own story, but instead allows others to be coauthors. To be impoverished of her "supply of self-esteem" is not only to lack a certain portion of dignity, but is also to lack the dominion over her life story that would allow her to experience and to act upon her "preciousness and value" without having to allow others into her narrative.

If she cannot tell herself that she is "okay," then the reader does not stand sufficiently at the center of her life story. She not only feels "not okay" about herself; she does not even know that it is up to her to tell herself how (or who) she "really is," to stop looking to a public space for the confirmation of her own story, and to become her own author instead. Beattie makes this point in explicitly narrative terms.

> The people who look the most beautiful are the same as us. The only difference is they're telling themselves they look good, and they're letting themselves shine through. The people who say the most profound, intelligent, or witty things are the same as us. They're letting go, being who they are. . . . The people who are successful are the same as us. They've gone ahead and developed their gifts and talents, and set goals for themselves. We're even the same as the people on television: our heroes, our idols. We're all working with approximately the same material—humanity. It's how we feel about ourselves that makes the difference. It's what we tell ourselves that makes the difference. (CNM, p. 113)

All the crucial differences among people result from what they tell themselves about themselves; and the unfortunate are those who do not recognize this "fact" about being human. If only we take our rightful place at the center of our own stories, we will be "who we are"; we will "shine through." The failure of the codependent is not only that she tells herself the "wrong" story, but that she doesn't understand that she is telling herself a story at all.

Of course, even the codependence writers are not coauthors. The importance of the isolated person's standing at the center of her own story is not presented as a claim about human being which has a history of contention, as some author's opinion or cultural agreement about the way things are or ought to be. Instead, one's ability to experience one's preciousness and value is held to be a "natural characteristic" that, if properly developed, turns into the adult quality of "self-esteem," of having that experience consistently (FC, p. 61). And self-esteem belongs to one by right: we are born with a supply of it, so it is an entitlement conferred simply by dint of being human. As Taylor (1989) reminds us, to talk about "rights" instead of about "laws" is to change "not what is forbidden but the place of the subject" (p. 11); a right belongs to the individual, while a law belongs to the community. Dignity, understood as a right, is neither to be earned from nor to be conferred by others, because it is something one already possesses. It is not granted by a community, and to be deprived of it is thus an unwarranted loss.

To speak in the language of "rights," then, is to reinforce the notion of sole authorship by telling the reader that her dignity is entirely hers. We can see the impact of this language when Beattie asks the reader, "Do you know you have the right to be as healthy as you want, no matter what your family does or doesn't do?" and urges her to understands "recovery" as a process of "demanding . . . our birthright, our right to be, our right to live, and our right to recover" (BC, p. 90). Later, in a discussion she calls "From Deprived to Deserving" (BC, pp. 113-24) she tells the reader what goods will come to her when she repossesses her rightful portion of self-esteem:

> healthy love, an identity, an underlying feeling of safety, a norm of feeling good, the ability to resolve conflicts, good friends, fulfilling work, enough money, and the unconditional love and protection of a higher power. (BC, p. 116)

To the extent that she does not possess her rightful goods, it is because the reader has been unduly removed from the center of her story. This de-centering can be so profound that, as Schaef puts it, codependents come to be "totally dependent on others for their very right to exist" (CD, p. 49). To be codependent—to be affected by others in a way that allows them to be coauthors—is for the reader to lose the right to tell her own story, which is tantamount to the right to exist. It is to lose her "natural" legacy of sole authorship, and all the bounty it promises.

Schaef suggests that telling one's own story is not only a right, but also a responsibility. She turns to an explicitly moralistic language when she argues that to be "externally referented" is not only to lose a right, but is also to be "dishonest": "The dishonesty of codependents is to be looking outside themselves for their value" (CD, p. 80). But the imperative to be "honest" is not a command to treat others in a certain way; rather, it is to know oneself.

> To be out of touch with your feelings and unable to articulate what you feel and think is dishonest. To distrust your perceptions and therefore be unable to communicate them is dishonest. (CD, p. 59)

Certainly, this "dishonesty" can have consequences for others. Schaef, for instance, tells the story of a woman who lies to her hairdresser about her visit to another hairdresser. But the priority is clear; the dishonesty is first to oneself, and then, only as a contingent result, to others. Honesty consists of a particular comportment not with others, but with oneself. It is not because one is obligated to others that one ought to be honest, but rather that one is bound to uphold one's own dignity.

The next chapter will further detail what can be glimpsed here: that even the texts's construal of obligation to others still eclipses those others by making the individual herself the object of obligation. For now it is important to see that for the reader to claim her "birthright" is an explicitly moral imperative; she is obligated first and foremost to uphold her own dignity. It is "dishonest" to act in a way that implicitly denies the "truth" of her inherent "okay"-ness, that fails to understand that it is "okay to be who we are." One's highest moral obligation is thus to withdraw one's sense of "value" from the realm of entanglements with others in favor of coming into full possession of one's own sense of value. The reader is here encouraged to understand her own story as a moral drama in which her ability to derive "value" from within—to be the sole author—is both her highest responsibility and the most important guarantor of her happiness.

The language of "rights" speaks of two important aspects of this dimension of moral space. First, because a "right" is understood here as entirely the domain of the individual (and the literature overlooks the historical developments by which we come to think we have "rights" in the first place), this language speaks of a radical split between self and world. The reader's dignity can only come from the story she tells herself about herself, a story flawed to the extent that it bears traces of an outside world, of a family or a community which establishes the conditions for attaining that dignity. This "right" exists regardless of what she does or doesn't do in the world of others.

Second, the "self" that is thus hived off from the outside world, as we will see in more detail in chapter 6, has these "rights" as a "possession," like private property. For the reader to ask if she feels "okay" about herself is to make an assessment of something that is hers in much the same way as a piece of real estate that she has inherited without encumbrance. It is to ask if she has possession of the most private of private property—a legacy bestowed not by human history or cultural agreement, but rather by "nature" or "God," by the very fact of her own existence, and which can only be validated by her own private feelings. The claim of the community is thus only an unwarranted lien against this property: "self-esteem" is an utterly private matter, utterly one's own responsibility.

This last remark might help us to see another important feature of this dimension of the texts' moral space. The reader who asks after her dignity in this fashion is already understanding herself as something that can be valued in economic terms. But self-esteem is not something that she produces or purchases with her action. Rather, in keeping with Bradshaw's distinction between "human doing" and "human being," it is her inherent worth, her value regardless of "market conditions" such as the extent to which others value her for what she has done. In this sense, self-esteem has a dual function. On the one hand, it is an inoculation against the tendency of free-market capitalism to reduce everything and anything to its exchange value. The reader finds out that her value is precisely *not* what is assigned to her by a society of others. At the same time, she need not leave the marketplace and its standards too far behind, as she still has a "value"—the God-given supply of self-esteem that only *she* can assess. Dignity understood as self-esteem, then, becomes the ultimate hedge against uncertain economic times, a property value that is constant precisely because there are no others who can confer it, revoke it, or depreciate it.

Dignity as the Expulsion of Others from the Reader's Story

Once the reader begins to question whether or not she is sufficiently in possession of the "right" story, all of her vital engagements are brought under scrutiny. She is urged to consider whether those engagements are further instances of the deprivation of her birthright to tell her story in such a way as to feel "okay." This questioning is guided by the understanding that such instances arise whenever a person is dependent on those engagements for her sense of "okay"-ness. Intimate relationships, for example, may reflect her impoverished authorship if she is looking to them to fill the emptiness that only her own sense of "self-esteem" can supply. Such relationships, however, can only deepen her poverty, as Schaef makes clear in this metaphor.

> Codependents are relationship addicts who frequently use a relationship in the same way drunks use alcohol: to get a "fix." Since codependents feel they have no intrinsic meaning of their own, almost all of their meaning comes from outside. . . . Persons who are so completely externally referented will do almost anything to be in a relationship, regardless of how awful the relationship is. Codependents have no concept of a self that others could relate to; whatever small vestige of the self does exist is easily given away in order to maintain a relationship because they feel like literally nothing without the relationship. I have seen many recovering codependents avoid intimate relationship in early recovery because they do not

know how to form them without giving away big pieces of themselves in the process. Frequently their partners are not asking them to give themselves away; codependents do it without being asked. (CD, p. 44)

Beattie uses a similar analogy when she discusses what she calls caretaking, which she defines as occurring "when we take care of people's responsibilities for them" (CNM, p. 78). We do this, she says,

> because we don't feel good about ourselves. Although the feelings are transient and artificial, caretaking provides us with a temporary hit of good feelings, self-worth and power. Just as a drink helps an alcoholic momentarily feel better, a rescue move momentarily distracts us from the pain of being who we are. We don't feel lovable so we settle for being needed. We don't feel good about ourselves, so we feel compelled to do a particular thing to prove how good we are. (CNM, p. 84)

I will take up statements like these in more detail in my discussion of the dimension of moral space comprised by our commerce with others. For now, they can tell us that a person who suffers the indignity of staying in an "awful" relationship or "rescuing" others from their own problems does so because she lacks the fundamental sense of self-worth that would tell her she is "okay" without "proving" it to, or hearing it from, the other person. Her "supply" is so depleted that she is desperate to be filled, and further depletes it in order to get the other to give her her "meaning." Because she is already impoverished, she rides a slippery slope to indignity and disgrace, much as does the alcoholic who drinks to quell the pain of his addiction.

The question of who is telling the story must be asked not only of one's intimate relationships, but of all involvements with the "external" world. To look outside the self for what only the self can supply is to attempt to gather what Mellody calls "other-esteem," which she says is "based on external things . . . either on one's own 'human doing' or on the opinions and behavior of other people" (FC, p. 9). The opportunities for the external world to break through and lead the reader away from the "truth" of her own story are manifold. She finds out that she is in danger every time she feels called upon to react to an external situation. Beattie tells us that

> codependents are reactionaries. We react with anger, guilt, shame, self-hate, worry, hurt, controlling gestures, caretaking acts, depression, desperation, and fury. . . . It is normal to react and respond to our environment. . . . It's part of interacting, and it's part of being alive and human. But we allow ourselves to get so upset, and so distracted. Little things, big

things–anything–have the power to throw us off the track. And the way
we react is frequently not in our best interests. (CNM, p. 62)

To be thrown "off the track" is to be led away from what Schaef calls
"whatever small vestige of the self" remains after the supply of self-
esteem has been depleted. But it is important to save this vestige, and
this salvage starts with an understanding that "reacting" is itself the
source of much misery. "Usually when you start to feel anxious, afraid,
worried, or confused, something in your environment has snagged you"
(CNM, p. 66). The indignity of such a state of affairs is that the person
finds him- or herself so susceptible to events in the world, when she
could (and should) be self-contained. In the language of strong evaluation, when the reader is questioning whether the environment "snags"
her, she is implicitly acknowledging the claim that she ought to aspire
toward being immune to being "snagged," toward the possession of
enough self-esteem to make the "environment" a minor character in
her narrative.

The reader of the codependence text, then, is encouraged to question to what extent the intrusion of others into her story has made it an
unhappy tale. A person who suffers the indignity of codependence, who
finds her everyday life to be characterized by the "symptoms," who is
"externally referented" and easily "snagged" by the "environment," has
lost touch with the "true" story of the human person. She has

> los[t] faith in that deep, important part of ourselves that feels appropriate
> feelings, senses truth, and has confidence in its ability to handle life's sit-
> uations. . . . We abandon ourselves and lose faith in our ability to take care
> of ourselves. (CNM, p. 95)

To restore that "faith," the reader must journey "inward," in search of
the "true" source of her dignity.

> We go back . . . and back . . . and back . . . through the layers of fear,
> shame, rage, hurt, and negative incantations until we find the exuberant,
> unencumbered, delightful and lovable child that was, and still is, in us.
> And once we find it, we love and cherish it, and never, never let it go. (BC,
> p. 90, ellipses in original)

This journey is the expulsion of others from the reader's narrative in
favor of an infallible author that she is told resides within her.

For the reader to "go back" is to take possession of her history in
such a way as to make it her own, and she does this by means of a technique known as "affirmations," which are statements like

> Today, I will practice accepting myself and my present circumstances. I will begin to watch and trust the magic that acceptance can bring into my life and recovery. (Beattie, 1990b, p. 93)

The repetition of affirmations is

> . . . how we change the rules, change the messages, deal with shame, and travel the road from deprived to deserving. . . . If negative messages have contributed to this havoc, imagine what positive messages can help create.
> Affirmations aren't silly little sayings or wishful thinking. They're the antidote to all the negative garbage we've been feeding ourselves for years. (BC, p. 128)

To guarantee that her narrative will become a happier story, all the reader must do is to find the "child" who can tell that tale, nurture her with affirmations that "neutralize" the "garbage" that has concealed her, and allow her "delightfulness" to emerge. The reader who asks after the welfare of this "inner child," who wonders if it has been abandoned, already understands herself as the sole source of her own dignity, and as a potentially omnipotent storyteller.

To "go back" is thus to eclipse others—in this case the liens on her "deed" to self-esteem constituted by her history—in favor of the innocent and unencumbered "child" within, who alone can secure the dignity that is a constituent of the good life. It is also, by extension, to eclipse the otherness constituted by what we might call the political realm. A child is, after all, a nonpolitical being, living in his or her own "present," free of the obligations of citizenship. The child serves as the model of the person who is not concerned with the "opinions and behavior of other people." To invoke such a model is to equate dignity with an indifference to the political world in favor of a concern with the "inner world." It is to see that world as merely an obstacle to the achievement of the "true" story, which is best told when one is free of the "falsifying" effects of historical and political "garbage."

The notion of the "within" as the source of "truth," at the expense of considerations of a socially constituted "truth," shows up in the stress these authors place on knowing and acting on one's "feelings," or, as Schaef puts it, trusting one's "perceptions" (CD, p. 52). This trust is necessary to a self-understanding that does not "abandon ourselves" and that will bring the authorial competence promised in a statement like Beattie's above. What a person loses when he or she does not have this faith is what Mellody calls the ability to "own our own reality." This possessing, however, must be understood as an apprehension that still eclipses the otherness of that "reality"; to "own reality" is to bring its otherness under the sway of the "recovering" self, as just another possession of the sole author. A lengthy excerpt will help illustrate the extent to which the ability to stand at the center of one's own narrative determines the destiny of one's life.

> Codependents often report that they don't know who they are. I believe that complaint is directly related to the difficulty of owning and being able to experience what I call one's "reality." To experience ourselves, we have to be able to be aware of and acknowledge our reality.
>
> Our "reality," as I am using this term, has four components:
>
> The Body: How we look and how our bodies are operating
> Thinking: How we give meaning to incoming data
> Feelings: Our emotions
> Behavior: What we do or don't do
>
> These four parts of our lives constitute our *reality* as I am using the term. When we are experiencing our bodies, our thoughts, our emotions, or our behavior, they make up what is real from our perspective, even if they are not what others would experience in the same situation. So these things are what make each person uniquely who he or she is, and are the "reality" of the person experiencing them.
>
> Codependents have trouble owning all or some parts of these components in the following ways:
>
> The Body: Difficulty "seeing:" our appearance accurately or being aware of how our bodies are operating.
> Thinking: Difficulty knowing what our thoughts are, and if we know, not being able to share them. Also, giving skewed interpretations to incoming data.
> Feelings: Difficulty knowing what we are feeling, or feeling overwhelming emotions.
> Behavior: Difficulty being aware of what we do or don't do or, if we are aware, difficulty owning our behavior and its impact on others. (FC, p. 21)

To "own our own reality" is to be able to make sense of what we experience, to "see" it clearly and without unduly "skewed interpretations." Free of the confusions of codependence, in full possession of the self's unique faculties, the reader will come into her "true" authorial power. She will possess her own story, and all the others in it. The texts do not show this as an ownership of some uniquely constituted world; the "recovered" person does not "own reality" as Wallace Stevens's man with the blue guitar owns his—through the radical transformations of imagination. Rather, when she is transformed into the sole author, she cannot help but see things as they really are, which is the way any "recovered" person, freed from the distortions of codependence, would see them. What she owns is thus no more or less than the intersubjective world, and her assessment of her current circumstances must be guided by the strong evaluation that says she ought to aspire to this acquisition.

Dignity as the Smooth Functioning of a Machine

Mellody's language makes it clear that this aspiration is toward a state of affairs that is explicable in terms usually reserved for devices. The self who is a sole author is a kind of machine whose smooth operation is impossible for the codependent. When it is functioning well, fueled by an adequate supply of self-esteem, sufficiently in possession of its faculties, when its "components" are in order, then that "self" is an accurate processor of "data," and tells the "right" story. And when it is not, when the feelings of others are more important, then there is a breakdown, and the machine becomes "dysfunctional"—that is, it loses its authorial function and takes on the indignity of codependence. The realm of the Other, in this metaphor, is understood as a realm of "data," that is, as lifeless information that awaits the vitalizing possession of the "processor." It has no presence of its own. Here we might recall Schaef's warning that "interpretation is the disease of codependence." "Interpretation" is pathological because "reality" speaks for itself: it is "out there" awaiting my "processing" it. If I need to interpret, if I cannot simply "own" the data that are already there, if they seem somehow beyond my complete knowing of them, then I need to consider the possibility that my "machine" has broken down.

This breakdown can occur not only when other people are let into the narrative, but also other things, and particularly drugs and alcohol. All of the codependence authors stress the importance of "sobriety"; Schaef, for example, defines addiction as

> the compulsive need for any substance or process outside the person that becomes more important than sobriety—the state of functioning in a way that is clear, healthy, and normal for the human organism. (CD, p. 24)

"Addiction" is problematic because it threatens our "functioning" by binding us to an agent (which, as we have seen, can be a person as well as a drug) outside of ourselves; and, although this is never made explicit, it is safe to assume that the mind-altering capabilities of drugs, their potential to render us "unclear" about "reality," is what makes them potentially dangerous. Whether our functioning is compromised by a "compulsive need" for other people or for drugs, it is impossible to "own reality," to "process incoming data" when we are under the sway of something "outside the person." The machine malfunctions when its hardware is breached in this fashion.

This "malfunction" shows up in the indignity that Mellody identifies as "difficulty experiencing and expressing our reality moderately" (FC, p. 35). Indeed, she argues,

> not knowing how to be moderate is possibly the most visible symptom of codependence. . . . Codependents don't appear to understand what moderation is. . . . The codependent believes a moderate response to a situation is not enough. (FC, p. 35)

When the machine breaks down, the authorial voice falters, and the codependent's story becomes one of extremes: "They are either totally involved or totally detached, totally happy or absolutely miserable, etc." (FC, p. 35). This immoderation, which is akin to Beattie's "reactiveness," shows up, as we have seen, not only when the "environment snags" people, but also in how they comport themselves in their daily lives: in the way people dress, in "how fat or thin people become," in their "personal grooming habits," in their tendency to have extreme opinions or emotional reactions, in "extreme behaviors" like "letting anyone touch them or no one touch them at all" (FC, pp. 35-38). A person's dignity consists of a kind of Golden Mean, but this Greek virtue is not to be understood as constituted by a civic understanding of "moderation," but rather as an inherent tendency of the person whose components are functioning smoothly.

Beattie helps to extend this metaphor when she tells the reader that her failure to possess her own perceptions and feelings leads her to follow the "rules" imposed by others.

> The rules position themselves in our control center. They jam things up and take over. They direct our behaviors, and sometimes our lives. Once situated, they program us to do things that leave us feeling miserable, stuck, and codependent. (BC, p. 93)

Just as turning to others for our sense of ourselves is an impoverishment of our birthright of self-possession, so too letting others' "rules" influence us invites a breakdown of the machinery. Our "control center" must remain ours, so the machine's homeostasis can be maintained even in the face of the claim of others. This aspiration toward homeostasis—what Mellody calls "moderation" and Beattie calls "detachment"—is toward a state of affairs in which the realm of the Other is eclipsed insofar as it might disrupt the "control center." That realm is never to hold sway, lest one become "diseased."

The machine metaphor makes it clear that confusions about emotional experience, about the body's appearance, about what we think, indicate a failure of the machine to operate in the way in which it is designed, which is to "feel appropriate feelings, sense truth," etc. To lose sole authorship is to lose that homeostasis, and to ask after one's confusions and doubts, or one's "immoderation," is to question the extent to which the machine is operating smoothly, rather than the ability of a person to carry out an identity that is historically or socially constituted, and to which there might be alternatives. This metaphor, of course, helps to remove the reader even further from any sense of coauthorship by construing her as the operator of a machine apparently designed to function best when it has a solo pilot, and which has this "design" of itself rather than because of some cultural understanding. In addition, the machine metaphor invites the use of terms like "functional" and "dysfunctional," which refer only to the machine's inherent capabilities and qualities, rather than to any evaluations that might be imposed upon it by others. Such terms, as we have seen, stand in for terms like "normal" and "abnormal," which are about "what most people do," that is, are publicly constituted, and therefore irrelevant, notions of dignity. A sole author can hardly expect to tell a dignified story if she is concerned about such things.

The Dimension of Dignity: A Summary

The reader of the codependence text is directed to ask a series of questions about her dignity. These questions can be understood as concerning the extent to which she is the sole author of her own story, and thus as inviting her into a narrative space that, she is told, can and should be entirely hers, a "right" that is like a "possession." If she finds that the vicissitudes of her life's vital engagements throw her off the track and make her question her own value as a human being, she is encouraged to understand this as a failure to possess the sole authorship toward which she ought to aspire. This failure shows up in, and is confounded by, her tendency to allow others a central place in, a coauthorship of, her narrative. As a result, she cannot "own" her reality; she is beset by doubts about herself; she "loses faith" in her own inherent ability to narrate her own life. And this indignity itself is not to be understood as a failure to live up to someone else's expectations, to some cultural norm or codependence author's vision of what dignity consists of. Rather, it is a failure to let the machine run the way it is intended to run. The "control center," to paraphrase Yeats, cannot hold. And when it does not, the reader finds out, she is prevented from entering the narrative that she can only dedicate to herself when she achieves dignity by expunging all possible coauthors and becoming the only source of her dignity. The story dedicated to herself is the paradigm of the good life.

6

The Sole Author
in the
Social World

I do not think that there is such a thing as personal wholeness, or integration, minus a direction, and that direction is
the unique direction discovered ever anew in one's response
to the world.

—M. Friedman, "Aiming at the Self: A Paradox," p. 10

The questions that shape the narrative space entered into by the reader
of these texts suggest that dignity resides in her taking her rightful place
at the center of her own story, and that her indignity consists of her
allowing others to tell her story for her. When the reader asks these
questions, she is given a direction in moral space by a strong evaluation which says she ought to aspire to having no authoritative voice in
her narrative other than her own. And this orientation is presented to
her as if it were consistent with that strong evaluation: it comes not
from some authorities, but rather from her inner being. Sole authorship

147

constitutes the best functioning of her machinery, and thus is simply what any "healthy" machine-person ought to aspire toward.

But, as I noted at the outset of chapter 5, "recovery is learning to function in relationships." The reader is being offered an account of the kind of relationships that constitute the good life, so the absence in the reader's narrative of other authorial voices cannot mean that there are no others in her story, or that relationship with them is *only* a threat to her narrative dominion. And, it would seem, to enter into relationships with other people is always to open the question of what is to guide one's comportment with others. In this chapter, I will continue our exploration of the narrative space of the codependence literature by taking up the question of how the exemplary texts suggest that the reader is to find her way in relationship to both other people and what the texts refer to as the "Higher Power." To ask this question, I will examine the dimensions of moral space that Taylor (1989) refers to as concerned with respect for and obligations to others, and with what makes for a full life.

GOOD FENCES MAKE GOOD NEIGHBORS: THE DIMENSION OF RESPECT FOR AND OBLIGATION TO OTHERS

Introduction: Obligation as Crossing Over into the Realm of the Other

To ask questions about what Friedman (1976) calls "direction" and "response to the world" is to raise the possibility of being related to others in a way that might easily compromise one's own narrative dominion. If there must be room in the narrative for others, and if that place must not compromise the reader's own dignity, questions will necessarily arise about what the reader is obligated to do with respect to others, about how she can enter into relationships without losing her rightful place as sole author. An examination of the account of obligation in these texts, then, is crucial to an understanding of the good life they propose. In this section, I will make that examination by sketching the dimension of moral space that Taylor (1989) describes as concerned with "respect for and obligation to others" (p. 15).

Of course, the distinction among the axes of moral space that Taylor (1989) is proposing is largely an artifice, and we might expect substantial overlap among them; each dimension really constitutes a different aspect of the same phenomenon. But, in the case of this axis and the one just discussed, there is an important and peculiar relationship. For, as will soon become clear, my obligations to others are really no more than my obligations to myself writ large. We might begin to see this in Beattie's account of the meaning of her first book.

> *Codependent No More* . . . has emerged primarily as a book about growing in self-love, and our ability to affirm and nurture ourselves. A serendipity of that process is growing in our capacity to love others and to let them, and God, love us. (BC, p. xii)

Clearly, in this account, the dignity of the reader is primary, and her ability to uphold any obligation to others follows as a by-product of that dignity. For the reader to ask questions about her comportment with others is not to stop asking questions about her own dignity; to the contrary, the latter must be seen as logically and morally prior to the former, just as one is bound to oneself before to others to be "honest." "If we love ourselves, we become enabled to love others" (BC, p. 133), and if we do not love ourselves sufficiently, then we *cannot* love others. The reader is thus told that to seek the well-being of the other, to recognize a dimension of obligation that exceeds her aspiration to sole authorship is to put the cart before the horse, so to speak, by trying to love others before she loves herself sufficiently.

This understanding of commerce with others raises certain difficulties for a discussion of the axis of moral space I am concerned with here, and this section will address those difficulties in order to discern the nature of the "recovering" codependent's obligations to others. Again, we must start with some definition, and this will immediately bring to light what those problems are. Taylor (1989) tells us that this dimension is primarily concerned with what we are obligated to do in order to respect others, and the *Oxford English Dictionary* defines "obligation" as "the action of binding oneself by oath, promise, or contract, to do or forbear something" (p. 1964). The word "binding" is crucial for this discussion: to be bound to something is to have to do it regardless of circumstances, and, presumably (at least in some cases) regardless of its implications for one's own dignity. It would require a person to be willing to leave behind his or her own narrative in order to be bound to another, "to do or forbear something" even if it does seem to fit into his or her story at a particular moment. And given that "health" is, according to the codependence literature, a condition in which one is bound to oneself *before* others it would appear to be "pathological" to be bound to others in this fashion. On this view, I would encourage codependence simply by giving an account of what the reader ought to aspire to be bound to do in her commerce with others.

An illustration might help show how obligation, understood as this kind of being bound, necessitates the opening of a realm of the Other, and how the understanding of sole authorship conceals that realm. When I drive, I am "obligated" to stay on the right-hand side of the road. But this is an "obligation" only to the extent that I am bound to do so in a way that transcends considerations of self-interest. Driving on the right might customarily be perfectly in keeping with my own narrative, something I do largely without even thinking about it. But in this case, it is not out of obligation that I do so; rather, it is out of convenience, or prudence, or habit, or, perhaps, a wish not to get arrested. My evaluation of driving on the right is what Taylor (1985) would call a weak one. But let us say that I am driving late one night on a familiar back road in the country. I am in a hurry to get home as I must get up early the next morning. I round a bend, and a slow-moving car is suddenly in front of me. I am in a no-passing zone, and I know that there will not be another opportunity to pass for five miles. At the same time, however, I know that there is virtually no chance that I would encounter a police car on this road at this hour, and I can see far enough ahead to know that I can pass safely. The only reason now for me to stay to the right is out of some obligation: to uphold a law regardless of my chances of being arrested, not to startle the other driver, or some consideration like this. I incurred this obligation when I obtained the right to drive, and thus entered the "narrative space" of the traffic laws. And if I decide not to pass because I am caught up in that narrative, then I am acting not solely out of convenience, prudence, or habit, but rather out of my sense of being bound by that law to forbear passing on this road, out of what Taylor calls a strong evaluation.

To act in this way, I must abandon my own narrative (in which I am in a hurry and would like to pass) and enter the space of the Other, in this case a law (and a government) which is largely beyond me: I certainly did not author that law or authorize that government which says a good driver is one who stays to the right. It is this being bound to cross over into another realm (which constrains me from crossing over into another lane) that makes an obligation of my staying to the right. Prior to that point, it is only an obligation in the abstract, a binding not yet binding on me. Without a realm of the purely Other into which I can cross, there would appear to be no sense in talk of obligation, which, by definition, requires one to enter just such a realm. If I am bound to treat you in a particular way, then that binding makes me subject to your story, and thus might easily remove me from the center of my own. And if I am not to be bound to others because it threatens my dignity, then it becomes questionable whether indeed I can be said to have obligations.

The fate of this problem in the codependence literature is complicated. Certainly, it is not possible to dismiss the question of obligations to others from this interpretation, to say that they are, almost by definition, entirely absent from these texts. The reader, as we shall see, finds that there is indeed a way in which she is obligated to others, a manner in which she ought to respect them. But even when that dimension of the literature is teased out, it still in an important way conceals the possibility that the Other to whom she is obligated truly exceeds her, that her obligations somehow go beyond her sole authorship in such a way as to bind her to others. The questions that a reader is urged to ask about her obligations to and respect for others reveal a dimension of her narrative that is still an eclipse of the concerns of that axis, and an instance of the concealing of the realm of the Other.

Obligation as a Serendipity of Self-Love

Our access to this dimension must be gained through an understanding of the way in which it is obscured. According to these texts, it is always a mistake for the reader to grant too much sway to her concerns for others, to be bound to them in a way that threatens her narrative dominion. To aspire to looking after others, to take on obligations based solely on a sense of how she "ought" to treat others, is to risk compromising her own dignity. It is to ask the wrong questions about one's engagements.

> The lives of codependents are structured by the question, "What will others think?" Codependents are insecure and have such low self-esteem that they must depend on others to prove their worth. Their main goal in life is to try to figure out what the others want and then deliver that to them, for codependents are people-pleasers. They have developed amazing abilities to learn about the likes and dislikes of other people, and they truly believe that if they can just become what others want, they will be safe and accepted. (CD, p. 48)

Beattie suggests that people who concern themselves with considerations like these have been given a false idea of what their obligations are.

> Maybe someone taught us these lies, and we believed them: don't be selfish, always be kind and help people, never hurt other people's feelings . . . never say no, and don't mention personal wants and needs because it's not polite. (CNM, p. 85)

And Mellody, as I noted previously, argues that to try to please people is to seek "other-esteem" instead of self-esteem. The problem with this seeking is that the source of other-esteem is outside the self and thus vulnerable to changes beyond one's control. One can lose this exterior source of esteem at any time, so other-esteem is fragile and undependable. (FC, p. 9)

So the very notion of a dimension of respect for and obligation to the other is inimical to the notion of sole authorship. The dissolution of self-interest in favor of some a priori understanding of another's concerns is never a viable way to carry out our commerce with others. The reader is urged to question the extent to which her understanding of that business is dominated by "lies" that tell her there is some set of concerns that exceeds the questions about her sense of her own dignity.

The self-interest constituted by the pursuit of sole authorship must then be the guide to assessing entanglements with others. To direct the reader to ask if her life is "structured" by questions about what others will think is to urge her to make an account of the extent to which she mistakenly gives up her authorship by entering into a realm in which there are obligations to others irrespective of considerations of her self-esteem. To help the reader understand how to make this accounting, the texts use language that construes relationships as economic transactions. Beattie, for example, suggests that the reader ask, "What hurts? What feels good? What's ours and what isn't? And what are we willing to lose" (BC, p. 170)? In a discussion I have already cited, Schaef tells us that

> whatever small vestige of the self does exist is easily given away in order to maintain a relationship because [codependents] feel like literally nothing without the relationship. . . . [Codependents] simply do not know how to form [relationships] without giving away big pieces of themselves in the process. (CD, p. 44)

"Pieces of ourselves" can easily be given away, and perhaps the greatest temptation is to do so out of a dishonesty masquerading as respect for others. When she succumbs to this temptation, the codependent brings her already impoverished self to the brink of bankruptcy.

> Caring about people and giving are good, desirable qualities—something we need to do—but many codependents have misinterpreted the suggestions to "give till it hurts." We continue giving long after it hurts, usually until we are doubled over in pain. It's good to give some away, but we don't have to give it all away. It's okay to keep some for ourselves. (CNM, p. 86)

Schaef extends this metaphor of giving away and keeping in her account of the "cling-clung relationship," in which neither party can survive without the other, a condition that provides the relationship with security. This kind of security, however, will be bought at any cost, is static and nongrowing. A great deal of energy is put into keeping a cling-clung relationship together, frequently at great personal cost to the codependent. (CD, p. 45)

Rather than asking, "what are my obligations to others?" then, the reader is encouraged to ask, "what is the cost of doing the business of relationships?" And if that "cost" is too high, if she is "giving it all away," then it is likely that she is codependent, and needs to "keep some" more for herself. To ask about "business" is already to understand "obligation" as something contingent upon self-interest, here measured in terms of the profitability of a given transaction.

There is a place in this financial plan for charitable gifts, but there are important constraints on this giving. As Beattie says,

I believe God wants us to help people and share our time, talents, and money. But I also believe He wants us to give from a position of high self-esteem. I believe acts of kindness are not kind unless we feel good about ourselves, what we are doing, and the person we are doing it for. . . . If we absolutely can't feel good about something, then we shouldn't do it—no matter how charitable it seems. (CNM, p. 87)

When the reader asks about her "giving" in this way, she is already understanding herself as never bound to sacrifice her self-interest—measured by how "good" she feels about what she is doing—in carrying out this obligation. She is never to get so carried over into another narrative as to bring pain upon herself. For this would be to give others unnecessary dominion over her own story, to be a bad businesswoman, profligate with her inventory of self-esteem.

Other metaphors can help clarify precisely what that inventory consists of, what the codependent ought to aspire not to spend in order to purchase her security. In her discussion (cited above) of a "cling-clung relationship," Schaef speaks of the codependent's squandering a "great deal of energy." Beattie tells us that in "recovery . . . we find our personal power. We become empowered to do the possible—live our own lives" (BC, p. 28). To ask about her "power" is to ask about something she "has" like a bank account, and which is expended only at great risk. To give up too much "power" is to lose energy, to become weak, and to allow others to tell her own story. She cannot "live her own life" if she expends that power in order to get close to others. The reader is urged to be vigilant about her power, to be mindful that "getting close to another person always offers the possibility of being swallowed up by that person" (CD, p. 47). Her "power" and "energy" must be conserved for the work of taking care of herself. They are so entirely her own possession that they cannot be replenished, but only depleted, through interaction with others.

The use of these metaphors to tell the reader how she is to comport herself with others also suggests the machine metaphor discussed above. For the reader to ask after the dimension of her narrative concerned with respect for and obligation to others is to inquire into her fuel supply. This in turn is already to understand that dimension as a dangerous aspect of being, one that threatens her machinery, and that must be approached with suspicion lest she find herself running out of fuel. Even to be concerned with respect and obligation exclusive of self-interest is to risk a fatal leak in the power supply.

May I See Your Passport, Please?
Obligation as Foreign Policy

One last set of metaphors will further clarify the nature of the questions the reader is to ask about her entanglements with others. If her dignity can be understood as a fuel supply, and her self as a machine whose smooth functioning can, but need not, be compromised by an expenditure of that energy on others, then it would seem necessary to find a mechanism which can both contain the "fuel" and allow for some kind of commerce with others. The reader who wonders if she gives away too much of her fuel supply can find out by asking about what these texts call "boundaries." Beattie explains this notion by expanding the geographic analogy it implies.

> In geography, boundaries are the borders marking a state, a country, or a person's land. In recovery we're talking about the lines and limits establishing and marking our personal territory—our selves. Unlike states on maps, we don't have thick black lines delineating our borders. Yet, each of us has our own territory. Our boundaries define and contain that territory, our bodies, minds, emotions, spirit, possessions and rights. Our boundaries define and surround all our energy, the individual self that we each call "me." Our borders are invisible, but real. There is a place where I end and you begin. Our goal is learning to identify and have respect for that line. (BC, p. 167)

Mellody writes of "boundary systems," and describes them as

> invisible and symbolic "fences" that have three purposes: (1) to keep people from coming into our space and abusing us, (2) to keep us from going

into the space of others and abusing them and (3) to give each of us a way to embody our sense of "who we are." (FC, p. 11)

(It is useful to point out here that Mellody has an expansive definition of "abuse," one that I will take up in detail later. She calls abuse "any experience that [is] less-than-nurturing or shaming" [p. 118, see also p. xx].) Schaef also speaks of the value of boundaries in the self's commerce with others.

> Codependents literally do not know where they end and others begin. One of my colleagues described this aspect of codependence as getting confused when others are confused. She said that she can be as clear as a bell one moment and then know she is slipping into her disease of codependence when she is around others who are confused and begins taking on their confusion as her own. This also applies to depression, anger, happiness—anything that one "takes on" from others without at the same time being clear that it is also coming from within. (CD, p. 45)

The reader who encounters this metaphor is being told that the best understanding of a person is as a bounded monad. In accordance with this understanding, she is directed to wonder if she indeed knows where she "ends" and others "begin." She finds that she is to see her being affected by others' moods and confusions as a sign of not knowing, and thus of being bound to them in a way that invites "abuse." The conservation of her authorial power depends upon her having strong "boundaries."

"Boundaries" thus protect the person's narrative from the unwanted influence of other people and help contain that narrative from intruding on their stories. Here again, it must be noted, the reader's caring for herself—in this case, by having strong "boundaries"— is the guarantor of her respect for and obligations to others. If the other's stories are safeguarded, it is as a serendipity of that strengthening; the reader must gather her "power" first. Schaef makes this clear when she tells us of a friend who had been "trained into codependence." This woman

> had never known a relationship that did not require her to give up herself in order to survive. It was not until almost five years into her active recovery that she began to feel that she had developed enough of a self even to have friends. She was still not ready for an intimate love relationship! She was just starting to learn what it meant to have a self with which she could relate to others. . . . (CD, p. 45)

To contain ourselves within boundaries is to have "enough of a self," which is to make it possible to enter into commerce with others; as Schaef says, "in order to be intimate, you need a self" (CD, p. 47). The bounded self is a "power"-ful instrument, one that can conduct the business of relationships without fear of being swallowed up in a hostile takeover.

The idea of "boundaries," then, can be understood as further obscuring any possible dimension of respect for and obligation to others that is not simply a byproduct of the reader's own dignity. To have "boundaries" is to be able to "give from a position of high self-esteem" (CNM, p. 87). A relationship is possible only when that dimension is obscured in this fashion, only when considerations of self-interest are never dissolved in favor of a sense of obligation to and respect for the other. Beattie sees an analogy to this imperative in U.S. foreign policy. While visiting a U.S. Air Force base in Panama, she saw a sign that

> made a statement about American foreign policy on Soviet expansion in Latin America [and] also made a statement about my new policy: "No ground to give."
>
> I'm no longer willing to *lose* my self-esteem, self-respect, my children's well-being, my job, home, possessions, safety, credit, my sanity, or *myself* to preserve a relationship. I'm learning how to appropriately, and with a sense of high self-esteem, *choose* to give. I'm learning I can occasionally decide to *give up* something during conflict negotiations. But I'm no longer willing to mindlessly lose everything I have for the sake of relationships, appearance, or in the name of love. (BC, p. 165, emphasis in original)

Relationships, like foreign policy, are best conducted when we, as Henry Kissinger has said, "negotiate from strength." In being urged to ask if she "gives ground," then, the reader is told to inquire about the extent to which she allows herself to be bound to others in a way that accommodates, or perhaps even invites, their "expansionism"; she already understands those others as potentially hostile "foreign countries."

If the dimension of respect and obligation is obscured, still there is a space in the narrative for "intimacy"; but, like all the business of relationship, it must be understood as an instrumental application of an individual's capacity to function. "Intimacy" is a special case of this functioning, which "happens when our boundaries soften and touch another's borders" (BC, p. 183). This blurring of boundaries does not pose any lasting threat to the reader's sole authorship because it does not require her to "give any ground." As Mellody says,

> Intimacy means that I can share myself with you and let you share yourself with me without either of us trying to change who I am or who you are. (FC, pp. 54-55)

The "self" remains mostly intact during this kind of contact, with no demand that it alter its territory in order to purchase security. Clearly, some "sharing" takes place; there is an opening in the border, but the breach is temporary.

> After we get close or intimate, we need to restore our boundaries and energy to normal, healthy, intact conditions. We need to close the gaps in our borders, and restore ourselves to a state of completeness and individuality. People cannot sustain permanent states of intimacy and closeness. That's not desirable, and would probably preclude getting anything done. We need to get our balance and selves back. (BC, p. 188)

"Intimacy" is an aberrant condition, one in which the machine cannot function for long, or, in keeping with the geographic metaphor, one that threatens domestic tranquility and productivity. So it must be seen as a temporary break from the usual business of authoring one's own narrative.

Because intimacy is such a dangerous condition, those "gaps in our borders" which allow for it must be treated like checkpoints at which visas spelling out the terms of the visit are issued.

> The other person needs to know we'll leave his or her territory when that's appropriate. Both people need the reassurance that when we blend territories, no invasion, shaming humiliations, trespassing or overextended stays will occur. (BC, p. 185)

And if this is the case in single instances of the "blending of territory," it is also the case for the series of such episodes that constitute an intimate relationship. The reader must question to what extent she is in control over not only individual incursions, but also the commitment that makes those incursions possible.

> A relationship must be mutual. That means both people are free to either stay or leave, and both are now in the relationship because they *choose* to be, not because they *need* to be or feel they *have* to be. (BC, p. 187)

Visas can be withdrawn, and so can the diplomatic recognition that makes them possible in the first place: people are not to be compelled to open their borders, nor questioned or opposed if they choose to close them. Obligation must never preclude choice; and choices, as we have seen, must be made solely on the criterion of what makes the reader "feel good" about herself.

To ask after boundaries, then, is to ask to what extent the reader is in possession of her own territory, and thus bound to no one else. Talk of letting someone else in or entering someone else's territory is not even possible until this territory has been established, and the rules guiding the incursion are spelled out. The reader, in asking questions about her boundaries, is being told that she ought to aspire to conduct her affairs of the heart like the foreign ministry of a sovereign country conducts its affairs of state.

Clearly, this understanding continues to speak primarily of the dimension of dignity, at the apparent cost of the concealment of any possible dimension of respect for and obligations to others. This concealment occurs because the reader can only understand the success or failure of her relationships as a function of how well she safeguards her own "supply" of "power," her own "territorial borders," her own freedom to choose. She is told to ask questions about an intimacy that must constantly be monitored lest it lapse into codependence, in which one person/nation-state is "swallowed up" by another.

Laissez-Faire Obligation

But, even in this concealment, some dimension of respect and obligation is revealed. If I have boundaries, then so do you, and my recognition of this fact, while it is contingent upon my own "recovery," is still a recognition of something that is entirely yours. When Mellody speaks of intimacy as "sharing" without undue incursion, she speaks of a kind of mutuality that hinges upon my recognition that you are "okay" the way you are. If I am to be close to you, then I must not want to "change" you.

This mutuality shows up in our commerce with one another, in a way that Mellody's language suggests is truly commercial.

> Intimacy . . . involves an exchange. One person is giving and the other is receiving. Sometimes both occur at once. When I say to you, "Can I give you a hug?" I am approaching you and nurturing you. When I say, "Would you give me a hug?" I am asking you to approach me and be intimate with me. During a hug both of us are being physically intimate, but one of us is giving and one is receiving, depending on who asked for what. (FC, p. 55)

The language of "exchange" implies that there are two parties on a level playing field, acting in ways that recognize and support each other's dignity, as if there were a contract between them. This "contract" specifies that when I "share" with you, I "allow you to be who [you] are" (CNM, p. 56), and you will do the same for me. These are our only obligations: to leave each other maximally free. This respect is described by Beattie as "a grand plan! We each mind our own business" (CNM, p. 57).

Our obligation to others is thus to respect *their* sole authorship, to ensure that they too are free of any binding to anyone else's story but their own. And the codependent cannot do this. Her "disease" is one that makes her fear abandonment, and she is thus concerned to ensure that others do not leave. In pursuit of this goal, codependents try to "change" others, or as Schaef puts it, to "control" them.

> Codependents believe that they can control others' perceptions . . . control how others see their families, and control what their children perceive and feel and how they will turn out. They believe that with just a little more effort, they can get their families back to normal and make things turn out the way they want. There is almost nothing that codependents will not try to control. (CD, p. 57)

For the reader to ask about her "controlling" is to understand that she is bound only to "mind our own business," and thus not to deny the other's dignity. This means that she is obligated not to "control," even if it appears to be in an attempt to "help" the other. "We adopt a policy of . . . hands off," says Beattie. "If people have created some disasters for themselves, we allow them to face their own proverbial music" (CNM, p. 56). Others must pull themselves up by their proverbial bootstraps, and this is not a coldhearted indifference, but rather an obligation to others, a gesture of respect for their autonomy.

This "hands-off policy" is the only understanding of obligation and respect that is possible given the literature's emphasis on authorial power. Such a "policy" helps to safeguard others from the ravages of codependence.

> When we love, accept and nurture ourselves, we're able to do the same for others. We can help them love themselves, and they're more apt to react to us with love and acceptance. It starts a great chain reaction. (BC, p. 133)

The codependent must learn to "love [herself] and stop controlling others" not only because to do so makes her diseased and compromises her dignity, but also because it contributes to the disease and indignity of others. She is obliged to secure this "health" for the other by "allow[ing] people to be who they are." This is why "each person affected by other people's problems . . . needs to find his or her own program of recovery apart from anyone else's recovery program" (BC, pp. 223-24) "Recovery" is, after all, the regaining of one's sole authorship, and to intervene in someone else's "program" would only be to recreate the conditions which gave rise to the illness in the first place.

Everybody minds their own business. The attempt to "stop controlling others" becomes the abnegation of responsibility for others. In this proposed understanding of the dimension of obligation to and respect for others, no distinctions are made that might tell the reader what responsibilities she might have to another, in what situations she *ought* to leave her own narrative dominion and enter the realm of the Other. "Responsibility" for the addicted spouse is the same as "responsibility" for the addicted homeless person, which is the same as "responsibility" for U.S. foreign policy: they are all processes beyond the reader's own control, others' own "created disasters"; they are therefore *not* concerns for which the reader can be responsible. The only relevant distinction is provided by the question of self-love, the question of whether or not one is upholding one's own dignity in assessing one's obligations to others. This self-love, here understood as the "obligation" to mind one's own business, is the only obligation.

This laissez-faire "obligation" is perhaps best seen in the codependence literature's understanding of childhood. This aspect of her life is held by the literature to be the primary causal agent of her "disease." In chapter 3, I noted the pervasiveness of this kind of etiological account in the predecessor books to the codependence literature: "adult children" carry the scars of an "abusive" childhood. And in the codependence literature, this "abuse" is thought to consist not only of

> the overt physical beatings, injuries, and sexual incest or molestation we commonly associate with the term. Abuse also takes emotional, intellectual, and spiritual forms. In fact, when I talk about abuse, I now include any experiences in childhood (birth to age seventeen) that is less than nurturing. In my lectures I often use "dysfunctional" and "less than nurturing" interchangeably with "abuse." (FC, p. xx)

The reader is here offered an account of her past that tells her this "abuse" is what "trained [her] into codependence." It accounts for "why . . . we feel so uncertain and vulnerable that we can't go about the business of living our lives" (CNM, p. 94).

To ask after her own "training" is to inquire about the extent to which the reader's own childhood was one in which her parents upheld their obligation to encourage and respect her sole authorship. The moralistic/legalistic implications of the word "abuse" at first make it seem that the violation of that obligation—the failure to keep a "hands-off policy"—is truly a concern that exceeds autonomy: it is not a choice or a matter of self-interest for the parent to do this. Rather, they have a binding responsibility to do so, and that is why it can be called "abusive" when they do not.

This obligation, like the one between adults, requires not indifference or obliviousness to the other, but rather a specific kind of contact. Parents are obligated to "support the value of the children" (FC, p. 77). Disrespect occurs when parents

> either ignore or attack children for the very essence of who they are, creating an intense experience of shame in the children. Inordinate shaming happens to children when they lose contact with the sense that they are adequate and have value from within, even when making mistakes, having needs or being immature. (FC, p. 75)

What Mellody calls a "shame core" (FC, pp. 100-109) replaces the child's "internal supply" of self-esteem. The parents' job is to give a child guidance without contaminating her fuel supply with shame. Mellody illustrates this principle with a story about "Billy," who is punished with a week's grounding for not going to bed on time. This, she says, is an "exaggerated consequence," and because of it

> Billy becomes sensitive to the idea that his behavior dictates his worth to his parents, and he believes that who he is (a child who does not want to go to bed) is worthless. Also, he sees eventually that when he can cheerfully and promptly go to bed (even if he has to hide his distress and pretend to be cheerful), he apparently has value and worth (though in fact this is other-esteem based on doing rather than on being) . . . Billy may develop the characteristic survival trait of working very hard at pleasing people because he does not know how to esteem himself. (FC, p. 79)

To discipline Billy in this fashion is to fail to uphold the obligation to respect his sole authorship.

Beattie makes an almost identical point with an anecdote about "Johnny" who has hit another child.

> One mother might say, "Stop that Johnny . . . I don't ever want to see you hitting someone again." In this case, Johnny learns it's not okay to hit, but it is okay to be Johnny. Another mother says, "Stop that, Johnny. And you're a bad, bad person for doing it in the first place." In this case,

Johnny learns that it's not okay to hit, and it's not okay to be Johnny.
The externally applied guilt becomes guilt for being [which is Beattie's definition of shame]. (BC, pp. 102-3)

Children who are told that they are "not okay" are "trained into codependence" through "lies" that specify conditions for their acceptance.
This "abuse" fails to accept the child for who he or she is, and leads
him or her away from an internal experience of preciousness and value.
The abused person is the one who is not encouraged to be a sole author,
but is instead told that she is bound to others' opinions of her, to the
effect of her actions on the world around her. "Abuse" is being compelled to move into the realm of the Other in order to gain self-understanding.

So a dimension of obligation to and respect for others begins to
emerge here, and it takes shape for the reader through a proposed
understanding of her own past. To ask about the possible "abuse" she
encountered is to attempt to understand how well her parents upheld
this obligation, which is not defined in terms of the parents' own sole
authorship, but rather in terms of what a child *is*, what a child deserves
based on his or her right to a supply of feeling precious and valuable. But
this definition of "abuse" makes a parent's intemperately expressed dis-
approval the same as a parent's repeated beating of a child. Such distinctions can be blurred because what is at stake is not a particular code
of behavior or a particular hierarchy of goods and rights, but rather the
command to leave the child alone. What allows Mellody to claim (and to
be given credibility in her claim) that "dysfunctional" equals "less than
nurturing" equals "abuse" is only this imperative. A child must be left free
to be who he or she is, and anything else is "abuse." Anything else is the
failure to uphold the obligation never to make a child feel obligated to
others, and so to help the child maintain a hermetic autonomy.

As impoverished as it is, this imperative is nonetheless presented as
something that exceeds sole authorship (at least that of the parents).
We might understand the obligation thus imposed as a special case, an
exception to the rule that one acts first to enhance one's own dignity and
is thus able to uphold one's obligation to enhance other's dignity.
Because a child's "boundaries" are not in place, he or she, perhaps more
than anyone else, must be protected from the undue influence of others,
lest he or she end up as an adult who gives too much sway to the realm
of the other.

Taking care of infants requires a person to forfeit his or her needs, to do
things he or she doesn't want to do, to squelch his or her feelings and

desires (4 a.m. feedings usually only meet the needs of the person being fed), and to assume total responsibility for another human being. (CNM, p. 85)

But even this obligation must be tempered by considerations of dignity. Beattie goes on, "But if that [infant's caretaker] doesn't take care of him- or herself, he or she may begin to feel the codependent blues." In the end, even this crossing over into the realm of the Other cannot be complete: no parent should get so carried away into that realm that she forgets herself. The important distinction remains self-love; the imperative not to "control" must take precedence over any consideration of responsibility or binding obligation.

This caveat does not constitute the only limit on the parent's obligation, nor indeed is it the most important one. We would expect, given the connotations of the word "abuse," that the failure to uphold that obligation leaves a parent culpable, just as my failure to stay in the right lane would make me culpable if I hit an oncoming car. But the literature is adamant that this is not the case: the "abusive" parent is not a "perpetrator," but is rather a fellow "victim." Mellody announces in capital letters that "WE CODEPENDENTS ARE SET UP TO ABUSE OUR CHILDREN AGAINST OUR WILL" (FC, p. 105). After all, "dysfunctional . . . family systems create children who become codependent adults" (FC, p. 4), and those adults cannot help but become the parents of codependents.

> As an adult the person continues to feel too vulnerable and also operates with nonexistent or damaged boundaries. This adult cannot properly protect himself or herself in relationships, nor prevent himself or herself from being offensive to others. (FC, pp. 81-82)

And, of course, the solution to this problem is for the parent to "recover":

> . . . it is clear that we [codependents] are almost guaranteed to be unable to parent our own children in a functional and supportive manner *until we face our own codependence* and move into recovery from it. (FC, p. 106, emphasis in original)

There is an endless cycle of codependence, which is not to be rectified by people binding themselves to certain obligations. Instead, they must enter a narrative in which the "obligation" of another is carried out as a serendipity, which is to say not as an obligation at all; this understanding of "obligation" forecloses precisely the possibility of crossing over into the realm of the Other which I have identified as constitutive of obligation.

There are no "perpetrators" of "abuse," only victims who cannot help themselves. This understanding obscures the realm of the Other in a number of ways. First of all, as I just noted, it puts out of play the possibility of obligation as a crossing over into the realm of the Other. Second, it understands those "obligations" not as the precipitate of some cultural agreement about how we are bound to act toward our children, but rather as the way any "healthy" adult treats any "healthy" child. Third, it proposes the child as the paradigmatic "self," and, in so doing, puts forth a depoliticized, asocial understanding of selfhood. And finally, by making everyone a "victim," it reduces us all to the same status (and 96 percent of us have this status), thus extinguishing the distinctions that would make it necessary (and possible) for there to be a realm of the Other into which to cross over in order to carry out an obligation.

It is worth noting that this notion of widespread, if not universal, abuse—sexual, emotional, physical, etc.—is a meme that seems to be eclipsing the "recovery" meme; the talk-show circuit burgeons with accounts not only of the descent into addiction but also with painstaking and graphic accounts of the abuse which is thought to underlie perdition. Here we can see the roots of the abuse meme in the "recovery" literature. If everyone is a victim and no one is a perpetrator, then there is no one against whom to lash out in anger; there is no person or group against whom to agitate, organize or rebel. This understanding of abuse and victimization obscures the Other not only as a locus of obligation and respect but also as a locus of political action. Any sense of victimization we might encounter is ours to sort out in the privacy of our own families and therapists' offices.

The Twelve-Step Group as the Arena of Obligation

So the questions a reader asks about her obligations to and respect for others prove to give a complex shape to her narrative space. At first glance, it seems that she is urged only to ask after her own dignity, and to see her obligations as incurred and carried out only as a serendipity of her enhancing her sole authorship. But this means that there is indeed an obligation that seems to stand alongside self-interest, in special and temporary cases (such as adult intimacy or parenting), even seeming to transcend it. The morally loaded word "abuse" is invoked to describe the failure to uphold this "obligation."

But what does this "obligation" amount to? If the reader is urged to ask about the extent to which she allows others to "be who they are," to be their own sole authors, then she is already understanding them as other "selves" just like her. The "obligation" is not really to any Other, but only to another who is the same as she is, another "victim" who has also been robbed of her sole authorship, and to whom she is obliged only to keep free of any binding to her. We can see the nature of this "obligation" in the explication these texts give of their universal prescription for "recovery": participation in a Twelve-Step program. In order to "recover,"

> a person has to make major changes in his or her attitudes, beliefs behavior, thinking and practice. . . . What the . . . Twelve-Step program does, I believe, is facilitate what I call a *systems change*. The . . . program is a set of tools to bring about a change from an *addictive system* to a *living process system*, which is a system that we all know but have been trained out of. (CD, p. 26, emphasis in original)

Joining a Twelve-Step program, at least according to the codependence literature, has two "central ideas: (1) going to meetings and being involved with other recovering people, and (2) working a program" (BC, p. 234). The "program" is to be central to the "recovering" person's life; Schaef describes it as "very much like breathing for me" (CD, p. 145). And the essence of the program is to help people to

> decide that who we are is okay. We love and accept ourselves unconditionally. When we do something that's inappropriate, we separate the behavior from our identity. What we did may not be okay, but we're okay. (BC, p. 107)

This "deciding" is best done in the fellowship of other people who are dedicated to their own sole authorship. This is why Beattie (1989) is adamant that "*we need to go to groups or meetings, to find some way to be involved with other recovering people, who have similar issues and goals*" (p. 234, emphasis in original).

The fellowship of the group is to become the most important "tool" in the reader's "recovery," but this is not only because such groups give her an opportunity to "be with people who are talking about the disease and recovering from it" (FC, p. 203). It is also because a Twelve-Step group is the most likely place to

> surround yourself with people who'll support you in your efforts, people striving to live by new rules. Support them in their efforts too. It's called recovery. (BC, p. 99)

A fellowship of sole authors, each committed to the other's sole author-ship, is the norm of the Twelve-Step group. It is the best place to enhance one's own dignity while upholding that of the other, because it is the most likely venue in which to find other selves who subscribe to the same understanding of selfhood as one's own. The "community" constituted by the Twelve-Step group is comprised of boundary-mak-ing, self-enclosing selves, all of whom value the "community" only inso-far is it enhances their own authorial power. In this "community," the whole must *never* exceed the sum of its parts; it must never be more than a "tool" for "recovery." In other words, it is a community in which others do not constitute a realm of otherness, where no one will expect anyone else to be bound to them in a truly obligatory fashion.

It is important to point out that the foregoing is not intended as a wholesale summary or critique of Twelve-Step programs, but rather as an interpretation of the codependence literature's presentation and use of the Twelve Steps. I am not claiming that Twelve-Step programs are inherently incapable of fostering a community in which the otherness of other people is upheld. Rather, I would argue, the codependence authors' explication of the Twelve Steps reduces that community to the status of a "tool," a means to an end, and not an end in itself; the "com-munity" thus becomes another arena for the obliteration of the other-ness of others, one that is clothed in language that claims the opposite. To return to Friedman's (1976) language, the group is there for the "use" of the individual, a forum for the "recovery" of one's authorial power, and not as an arena which "demands response" that might con-stitute the giving up of that power. It is a group dedicated precisely to *not* being an "environment" that can "snag" its inhabitants, an instru-ment of the "recovering" self, rather than a transcendent end in itself.

The Twelve-Step group, as it is understood by the codependence literature, thus comprises a public space free of people who might *not* understand themselves as sole authors of their stories, and therefore one in which the obligation to others is always the same obligation: to mind one's own business. Of course, the literature's naturalist episte-mology and universalist claims make it seem as if this is not just one pos-sible understanding of one's obligations; and if anyone is excluded from them, it is only by virtue of their own "illness": they have yet to "get with the program." To carry out one's obligations, one must wait for those others to achieve "recovery" and thus be the kind of others for whom that obligation is meaningful.

So the obligation to others is only to "recovering" others, that is, those who are most like me if I am "recovering." This "obligation," how-ever, turns out still to be a concealing; for those others are understood only as other selves like me, who will presumably act in ways that uphold my sole authorship, and thus in my self-interest. There is no obligation to someone who sees herself as something other than a sole author, who cannot be instrumental to my own "recovery." That kind of person is not worthy of my respect until she begins to pull herself up by her bootstraps and to "recover" from the illness that makes her see herself, perhaps, as someone who needs to get her self-esteem from her involvements with others, from her "human doing" rather than from her "human being." In this sense, she does not exceed me at all, nor does my obligation to her exceed my self-interest.

The Dimension of Obligation and Respect: A Summary

Questions posed to the reader about her obligations thus reveal a strong evaluation which says that she ought to aspire to respect others' boundaries, that she is obligated to help them keep their machinery operating smoothly by "allowing them to be who they are." And this strong evaluation, in turn, only strengthens the contention of this literature that the "self" must occupy its own space. The obligation to others that emerges here does not imply stepping out of that space or letting others into it in any substantial way. Rather, if the codependent's narrative is to be dedicated to herself, it is also to be dedicated to helping others in their own attempt to be so self-dedicated. It is a central characteristic of this dimension of the narrative that there is no obligation other than keeping others free from any obligation or necessity to waver from their place at the center of their own story. The imperative to "mind one's business," to act only on the basis of "self-love," provides the only distinction for the reader to assess her responsibilities; and she is not to be responsible for anything she did not herself author. This kind of "obligation" serves, in the end, to eclipse further any possible realm of the other.

We might understand this "obligation," and some of its problems, in the terms of a metaphor used by Robert Frost (1949), who describes his neighbor's annual checking of his stone wall boundaries. The neighbor insists that "good fences make good neighbors" (p. 48), and he might well be understood as "patching any chinks in [his] borders" (BC, p. 170) in order to uphold this obligation to his poet-neighbor. Of the farmer's devotion to this practice of setting boundaries, Frost says,

> Spring is the mischief in me, and I wonder
> If I could put a notion in his head:
> "*Why* do they make good neighbors? Isn't it
> Where there are cows? But here there are no cows.
> Before I built a wall, I'd ask to know

What I was walling in or walling out.
And to whom I was like to give offense.
Something there is that doesn't love a wall,
That wants it down." (pp. 47-48)

The farmer stands firmly ensconced by his walls, obligated only to keep them strong in order to respect his neighbor. Because the farmer only asks questions about good fences, there is no room in his world for questions like Frost's, for distinctions that might tell the landowner when and where a wall is necessary and when it is not. The farmer "will not go behind his father's saying" (perhaps because he is as wary of "interpretation" as are the codependence authors), so the poet can get no answer. But, as Frost's questions make clear, the farmer's obligation only makes sense if his neighbor understands the necessity of "walling in or walling out," and of thus eclipsing the possibility of somehow being bound to cross over into someone else's territory.

But the codependence literature does offer an answer: good fences make good neighbors because, objectively speaking, a human being *is* a bounded, autonomous being, one that authors its own stories, and is at its best when it helps other such beings do the same. The texts' own metaphors support this understanding of the self as a self-enclosing unit: we are "machines"; we engage in "business"; we are "countries." Moreover, and as we have already seen, the metaphors do this in a way that conceals that they are metaphorical, that is, that they might have any meaning that is not immediately obvious. Schaef says, "Codependents do not know how to have clear, straight interactions. There is always much more going on than meets the eye" (CD, p. 51). The texts, however, present themselves as "clear" and "straight," to be taken exactly at their word, with no attempt to "go behind" the author's saying or to exercise the "symptom" of "interpretation" (CD, p. 90). In the case of the question of one's obligations to others, this means that to be told to ask about a bounded self that engages in exchanges with others that are like foreign relations is *not* to be told to ask about a certain author's understanding of being, an ontology with certain presuppositions and implications, or a particular history. Rather, it is to be told that this is who we are, and that the proof of this is not to be had through debate among various possible ontologies, or interpretation of various metaphors, but through the "fact" that it is "healthy" to be this way; "recovering from codependence feels better than not" (BC, p. 11). And this feeling better is, of course, the only useful distinction for the reader who is trying to "stop controlling others and start caring for [her]self."

This understanding of obligation, it should by now be clear, constitutes the dimension of moral space under consideration here as an utter concealment of any possible realm of the Other. Whether that concealment shows up in what the reader is told her obligations are, or how she is told this, the effect of it is to lead her to understand herself as the sole source of her own narrative, and therefore of her own being. *Nothing* is beyond her in a way that requires her to bind herself to it, and this means that "obligation" is not really obligation at all. To "recover" from codependence is to come into possession of one's own story in the same unquestioning way that Frost's neighbor has possession of his private property.

THE DIMENSION OF A FULL LIFE

Introduction: Horizon as Inescapably Other

To say that nothing is beyond the reader in a way that binds her is to say that there is no necessary horizon before which she must stand, and which thus has authority over her narrative. Indeed, the kind of "freedom" the reader encounters in these texts is a freedom from any determining force "outside the person." Dignity is to be gained through casting all possible coauthors out of her narrative; obligation is the commitment to remain firmly bound only to the maintenance of her own walls. The questions she is urged to ask about her life indicate to the reader that she ought to aspire to this kind of "freedom" and to a life among other similarly "free" people. Each person is to live within her own walls, firmly in control of her own machinery, crossing boundaries only when, where, and how it is mutually agreed to do so; and any other kind of incursion is, at least potentially, "abuse." No one is to try to become a horizon for another to stand before, nor does a "mature" or "healthy" person seek to be bound in this fashion. This is true not only of the reader's interpersonal life; she is to eschew *all* possible horizons that might force her into the indignity of codependence, into setting aside her pursuit of "feeling good about herself" or "being who she is" in favor of some background imposed from outside her own narrative.

I introduce this metaphor of horizon in order to take up the third axis of moral space identified by Taylor (1989), the dimension which he claims is constituted by questions about "what makes a full life." Even in a literature hostile to the notion of what it calls "external referenting," it would seem to be impossible to talk about these questions without discussing the "frameworks" by which we can "judge our lives and measure . . . their fullness or emptiness" (p. 16). If a discourse claims to tell us about such things as "maturity" or "fulfillment," then it must somehow invoke a background against which those qualities can show up as more or less present or absent.

That background—what I am calling the "horizon"—has a number of functions, which might be enumerated if we think of the horizon that we might see before us when looking out over the ocean. First, the horizon determines how things show up, makes one object more significant than another in my field of vision. A sailboat that is closer to me will appear larger than one that is on the horizon; if the sky is a deep blue, a red spinnaker may show up more vividly than a blue one. Second, the horizon determines what things will show up. On a clear day, for instance, I might be able to see an island that is not visible when it is stormy; even on a clear day there are objects "over the horizon" which I cannot see. The presence of the horizon limits what I can see, and, while that limit may change if I approach the horizon, or if the weather changes, there will always be another horizon, which allows some objects to show up and conceals others. Finally, the horizon stands before me in such a way as to provide me with a sense of direction or orientation. If I am looking out over the sea toward the horizon, then I have a sense of what is "here" and what is "beyond." I have a sense of where I stand, and I can know if I am moving toward or away from that limit.

To have a horizon, at least in my visual field, seems an integral part of being alive in this world. To imagine a visual field without a horizon, I would have to imagine something like being in outer space, where there is no curved earth's surface to limit what I can and cannot see, to make certain objects show up in certain ways, and to determine my orientation; I can only imagine this to be a disconcerting experience, one that might even be terrifying. And it is important to see that the horizon can only give an orientation because it is "out there." We stand before it and are thus commanded to see certain sailboats and not others, to see them as closer or further away, to experience ourselves as moving toward or away from them. To speak of horizon is always to talk of an Other which is only what it is by virtue of its being Other.

The horizon is thus necessarily imposed from "outside the person." And yet, to return to the metaphor of narrative, because it imposes the constraints against which any story can show up as full or empty, coherent or incoherent, significant or trivial, it is also constitutive of the person. The inescapable otherness of the horizon would appear to present a problem for a discourse which insists that nothing should come from "outside." A horizon, as Taylor (1989) puts it, provides an "unchallengeable framework [which] makes imperious demands" (p.

18); and it is just this kind of demand that the reader finds she is to counter with her own self-reliance. Of course, it might be said that the overall concern of this book is to show what that framework is, which, given the various concealments of the literature, is to bring the horizon out of hiding. But to take up this axis of moral space is to take up a much more specific question. Here we must ask not what horizon lurks behind certain claims, and holds sway despite its being obscured by those claims. Instead, we must ask what the literature itself openly proclaims to be the "out there," the Other before which the reader ought to aspire to stand. We must question this "horizon" to see what it might tell us about the narrative space the codependent enters when she reads these books.

The "Higher Power" as the Source of a Full Life

The texts openly present a horizon, or at least they claim to do so, and they do this in a traditional way; they talk about "God" and a reader's spirituality, which is understood as her relationship with that God. This "spirituality" is held to be crucial to "what makes a full life." In the rest of this section I will argue that it, like the other dimensions of moral space I have discussed, serves to eclipse any possible realm of the Other in the codependent's narrative.

The texts, of course, do not do this with an outright denial, any more than they simply announce that the "recovering" person has no true obligations. Rather, and in keeping with the concealment of authority which is crucial to these books, they lead the reader to question her orientation to what is presented as a horizon, but which, on further examination, proves not to be an "out there" at all. The horizon that is openly invoked turns out to be only an artifact of the "in here," and thus remains under the sway of the reader's authorship, instead of holding sway over it. This "horizon" does not determine what shows up in that story, nor how it must show up; neither does it give the reader a necessary orientation for her story, any sense of in what direction her story might be moving. It does not command her so much as beckon her onward to some limitless future, where she cannot help but get "better all the time."

At first glance, to talk of "spirituality" is necessarily to talk about a horizon. The *Oxford English Dictionary* calls "spiritual" concerns those having to do with "higher moral qualities, especially as regarded in a religious aspect" (p. 622). The "higher" is the "out there" in this definition, the background against which certain "qualities" are included or excluded, held to be greater or lesser; "higher" gives the direction of spiritual aspiration. And, as the codependence literature makes clear, some aspiration which it calls spiritual is a crucial aspect of "recovery," just as the loss of that "spirituality" is central to the "disease." Schaef, for instance, asserts that "recovery from the disease of codependence is impossible without recognizing and working with spiritual issues as healing issues" (CD, p. 92); and Mellody tells the reader that ". . . being in touch with our own spirituality is crucial to recovery in a Twelve-Step program" (FC, p. 95). We have already seen Beattie's contention that a loss of faith is part of the codependent's experience, and its restoration a "by-product" of "recovery."

To understand the nature of this "spirituality," it is helpful to turn to the Twelve Steps, from which the codependence authors take the notion that no progress can be made in the battle against addiction until a person begins to develop a relationship with what is called the "Higher Power" or "God." Precisely what is intended by these terms in their original formulation is not within the scope of this book. What can be discerned, and is highly relevant, is how the codependence literature urges its readers to understand them.

These are the first three of the Twelve Steps for Codependents (Beattie, 1990b).

1. We admitted we were powerless over others—that our lives had become unmanageable.
2. Came to believe that a power greater than ourselves could restore us to sanity.
3. Made a decision to turn our lives over to God as we understood God. (p. 270)

The "unmanageability" of the codependent's life (and here it is worth noting that words like "unmanageable" and "power" serve the "machine" metaphor I have already discussed) might be understood as the result of her standing before a horizon that commands her to lose her "sanity." That command is issued when others show up as larger than she is, when the possibility of her sole authorship is excluded, and when she is oriented to moving toward others instead of toward herself. When the horizon is constituted in this fashion, the codependent is bound to try to have "power" over others lest they have "power" over her. The ensuing machinations and manipulations make her life "unmanageable." To "make a decision to turn her life over to God" is to decide to stand before a different horizon, one against which, presumably, the qualities of "recovery" cannot help but show up.

In asking after her own "spirituality," then, the reader is wondering not so much whether she stands before any horizon at all as whether she stands before the horizon that can "restore her to sanity." It is as if, in her "disease," she has worshiped false idols, and, in "turning her will and life over," she comes to a worship of true gods. We can see this imagery in excerpts like these:

> Resentment is holding onto anger at someone, clinging to a need to have the person hurt or punished to make up for the suffering I think he or she has caused me. The person I resent becomes my Higher Power as I think obsessively about what he or she did to me and how I can get even, all the time recreating the shame-filled or pain-filled episode in my mind. (FC, p. 47)

> . . . if we are arrogant and grandiose, we become our own Higher Power and do not need an external Higher Power. . . . We sabotage our hope for spiritual recovery. (FC, p. 51)

> When parents cannot admit their mistakes and be accountable for them, they assume the role of the Higher Power for the child, blocking the way to a true Higher Power. (FC, p. 68)

The reader need not eschew all possible horizons "outside the person"; she must, however, take care that she not place herself or others in the place of the "Higher Power." She must not worship false idols.

Once she is oriented to the "true Higher Power," many of the reader's behaviors and dispositions that are held to be "symptoms" take on a new meaning. Shame, for instance, when it takes place in front of the horizon dominated by other people, is what poisons or depletes the "supply" of self-esteem. But it is intrinsic to the experience of standing before the "Higher Power."

> . . . when our natural shame tells us we are not the Higher Power, this awareness allows us to be spiritual and humble enough to receive help from a Higher Power. Shame is a built-in regulator to keep us from getting too grandiose about our abilities and from forgetting our status as created beings rather than the Creator. (FC, pp. 94-95)

More generally, to "come to believe" appears to be to discover the only legitimate coauthor of one's own story. At this point, the reader is told, it is safe to "lose her boundaries," in an act of what is called "surrender."

> I had turned my will and my life over to the care of alcohol and other drugs; I had turned my will and my life over to the care of other human beings. . . . I had spent many years trying to impose my own plan onto the scheme of things. It was time to remove myself from anyone or anything's control (including my own) and place myself in the hands of an extraor-

dinarily loving God. "Take it," I said, "all of it—who I am, what's happened to me, where I shall go, and how I'll get there." (BC, pp. 172-173)

The reader is urged to ask whether she has "turned her life over" to a worthy "power"; and clearly, to ask this question is always already to hold open the possibility of an "out there," of a "power greater than self which transcends understanding" (FC, 1989, p. 50).

The reader thus finds that the "symptoms" of codependence are only symptomatic in front of a certain horizon, only when the "way to the Higher Power" is blocked and others occupy that place instead. But if she is oriented to the horizon which makes of those "symptoms" something "natural," then she stands before the only "out there" before which she can be something other than a sole author, and to which she can be bound, without being codependent. Indeed, she finds that she *must* seek that horizon in order for her life to be full. To understand what kind of background can turn the stuff of codependence into the stuff of "recovery," it is important to get a sense of what the literature means by "Higher Power." What kind of Other ought the codependent to aspire to stand before?

The "Higher Power" as the Divine Within

Certainly, it is not to be the Other proposed by traditional religions. Institutional religions are inimical to the kind of fulfillment sought in "recovery" because they constitute a horizon that is held to be universal to all, and against which certain actions and dispositions always show up as more or less valuable, regardless of the individual's narrative authority. According to Schaef, "the church" is one of the institutions (along with "the family" and "the school") that

> form[s] us into people who will fit into an addictive system, find persons with whom we can develop codependent relationships, and perpetuate the system by passing its characteristics on to our offspring. (CD, p. 68)

And "the church" does this precisely because it imposes a horizon on all people, forcing them to submit to its teachings.

> The characteristics of the good Christian person may or may not have anything to do with who an individual really is. Instead "niceness" [which she has already argued is the paradigm of those characteristics] is determined, abstractly, to be a virtue. (CD, pp. 81-82)

By insisting that its adherents are obligated to its teachings, "the church" becomes "unhealthy," particularly because a person can easily feel ashamed when standing before that abstractly determined standard. To illustrate this point, Beattie gives us the account of "Len," who is a "recovering codependent":

> I went to church on Sunday feeling good. I left feeling ashamed. I never felt good enough, no matter what I did . . . I couldn't tell if I was giving money because I wanted to or because I felt guilty. I was fine all week. But I felt crazy in church.
> . . . I need to hear God loves me, not that he's waiting to punish me. I've lived with fear and condemnation all my life. Looking back, I think that church was as shame-based as my family. I just didn't realize it until I got healthier. (BC, p. 55)

To ask if she gives allegiance "because she wants to or because she feels guilty" is to ask whether or not she remains autonomous before the Other. Clearly, a "healthy" person does not allow God to hold sway over her narrative in a way that goes beyond her own choosing.

The preservation of sole authorship, then, extends even to the realm of concerns about the "power greater than self." In order to ensure that the "Higher Power" is truly worthy of her "turning over her will and her life," the reader must make certain that it is "God as *she* understands God," rather than a God imposed abstractly, who commands her to a particular comportment and condemns her when she fails to follow that command. Schaef's gloss on the Third Step makes clear how idiosyncratic the constitution of this horizon can be.

> Some people say our Higher Power or Power Greater than Ourselves; some say our living process; some say our spirituality. Whatever works. The original wording is sexist and limited. (CD, p. 28)

In place of an abstractly determined understanding of God, the reader is to seek her own horizon, the one that "works" for her. The Other before whom she need not fear being condemned or ashamed or otherwise threatened with the "symptoms" of codependence must be the one that she chooses and gives a name, whose place in her narrative is determined by her alone.

But the reader's seeking after an adequate "Higher Power" is not entirely open-ended. To say "whatever works" is not to say that anything goes; rather it is to raise a question that gives a specific contour to the horizon. It is clear that "Len's" understanding didn't "work," because it left him feeling guilty and ashamed, which are already understood as "dysfunctional" feelings. For the reader to ask if it "works" is to ask if her understanding of her "Higher Power" makes

her feel good about herself. Indeed, this is the most important characteristic of the "Higher Power" proposed by these books.

> Authentic spirituality is about being accepted, loved, and valued in a rela-
> tionship with Ultimate Reality—our value and self-acceptance are experi-
> encially [sic] verified as we relate to Truth itself. (FC, p. 95)

The "authentic" Other is one with whom a relationship will make the
reader feel "accepted, loved, and valued." It is a benevolent Other, one
which makes no demands and issues no commands; and because of
this, it is an Other to which the reader can surrender without compromising her "health." She finds that the best understanding of God is
the one that fits her own narrative, the one she chooses on the basis of
its verifying her own self-acceptance; the "Higher Power" is yet another
"tool" for "recovery."

For the reader to enter into a relationship with this God is not to
strive toward something beyond her, or to surrender to something that
will have dominion over her; rather, it is only to strive to love herself.
"God hasn't abandoned us. We abandoned ourselves. He's there and he
cares. But he expects us to cooperate by caring for ourselves" (CNM,
p. 99). The reader's path to a full life is through the enhancement of her
own story. Any surrender this entails is not a giving over to a commanding Other; rather, it is a "cooperation" with something which
already has her best interests at heart. Indeed, that "Other" is indistinguishable from the "deep, important part of ourselves" that always
knows what is best. To abandon that "part" is also to lose contact with
God, which implies that God is only the "Divine Within." In theory, this
means that there is no conflict between the reader's autonomy and the
"Higher Power's" authority, no possibility that "surrender" will lead to
further suffering.

Indeed, this congruence between the "Higher Power" and the
"recovering" codependent means that the sacrifice and renunciation
often associated with traditional Judeo-Christian notions of spirituality
are unnecessary. Establishing a relationship with this Other

> does not mean we resign ourselves to a bunch of shoulds and ought tos
> and don our sackcloth. The exciting thing about this Step is it means
> there is a purpose and a plan—a great, perfectly wonderful, usually enjoy-
> able and worthwhile plan that takes into account our needs, wants, desires,
> abilities, talents and feelings—for each of our lives. (CNM, p. 173)

In asking after her own spirituality, then, the reader must already understand that the "Higher Power" that makes her life a full one is not—

indeed cannot be—an Other that demands compliance with a "bunch of shoulds and ought tos" or that places constraints on the validity of certain narratives or that stands beyond her in a way that commands her to move toward it. Instead, "Ultimate Reality" only "verifies" what she already is; only signifies the plan that is already there for her. As Beattie says, "We are here to live as long as we are alive, and there is a life for each of us to live" (BC, p. 173). And, of course, that good life is to be found only by journeying "within."

The "Higher Power" as Santa Claus

The horizon constituted by the "Higher Power," then, is, in an important way, not so much an "out there" as an artifact of the "in here." The reader is not to strive to transform her story into the one that shows up against a particular horizon as the narrative of a full life; rather, she is to seek the horizon against which her life will show up as already full. The "Higher Power" that "works" is the one to which she must be "open to feeling connected" (FC, p. 51), in front of which she cannot help but know that "it's okay to be who I am. Who I am is good, and I am good enough" (BC, p. 128). And she finds this horizon only when she stops striving to meet the demands of an implacable, alien God, and starts instead to care for herself. Indeed, that the "Higher Power" makes no demands is the measure of its "Truth." God doesn't call forth with "abstractly determined virtues" so much as stand by awaiting the codependent's discovery of the "worthwhile plan" that is already there for her.

The fullness of the life achieved by discovering this horizon need not be measured in what we might commonly think of as spiritual bounty. To stand before the horizon against which she is already good enough is to discover that "[she] deserve[s] the best life has to offer" (BC, p. 121). "Cooperation" with the "Higher Power"

> is connected to our deepest belief about what we deserve. It's connected to our desire and His [God's] desire that we be and have the best possible. It's connected to our willingness to let go. (BC, p. 243)

But to "let go," the reader must remember, is not to "don sackcloth"; to the contrary, it is to "let go" of the shame that prevents her from finding the worthwhile plan that the "Higher Power" has in mind for us, and "desires" us to take up. This "belief about what we deserve" is tied to prosperity. Beattie recounts a "recovering man" who

> tells the following story. "I always wanted a Mercedes," he says. One day, I bought one. I ordered the car, picked it up, and immediately the worst

feeling flooded through me. Whenever I went someplace, I parked a block
or two away. I didn't tell anybody I got the car. I felt like wearing a paper
bag over my head when I drove it. I didn't know what was wrong; I just
knew I felt uncomfortable about the car. One week later, I took it to
another car lot and started to trade it for a car of far less value. I was
going to lose money! Then it hit me. What was wrong was shame. I didn't
believe I deserved that car.

"I kept the car," the man says. "I'm working on my shame. I'm
working at changing what I believe about myself, and my right to have nice
things." (BC, p. 106)

A person who is "connected to her Higher Power" knows what her
rights are, and if she doesn't aspire to have "nice things," or feels some
shame about having them, she must question the horizon she stands
before.

This is true not only of luxury cars, but of more basic consumer
goods, as Mellody makes clear with this story about herself.

I was unaware that I needed clothes. I hardly had anything in my closet to
wear. I have a surrogate mom who has been teaching me how to tune
into my own dependency needs. One day . . . she confronted me about
not having any clothes. She said, "Pia, where are your clothes?"

I said, "In my closet, Jane."

"No. They're not there."

"I just hung them up five minutes ago. Go in there and look."

Finally I walked to the bedroom, opened the closet, and said, "Jane,
there are my pair of jeans, my T-shirt, my one good blouse, my pair of
slacks, and my five uniforms."

She said, "that's not enough."

"What do you mean that's not enough? That's enough for me." I
honestly didn't know what my need was. Eventually I moved up to
being too dependent, knowing that I needed clothes but not buying
them. Now I buy them, but periodically I still must make myself think
about the question of whether it is time to buy some new clothes. (PC,
p. 33)

Jane's advice here is not an opinion about Pia's wardrobe. It is a statement of "fact" about what a person's "needs" are. And that those
"needs" which must be satisfied include an ample wardrobe is verified by
nothing less than "God's desire that we have the best possible."

To ask after her own prosperity, then, is to ask if she stands in
front of the "Higher Power" who is the "authentic" Other, which is the
one that lets her know that she "deserves to have nice things." The
shame that the man in Beattie's story feels is the "shame [that] holds us

back," from which one can "break free by surrendering" (BC, p. 102). But this "surrender" is only to the inevitable goodness of what one already is, which in turn is only the benevolence of God working through that being. The "Higher Power" that "works" is the one that tells the reader to "have the best possible," and this can only be achieved by taking care of herself. If self-care requires her to buy a Mercedes or have a full closet, then it is incumbent upon her to buy them and to display them proudly. A full life is one lived against the horizon which makes a virtue of this kind of self-care, and in which the reader must question any reluctance she might have to partake in the bounty of a consumer society as a "symptom" of her illness.

It may come as a shock to find that God "cares and knows about all our needs and wants" (CNM, p. 214); and in reading over the reader's shoulder, we may be put off by this notion of a God who, like Santa Claus, only wants to help us help ourselves to the abundant goods of our shopping malls. But my concern here is not so much over whether this notion of what makes a full life is offensive, but rather whether it opens up any realm of the Other in the narrative space of the codependent. Is that benevolent horizon against which a proudly driven Mercedes is the fulfillment of a life truly "out there"? Or is it yet another instance of the concealment of otherness which I am arguing is pervasive in these texts? Surely the "Higher Power" is presented as an Other, but we have already seen that the concealment of otherness is itself concealed behind the texts' claim that they are offering the reader a technique of being-with-others.

It should be clear by now that the "Higher Power" presented in these texts is not an "out there" at all. Indeed, it is possible to "surrender" to the "Higher Power" precisely because it is not "abstractly determined," but rather is only God as I understand God, as God fits into my narrative. This God does not determine that one narrative is any better than another; the reader is only to question whether she has the "positive connection to a Higher Power" which allows her to feel already "good enough." Nor does this God limit the possible narratives that can show up; the reader finds that if she wants a Mercedes, wants to devote her life to getting one, then God wants that for her too, and can help her do this. The "true" God, she finds, is the one who would not think to make her feel ashamed for wanting a particular commodity or a particular kind of life, but who wants her to have the "best." And this God certainly does not stand as some immutable "beyond", a horizon toward which she ought to be oriented, or a direction in which her narrative journey ought to proceed. Rather, as Beattie says,

> Recovery is . . . a journey, not a destination. We travel a path from
> self-neglect into self-responsibility, self-care, and self-love. Like other jour-
> neys, it's one of moving forward, taking detours, backtracking, getting
> lost, finding the way again, and occasionally stopping to rest. Unlike other
> journeys, we can't travel it by forcing the next foot forward. It's a gentle
> journey, traveled by discipline, and by accepting and celebrating where we
> are in that journey today.
>
> Where we are today is where we're meant to be. It's where we
> need to be to get where we're going tomorrow. And that place we're
> going tomorrow will be better than any place we've been before. (BC,
> pp. 39-40)

But this guarantee of "getting better all the time" can only be
made because there is no necessary horizon against which one action,
one disposition, one life's narrative, can show up as any better than any
other. Even the "Higher Power" that is held forth as a necessary horizon
is only the "true Higher Power" because it does not issue any command
to the reader which would make her "getting better" a matter of anything else but feeling better about herself for who she already is. The
"Higher Power" is a worthy god only to the extent that it does not act as
an Other who demands response. To live before this horizon is never to
evaluate oneself by one's actions and comportment with others, but
only by one's "being," which is already recognized by the "Higher
Power" as good enough. Wherever "recovery" takes the reader, so long
as she has eclipsed concerns about the Other, God is sure to be on her
side and help her to a better place.

SUMMARY AND CONCLUSION

To understand the codependence literature as a moral discourse, then,
is to read its exemplary books as texts that suggest that the good life
involves relationships with a community of others, but only when those
relationships do not compromise the autonomy of sole authorship. And
the only way to achieve this good life is to make certain that others—
other people, a culture at large, the "Higher Power," and so on—never
hold sway, never constitute a horizon that commands the reader, but
rather remain under the sway of the reader/author herself. This is what
it means to say that the otherness of others is obliterated, and we can see
this obliteration in each of the axes of the narrative space of the codependence literature we have explored, as well as in the concealment of
the texts themselves as others. Nothing in that space exceeds the reader
in a way that demands she abandon her sole authorship, which is itself to

be understood as her own property, conferred upon her not by a culture or a tradition or even by the texts that tell her that it is hers; it belongs to her by sheer dint of her being alive. The reader questions her relationships in a way that reveals that only when she is the sole constituent of her narrative space can she have any commerce with other people, any sense of dignity, or any hope of living a full life. To be codependent is to experience oneself as "dependent upon others for [one's] very right to exist"; and to "recover" is to be dependent upon nothing and no one for that "right."

The reader of the codependence text thus enters a narrative space in which her downfall is understood as her failure to understand that she is the source of her own being, that nothing "outside the person" has the "right" to demand response from her, and that she must therefore take care of herself before anything or anyone else. Her redemption is to be found in a technique of self-care that allows her to take up her "rightful" place as the source of her own being. And this self-care is the key to being with others: "self-care is the one thing I can do that most helps me and others too" (Beattie, 1989, p. 38). To be in this way, however, is to be with others whose otherness is concealed, who can occupy the reader's narrative only so long as they do not stand beyond her in a way that exceeds her authorship, which is to say so long as they are not truly Other: they are only instruments of her narrative authority. Indeed, it is only by virtue of this concealing that the kind of relationship proposed by these texts is adequate to "recovery." Only when *she* determines the horizon can she "break free" and move toward the limitless future of abundance that her codependence is held to prevent her from attaining.

As I noted earlier, Beattie suggests that her book answers a crucial question: "How do we extricate our emotions, mind, body, and spirit from the agony of entanglement" (CNM, p. 58)? The reader who asks this question is already experiencing "entanglement" as "agonizing," and finds that "extrication" is achieved only when she can be in relationships that do not entangle her story with that of others, in which the otherness of others is obliterated by the "power" of her sole authorship. This extrication, of course, is held to be a panacea because who she (and all the others with whom she might be entangled) "really is" is a self-contained sole author; other understandings of her being are mistaken or misguided, particularly if they suggest her moral destiny is inextricably entangled with that of others. Relationships need not demand a choice between self-determination and relationship, between autonomy and community; but the fact that the codependence literature has achieved such popularity (not to mention the texts' own claim that

96 percent of us find agony in our entanglements) indicates that precisely such a choice arises for those among us who have not "recovered" but seek relationships anyway. Moreover, the books' popularity indicates that the solution they advocate—the absolute strengthening of the sole author's autonomy and the concomitant obliteration of otherness—is a compelling one.

It is at least ironic that a literature which claims to tell us how best to be with others ends by telling us how to eliminate their otherness from our lives, and thus achieve a good life. But I do not think this is an accidental outcome, some unintended meaning that randomly finds its way into the texts. Rather, as I suggested in the last chapter, and will argue in the next, I think it is possible to understand in an alternative way the texts' claim that agonizing relationships are the signs of an epidemic, namely, that the claim and its evident appeal indicate not so much a disease as a widespread confusion about how we are to comport ourselves with others. The ongoing presence of others in our narratives seems to present certain problems to people who have come to think of "maturity" and "health" as constituted largely, if not exclusively, by the hermetic autonomy signified by sole authorship. These problems are certainly not the bailiwick solely of the codependence literature; neither are they its invention: Beattie did not discover the "agony of entanglement." The texts, I am arguing, can be seen as a snapshot of how these problems show up in late twentieth-century U.S. popular culture. In the next chapter, I will try to account for the arising of that agony by locating it in the modern understanding of the human agent as a self-determining, self-contained sole author who must somehow find a way to bind itself back to a community of other such selves.

But before I turn to that account, I think it is necessary to point out that what I have been calling here the concealing of otherness can, and must, be seen as a problem that reaches into the heart of everyday life in contemporary U.S. culture. Elsewhere (Greenberg, 1989), I have argued that such concealing is the ontological basis of mass-death technology; it is the sine qua non of the construction and proliferation of devices like nuclear weapons which are designed to destroy wholesale large numbers of people. I argued there that unless others have already disappeared qua others, it is impossible to engage in practices like a nuclear arms race, to take on what Lifton (1979, 1982), along with other psychologically minded thinkers, has called "psychic numbing."

To recount this entire argument (which is indebted to Wyschogrod [1985] and Borgmann [1984], as well as to Heidegger's

[1954/1977] account of the ontology of technology) would take us far afield of the subject at hand. But we might glimpse its broad contours and its relevance if we consider some elements of what we have found in our exploration of the narrative space of the codependent. Take, for example, Beattie's (1987) claim that a person's downfall is his or her own "responsibility," that he or she must "face the proverbial music" (p. 202), and that if he or she wants to attain the good life (and help others to attain it), he or she must question, if not still, his or her impulse to help out the downtrodden. Now consider the everyday act, far too common, of walking down a city street past an array of homeless people, avoiding their imploring gazes, remaining unresponsive to their demands even as I hurry home to my own shelter. The concealing of otherness can be seen as the sine qua non of this (unfortunately) everyday act. Of course, there are many other possible valid interpretations of the "homeless" phenomenon; for example, it might be seen as the inescapable by-product of free-market capitalism. Here I am claiming only that my ability to walk on by without being "snagged" bears witness to my having already erased that other person as an Other, as a being who demands response from me. And this erasure is precisely what the codependence literature tells its reader is the cornerstone of the good life.

Consider a less emotion-laden everyday experience. Beattie (1989) claims that the shame a man feels about his newly purchased Mercedes is a "symptom" of codependence (p. 106). She suggests that being concerned with owning and driving such a car is the sign of having achieved the good life. Clearly, to understand the acts of buying and driving a luxury car as a "right" of the sole author/self is to say that it hardly matters how others might be affected by those acts. Even if the amount of money spent on the car would house a homeless family, this is a consideration which must take a back seat, so to speak, to the individual's pursuit of the fulfillments of "recovery." The otherness of others must already be eclipsed for this concern to emerge as a priority in the first place.

Indeed, it is not only the question of purchasing and feeling good about luxury cars that discloses that concealment. Simply to drive is to enter a web of practices that involve the exploitation of, and wars against, third world countries, the despoiling of the environment in the oil fields, the paving over of large portions of wetlands and wilderness, the increasing threat of the global catastrophe known as the "greenhouse effect," and so on. In order to drive despite these implications, I must already be a sole author, closed off from those others who might call forth from me a response that could likely lead me to experience (and perhaps eschew) driving as something at odds, instead of congruent, with the achievement of the good life.

The next chapter will argue in detail what I am only sketching here: that the concealing of otherness is an inescapable aspect of the understanding of the self as a sole author, a problem that emerges when the self is cut loose from any necessary moorings in a social world, and left free to tell its own story about that world. For now, I note some concrete implications of that concealing only to indicate that when the codependence literature is understood as a moral discourse, its solution to the problem of how the self is to be related to others raises some troubling questions. The obliteration of the otherness of the Other as a proposed underpinning of the good life does not bode well for a society that possesses instruments of mass destruction like nuclear weapons, and which seems to depend for its very survival on certain practices, like driving, which threaten an irreversible and complete annihilation of others. The notion that I have no responsibility for a homeless person, that his or her evoking a response in me is only the environment's "snagging" my diseased self, is alarming when we consider the widening gap between the rich and the poor in this country, the institutionalized foreclosure of opportunity to people of various ethnic and socioeconomic groups, and the ongoing threats, both technological and military, to the global environment.

Such problematic practices, it would seem, can only arise when the desire to drive a Mercedes has already eclipsed any concern with how the individual's procurement and use of that car might affect others adversely, with how the driver might indeed be responsible for those implications. To argue that any guilt or shame which might impose a limit on an individual's "self-esteem" has no place in the good life is to threaten to give a legitimacy (which, of course, in the codependence literature is granted by invoking standards of "health") to practices that ought at least to be questioned, if not eschewed. The radical split between being and doing embedded in this notion of self-love, and its concomitant insistence that our value is not based on how we act in the world of others, suggests an inaction bordering on apathy. For if our value as people does not depend on how we act at crucial moments, on how our comportment measures up against some transcendent horizon, then why would or should we take the difficult actions that might be necessary to ease the crises of our time? Why should we interpret our discomfort as anything other than the failure to secure ourselves within our boundaries well enough to be immune to getting "snagged"? Moreover, if everyone is a victim, and no one a perpetrator, then why should we act against any particular person or political interest? The thorough eclipse of the Other advocated by these texts threatens to conceal the very existence of problems like homelessness qua social and political problems behind the claim that one's destiny is merely a matter of one's own colloquy with oneself.

7

The Codependence
Literature as an
Instance of Nihilism

Wake up to find out that you are the eyes of the world,
But the heart has its beaches, its homelands and
    thoughts of its own
Wake now, discover that you are the song that
    the morning brings
But the heart has its seasons, its evenings and songs
    of its own

—Robert Hunter, "Eyes of the World"

INTRODUCTION

The good life proposed by the codependence literature turns out to be
attained when a person aspires to obliterate the otherness of other people. Whether they are intimates, codependence authors, or the horizon
constituted by a culture at large, these books, in form and content, suggest that those others ought to remain under the authorial sway of the
person seeking "recovery." This concealment—which, of course, is presented in the texts as an upholding of others' sole authorship—is held to
be the best way to overcome the "agony of entanglement." And it is
clear that the opportunity for these books to achieve their popularity

187

arises only because it is a widespread experience—if not an "epidemic"—
in our culture that relationships are painful and that the good life eludes
people who seek to conduct them. Indeed, the books claim that 96 percent of us suffer this agony; their sales, while not approaching this level,
indicate that many people find this claim, and the texts' way of addressing it, compelling.

If we take these books as a moral discourse, then we must discard
their contention that they are merely presenting a "diagnosis" and a
"cure" of a "disease," except insofar as their telling us this is itself constitutive of that discourse. This means that we must find some framework other than the medical/naturalist in which to place their claims,
some way to assess the good life they propose.

We can already say that the literature bears witness to a breakdown, deeply embedded in the culture, between self and Other: to say
that 96 percent of us do not know how to conduct relationships without
becoming unduly "entangled" (and to recognize that there is a significant opening in the culture for such an utterance) is to say that something is amiss in the cultural understanding of how we are to be with one
another. And we can also say that the proposed repair of this breakdown seems only to raise more questions about that understanding: to
claim that we can best engage in relationships with others when their
otherness is obliterated seems to open the way to the perpetuation of
certain practices which we can perhaps all agree are troublesome, if not
worthy of condemnation. But what is not yet clear is how both the breakdown and the proposed repair arise with such compelling power in the
first place, and what their wellsprings are.

I do not mean this as a question about the "psychology" of the
reader, but rather about her ontology. The question I am asking might
be stated in this way: what is the horizon against which the understanding arises of the good life as the life lived in front of no necessary horizon? In this chapter I will argue that the ontology of this claim is an
apprehension of being which is nihilistic. This nihilism—a word I understand to mean as the loss of seriousness and meaning which follows
from the leveling of significant distinctions—can be found in the breakdown the codependence literature addresses. But it remains the concealed background of that literature. It shows up in the proposed repair
that the texts call "recovery," perhaps most clearly in the absence or
insignificance of distinctions other than those arising out of the reader's
author-ity (understood as that which makes her feel "okay" about herself). To end the "agony of entanglement" by turning others into mere
instruments of my own authorship, I will argue, is only to deepen the
ontological conditions which give rise to that "agony" in the first place.

I intend to disclose this ontology by doing what the codependence authors, in their zeal to be "effective," fail to do: to place the literature's central tenet—that the good life is the life of sole authorship—in a philosophical and historical context.

In the course of this analysis, we will find that the codependence literature stands as a concrete instance of a breakdown that is implicit in what Dallmayr (1984) calls the "metaphysical pillar" of the modern age, namely, its claim that the human subject is a self-directed, self-contained narrator of its own story. We will see that this understanding is always already a concealing, if not an obliteration, of the otherness of the Other, whether other people or a culture at large. The "self" which is thus freed from necessary entanglements will show up as purely technical and efficient, that is, as a self that can live the good life when it learns certain techniques of self-management like those offered in the codependence texts, or other kinds of "therapy." Such a "self" can arise, I will argue, when the human subject stands before a horizon which is concealed qua horizon. Finally, we will see that so long as the self is understood as a "powerful" sole author, holding all otherness under its sway, entanglement will very likely be agonizing, and a narrative space which entirely erases those others—and, therefore, that agony—will hold a compelling appeal.

My strategy for carrying out this analysis will be somewhat circuitous. First, I will sketch the contours of the breakdown addressed by the codependence literature as they appear in certain accounts of the emergence of the "metaphysical pillar" of our age. I will argue that the construction of the edifice upheld by this pillar might be understood as an attempt to safeguard against a certain kind of agony—that caused by subordination to a tradition—but opens the way to a different kind—that caused by the wiping away of all tradition. I will illustrate these possibilities of agony with a reading of Shakespeare's *Othello*,[1] in which I will argue that Othello is so entangled in a tradition that he can have no sole authorship, while Iago is so much a sole author that he has no entanglements whatsoever. Each character commits a distinctive kind of atrocity, and we will see that these atrocities disclose the nihilism that haunts the background of the rupture for which these characters stand. If sole authorship arises as a way to safeguard against Othello's emptiness, I will argue, it also poses the possibility of the emptiness embodied by Iago. We will see that in both cases, there is no necessary shared understanding which preserves the possibility of meaningful relationships among individual narratives about being-with-others, or what I will call conversation.

I will then discuss the attempt to restore a horizon that allows for an overcoming of fragmented conversation, for entanglements that are not agonizing, through what has been called "metaphysical ethics" (see Caputo, 1989). This effort, which sounds many of the same themes as the codependence literature, cannot help but fail to repair that breakdown. The reasons for this will help us understand why the codependence literature—and some other "therapeutic" discourses—wrecks on the shoals of nihilism, failing to safeguard the interpersonal world from atrocity, perhaps even courting disaster. Finally, in an attempt to understand the apparent irreparability of the rupture embodied by the codependence literature, I will turn to Heidegger's account of nihilism, and in particular to its indictment of the notion of sole authorship as always already a concealing of the otherness of others. This account will help us to see both how the codependence literature emerges as a popular genre in our culture, and how its understanding of what is wrong with our love lives, and how they might be set right, is a dangerous one.

One way to understand my strategy here is to say that I am telling one story to help explicate another. The latter is, of course, the story, found in the codependence literature, of the sole author overcoming the agony of being-with-others by transforming that being-with into a narrative device under its own authorial power. The story I will use as an interpretive context is one that draws upon a number of sources, each of which is relevant because it also takes up the ontological dimensions of the problem of being-with-others in the modern age. My account relies at the outset upon Taylor (1989) and MacIntyre (1984), who have investigated the historical, cultural, and philosophical determinants of the *ego cogito*. Taylor's account is a more comprehensive attempt than MacIntyre's, and there are many differences between their respective works, but what they share (and what makes them relevant here) is a preoccupation with the question of what happens when the prevailing understanding of being is one in which self is declared sovereign. They take up specifically the implications of that ontology for the self's relations with a social world.

I have tried to synthesize these accounts into a coherent story about this problem, a story of a character who emerges with the Enlightenment into an understanding of him or herself as a being who can stand back from and reflect upon the world of others. By deferring to Taylor (1989) and MacIntyre (1984), I do not mean to imply that their accounts of this character are the only ones, or that they are without their own problems. Indeed, both writers might be seen as having their own prejudices, as setting a conservative, if not a regressive, social agenda. But it is not their conclusions, or their social programs, with which I am concerned here. Rather, it is their clear laying out of this problem of modernity, namely, that the *ego cogito* is left without necessary moorings in a social world, that for all of what Taylor calls its epiphanies (see pp. 456-93), its bestowal upon humanity of such legacies as the notion of "human rights" and the "integrity of the person," modernity, when understood as the age of the self-contained individual, also leaves the self without a clear way to be bound back to others. This problem, then, underlies both the codependence literature and the story I am about to tell.

THE GORDIAN KNOT

This story, as I have said, concerns the prospect of carrying out our commerce with others in a way that does not bring about an agonizing loss of autonomy, and yet still preserves some community. This story starts, that is, with a question similar to that of the codependence literature: how is the "self," understood as a sovereign agent, to relate to the "world," understood as the location of that which is "outside the person"?

We might find our way into the larger story, and begin to see its connections with the codependence literature, by recalling our exemplary texts' own attempt at "moral theory," perhaps best captured by Beattie's claim that "if we're working toward recovery, we have an internal moral code that will send us signals when it's violated" (BC, p. 107). First, we are to achieve the good life; ethical action, she is arguing, will "pop up" as a matter of course. The former is not necessarily achieved through the latter; indeed Schaef's analysis of the "good Christian" (discussed in the previous chapter) makes it clear that what is usually understood as right action can actually impede progress toward the good. It is more important, then, to pursue the good life of "recovery" than it is to consider the goods that constitute the "internal moral code."

This distinction—between what Taylor (1989) calls "constitutive goods" and "life goods"—is, according to him, an important part of the history of Western moral philosophy, and it points us toward the breakdown that characterizes the understanding of being from which phenomena like the codependence literature emerge. Before Schaef and Beattie can establish the priority of the achievement of the good life over the carrying out of certain kinds of action, life goods and constitutive goods must already be sundered. But what is the groundwork of that distinction? What is the ontology that makes possible an understanding of the right without necessary recourse to the good?

Taylor tells us that this sundering can be seen as emerging along with the conception of the person as an autonomous moral agent, one whose understanding of and assent to constitutive goods is more fundamental than those goods themselves, whose sole authorship is the highest moral priority. This character can be traced historically throughout Western philosophies of the self, as Taylor (1989) has done, but it emerges most clearly at the time of the Enlightenment, and particularly in this shift that Taylor describes:

> Instead of looking at the world as a providential order, we can look at it, and indeed, at our own natures, as a neutral domain, which we have to understand in order to master it, and whose causal relations we have to make use of in order to produce the greatest amount of happiness. (p. 321)

In terms of the narrative metaphor I have been using here, this shift means that constitutive goods hold sway not as the result of a taken-for-granted "providential order" which authorizes them, but rather only when they are author-ized by the individual's understanding of the good life.

There is a problem at the heart of this conception, one that can be seen in Taylor's summary of the ideals which he claims constitute the life goods of the *Aufklarer*:

1. The ideal of self-responsible reason. This entail[s] . . . a freedom from all authority, and [is] linked with a notion of dignity.
2. The notion that the ordinary fulfillments that we seek by nature, the pursuit of happiness in the characteristic human way, through production and family life, have a central significance. . . .
3. The ideal of universal and impartial benevolence. (p. 322)

While the autonomy and dignity of the individual in his or her daily life are important, according to this scheme, so too is the presence of some universal benevolence to which all persons can subscribe. Alongside the agony of entanglement stands the agony of fragmentation, of being cut loose from a background which somehow holds together—universally and impartially—a world of sole authors. The autonomous agent still aspires to some certain mooring in a social world, in which something of the universal is preserved. In this sense, the person who subscribes to this understanding of the self (which, I am claiming, is most of us moderns, including readers of codependence books), wants both to have his or her cake and to eat it. Ideal (3) above inscribes an ongoing dream in which the individual has autonomy and still continues to inhabit and be bound to an orderly political and social world. The difficulty is that if the good life is to be found by appeal to sole authorship independent of any authority "outside the person," then how can any individual agent be bound by any particular rule or set of rules? What kind of universals—what we might call "metanarratives"—can be found to which the individual can be bound without compromising his or her narrative sovereignty?

These questions have proved to be a Gordian knot. As Taylor notes, attempts to unravel it have tended to concentrate on questions of right actions rather than on the good life, but this simply begs the question. No list of what it is right to do can compel compliance without appeal to an authority that exceeds that of the sole author, and for the *Aufklärer* the good life is one lived outside the shadow of this kind of authority. The person who would resolve this dilemma is faced with the task of specifying "how the autonomy of the moral agent might be consistently combined with a view of moral rules as having an independent and objective authority" (MacIntyre, 1984, p. 65).

This question becomes particularly vexing when the existence of God is called into question, as it must be, at least according to Taylor (1989), as soon as something like Descartes' cogito is posited. Descartes, of course, was at great pains to preserve a realm of authority by arguing for the insuperable place of God as the basis of knowledge that is certain. But, as Taylor (1989, p. 324) says, to posit a cogito which can doubt all except certainty, and then to limit the scope of its inquiry and subsequent authorial power, is to stop halfway on the road to enlightenment. When that road is followed to its end, and the scope of inquiry includes the existence of God, then all that is left that is capable of determining the good is self-responsible reason. Eventually, "any appeals to a Law of Nature, or the 'Law of Reason, Right Reason, Natural Justice, Natural Equity, Good order,' or the like, have to be set aside" (p. 321).

For us moderns, it would seem, there is no teleological or categorical reason to compel us to adopt certain standards; but neither has the attempt to find such a grounding, to tell a story which upholds both the autonomy of sole authorship and the understandings that authorize certain narratives and proscribe others, been abandoned. Whether that grounding is to be found in the "invisible hand" of the marketplace, in the utilitarian principle of the maximum good for the maximum number, in Darwinian theory, in a categorical imperative, in "ideal speech situations," in "codependence" and "recovery," or in other such metanarrative devices, the attempt is to find some standard or criterion that is both nonauthoritarian and universally commanding of respect.

If this standard is found, then the autonomy of the individual person and the demands of the community will not be in conflict; entanglement will not be the agonizing loss of sole authorship. Kant's categorical imperative, for example, is the rule to which any reasonable person would freely subscribe to because of his or her own reason. In this kind of unraveling of the Gordian knot, there would be no forced choice between sole authorship and being-with-others. Instead, there would be an understanding of the good which neither violates autonomy nor consigns human interaction to inescapable solipsism. The character that would occupy such a story could live with the competing claims of autonomy and community without losing either.

Understood as a moral discourse, the codependence literature can also be seen as taking up this concern, at least to the extent that it starts with the same problem. The literature's claim that the "agony of entanglement" is a preoccupation of "96 percent" of us might now appear in a different light. The size of the target audience is not the evidence of a new "disease" of epidemic proportion, but rather an indication of the enormity of the literature's concerns. To enter a narrative space whose questions are largely about the how a person is to engage in relationships with others without "losing" himself or herself is to take up the question of how the sovereign self is to live in a community without having to subscribe to a common understanding of the good life which it does not itself author-ize. The story of "disease" and "recovery" that the codependence literature tells can be recast as a story about the "metaphysical pillar" of our age. And the vicissitudes of that older story thus provide a fitting context in which to understand the codependence literature's claims about the good life, and in which the difficulties and dangers of that good life can show up.

MacIntyre (1984) summarizes the problem that gives rise to these stories in this fashion:

> On the one hand the individual moral agent, freed from hierarchy and teleology, conceives of himself . . . as sovereign in his moral authority. On the other hand the inherited, if partially transformed rules of morality have to be found some new status, deprived as they have been of their older teleological character and their even more ancient categorical character as expressions of an ultimately divine law. If such rules cannot be found a new status which will make them rational, appeal to them will indeed appear as a mere instrument of individual desire and will. (p. 51)

The discovery of the life goods that Taylor (1989) has outlined leaves an ambiguous legacy. The modern invention of the individual, with its emphasis on the dignity of each person's quotidian life, is the wellspring of some of our most cherished beliefs about equality and justice. At the same time, however, that invention is made possible only at the expense of the very bonds that otherwise hold the person to his or her social world so tightly that individual reason and dignity cannot emerge. If there is to continue to be a meaningful social world, a world of others, in which certain practices can be distinguished as "better" or "worse" than certain others, a way must be found to bind the individual back to the social world, to find a "new status" for the agreements about what constitutes the good life. Most attempts to do so have involved what Caputo (1989) calls "metaphysical ethics" (p. 55): the attempt to provide a first principle, some new categorical or teleological distinction, that gives a compelling quality to a certain understanding of the good.

This is not the place to recount all of the various attempts to salvage universal morality by means of practical reason or the discovery of a nonauthoritarian teleology. Rather, I would like to turn to the endeavor itself, to the attempt to discover and elucidate that "new status" as it is recounted by Taylor (1989) and MacIntyre (1984), and to ask what the persistence of that endeavor (of which the codependence literature is an example) itself discloses.

One way to open up this question is to return to Taylor's (1989, pp. 4-5) suggestion that our moral reactions to various situations can be understood as "instincts" whose contours may be defined by culture and upbringing but whose existence qua instinct is not. The human subject must be understood as a capability for moral reaction; it must make strong evaluations about what makes life worth living, and this, he argues, is what makes it human. From those strong evaluations, in turn, can be deduced the understanding of being which makes those particular goods of value. What we strongly value, Taylor is arguing, can be viewed as the finger pointing to the understanding of being that already constitutes our everyday lives.

It is my contention that the endeavor of philosophers to answer the question that haunts the strain of moral discourse under discussion here discloses one of those reactions. Radical relativism, the notion of morality as a "mere instrument of desire and will," apparently evokes a negative reaction which is compelling in the same way that Taylor (1989) claims disgust is. The attempt to salvage universal morality from "individual desire and will," or a calculus of pleasure and pain, arises contemporaneously with the idea of the self as an autonomous agent and a concomitant radical critique of religious tradition. It is not just that we are driven to make our lives worthwhile in our own terms, to evaluate them in terms of (conscious or unconscious) strong evaluations. Moreover, we need to know what standards justify those evaluations, and, in turn, what justifies those standards. This "need to know" is not simply a matter of having some technique for adjudicating among moral claims. Rather, one of the goods that we autonomy-seeking selves strongly value *is* the moral grounding that makes strong evaluations possible and meaningful in the first place.

It might be said that one of the things that makes life worthwhile, at least in our age, is knowing what grounds our judgment, that is, knowing by what measure a life can be said to be worthwhile. This knowledge is what we ought to aspire toward in order to secure a good life, or to know what actions are right. Moreover, in keeping with Taylor's elucidation of the moral sphere, an inquiry into this particular evaluation, like any other, should disclose the understanding of being from which it emerges. Against what background do attempts to find valid moral principles arise and make sense? What can an illumination of that background tell us about those attempts? And, in the particular attempt made by the codependence literature, how can asking this question help us to understand the apparent impossibility of overcoming the agony of entanglement without encountering the agony of fragmentation? To address these questions will be to open the way to an understanding of the problems raised by the codependence literature's understanding, grounding, and validation of its definition of the good life.

OTHELLO AND IAGO

My object is to follow the thread of the quest for moral coherence to its ontological ground, and a pre-Enlightenment example may give us a preliminary direction for this project. In *Othello*, Shakespeare gives us two characters on opposite sides of the breakdown which that quest seeks to overcome. Othello knows all the rules, but is tragically limited in his ability to understand them in a way that allows him to respond to the demands of a particular situation. Asked what should be said of his fall into dishonor, he reveals his ongoing naivete:

> Why, anything:
> An honorable murderer, if you will;
> For nought did I in hate, but all in honor. (V, ii, 293-5)

Honor has, however, turned out to be an inadequate first principle, a foolish consistency that has turned into his hobgoblin and has led him to the absurdity of being an honorable murderer.

In Othello's commitment to honor can be glimpsed one of the problems that faces the person incapable of autonomous moral judgment, who has not taken up the mantle of sole authorship. He cannot deliberate on his predicament and weigh the relative merits of murder and losing honor. Othello is no *Aufklarer*, he, of course, could not have heard the Cartesian gospel of disengaged reasoning. And although he appears to mean well, to do all "in honor," his inability to separate himself from the background of honorable practices makes him incapable of making for himself the distinctions necessary to understand and to enact (or restrain from enacting) his strong evaluations. He is too tightly bound to that background to gain the distance necessary to carry on such a conversation; or, in terms of the "narrative" metaphor, he is too much a character in a metanarrative to tell his own story. His moral world cannot emerge as an object of inquiry, and he cannot emerge as an inquiring subject, as a sole author. When he describes himself as "one who loved not wisely but too well," Othello tells us of his failure to develop the "wisdom" that is inherent in the practice of disengaged reason. His lack of enlightenment brings him to a disgraceful and agonizing end.

Othello shows us what is dangerous about the failure of the individual to emerge as a person who exercises "self-responsible reason": without his knowing assent to it, the understanding of the good life, embodied in the rules he lives by, becomes empty of wisdom. It collapses in the meaninglessness of Desdemona's death and his suicide. Honor is empty not because it is an intrinsically bad practice or somehow *not* virtuous. Rather, it fails because Othello has not author-ized it in his own narrative. He fails to fill the notion of honor with his understanding of its place in his story, so he cannot put it aside in favor of some other virtue such as temperance. He is, in this sense, too entangled in his love—of both honor and Desdemona—to love wisely.

Iago, on the other hand, shows us a different kind of emptiness. Just after Othello speaks of his commitment to honor, he attempts to find out what force has shipwrecked him, what different principle has rendered his own absurd. He asks Cassio to

> demand that demi-devil
> why he hath thus ensnared my soul and body,

to which Iago replies

> Demand me nothing. What you know you know:
> From this time forth I never will speak word. (v, ii, 301-4)

Iago's villainy is not only his manipulation of Othello, his role in the violation of the moral precept against murdering. Indeed, we must remember that Iago is the villain and Othello the hero of this story. The sheer murder of Desdemona—based on love, albeit a foolish one—is less chilling than Iago's silence, which has nothing of love in it. The murderer is, in this case, morally superior to the conspirator because the Moor at least attempts to occupy a moral world, while Iago refuses any moral stance. Iago's crime is made truly evil by his refusal to account for himself, to give some meaning to his actions by placing them in a story that can be told to others. By leaving only unexplained death and disorder in his wake, he withdraws from the realm of strong evaluations embedded in narratives, and thus from the truly human world.

If Othello is tragically limited in his (authorial) ability to participate in a meaningful moral conversation, Iago is villainous in his outright refusal to do so, his renunciation of narrative. By rejecting the demand for meaning, he refuses to participate in a conversation that would make him part of a community by making him intelligible to others. If Othello stands for the emptiness that results from the individual's failure to be disentangled from his social world, Iago stands for the emptiness that follows upon absolute detachment. He is entirely a bounded monad, severed from others not only because he has (apparently) figured out and is living by different strong evaluations from theirs, precepts that might make him want to kill for a principle, but because he refuses to place his evaluations (if, indeed, he has them) in conversation with theirs. He refuses to make an account of his differences. It's all the same to Iago: there is no more point in his telling his story to Cassio and Othello than there was in setting Othello against Desdemona. Refusing conversation, refusing strong evaluation, refusing entanglement, he refuses humanity, and his refusals evoke our horror.

THE DANGLING CONVERSATION

Iago keeps any reasons he might have to himself, and Othello has reasons that are so unreasoned they bring about a disaster. In *Othello* we can begin to glimpse the background against which attempts at metaphysical ethics arise and make sense. Shakespeare shows us two kinds of emptiness here: the one in which rules imposed from "outside the person"—in this case the virtue of honor—are taken so much for granted that their meaning is lost; the other in which they have no part to play at all. Either way, the involvements of the person with his or her world threaten to become agonizing by becoming empty of meaning and seriousness; the spectre of nihilism is raised.

Clearly, the "invention" of a self that is an autonomous sole author addresses this danger in its first aspect. Meaningful distinctions cannot emerge when we love so well that we cannot be wise, when involvements are held so closely that they sweep us into stories over which we have little or no authorial sway, stories that, in effect, "tell" us: Othello "loses himself," and his life, when honor makes him its servant. To say that the individual is inherently dignified, his or her daily life important, and his or her autonomy sacrosanct, is to say that this servitude should not occur, that the individual's ability to stand back from and tell his or her own story about the social world is paramount. That disentanglement safeguards the moral realm from becoming a world filled with Othellos, in which one taken-for-granted narrative provides all meaningful distinctions, all individuals' understandings of the good life. The promise that is held out by the aspiration to sole authorship is that meaning will not disappear in an atrocity like Desdemona's death because it is the individual's business to weigh his or her actions against a rational understanding of moral precepts.

But this invention and celebration of the individual's ability to engage in meaningful conversation with his or her social world, the shift that Taylor (1989) claims signals the onset of the Enlightenment, raises the distinct possibility of a world of Iagos, of private narratives about the good that are so detached from one another as to be incapable of being placed in conversation with other private narratives. The second kind of emptiness threatens an agony more silent than Othello's, in which the sole author is a person with no occasion or ability to "speak word" with another, even if that is what the situation seems to demand, and even if that is what the person wants. A person need not hold the apparent malice of Iago to be the bearer of his kind of nihilism, or to suffer the agony of fragmentation and isolation. As Dreyfus (1981) points out, when there is no basis for serious conversation,

> there is no meaningful difference between political parties, between religious communities, between social causes, between cultural practices—everything is on a par. That means there are no shared commitments, and, as a result . . . individuals feel alienated and isolated. They feel their lives have no meaning because the public world has no meaning. (p. 508)

The attempt to overcome the emptiness embodied by Othello's unquestioning entanglement with his background yields the detached, reflecting cogito, author of its own story.

But this leads to a different kind of emptiness, one in which meaningful conversation is impossible precisely because there is no shared background. Taylor (1989) gives an account of the significance of this emptiness.

I am a self only in relation to certain interlocutors: in one way in relation to those conversational partners who were essential to my achieving self-definition; in another in relation to those who are now crucial to my continuing grasp of languages of self-understanding. . . . A self exists only within what I call "webs of interlocution." . . . It is this original situation which gives its sense to our concept of identity, offering an answer to the question of who I am through a definition of where I am speaking from and to whom. (p. 36)

Without the conversation that gives the person his or her orientation in a world of others, Taylor is claiming, there is no self. Light might be shed on this broad claim if we recall Cushman's (1990) argument that a self, no matter how it appears in a particular historical setting, is always a social construction: it can only exist in a network of relations, and gather its orientation through what Taylor is calling "interlocution."[2] Even if we achieve the detachment Othello lacks by inventing an autonomous individual, still we are not guaranteed a place in a web of interlocution, a moral orientation that will guide us between the Scylla of unreflective involvement and the Charybdis of uninvolved reflection.

If meaningful conversation is impossible, then a detached self is impoverished in a way quite different from, but perhaps no better than, the person naively committed to honor. In the latter case, each individual might be so different from every other that they are the same; the sole author fails to find his or her place in a web of interlocution, and remains empty. The individual who arises in an attempt to safeguard meaning against the agony of Othello faces a new kind of meaninglessness. The celebration must be tempered, at least until some prophylactic measure can be taken to ward off nihilism.

Kant explains his preoccupation with finding a universal basis for morality as just such a prophylaxis.

A metaphysics of morals is . . . indispensable . . . because morals themselves remain subject to all kinds of corruption so long as the guide and supreme norm for their correct estimation is lacking. For it is not sufficient to that which should be morally good that it conform to the law; it must be done for the sake of the law. . . . [T]herefore, this (i.e., metaphysics) must lead the way, and without it there can be no moral philosophy. (Kant, 1795/1969, pp. 6-7)

For Kant, the individual is not freed from systems of obligation, from all compulsory entanglement with others. To the contrary, the *Aufklärer* has taken on a new burden: it is no longer enough to obey rules without knowledge of that which makes them correct, without authorizing them;

but he must find his own way to obey rules. He must have more wisdom than Othello, and actions taken with the Moor's naivete cannot properly be considered moral. It is the thought-about intention that counts, but not only because that increases the likelihood of taking right action. More important, rational moral thinking, in the sense that Kant intends, is what we all can do. Unless we are thinking rationally about them, our narratives do not bear the traces of universality without which there is no objectively binding morality.

Without that kind of thought, according to Kant, there is no possibility of the conversation that binds enlightened individuals one to another by allowing them to talk about the differences among their stories. If human interaction is to be rescued from the dangers of "individual will and desire," Kant argues, it will only be through the discovery and affirmation of a metaphysics—which, of course, for Kant, was to be provided by the universal exercise of pure practical reason, which alone provides the common basis for our taking up of our obligations. The moral *is* what we, as rational beings, all can share, no longer because it is inscribed in religions which we are compelled to believe, but because it is achieved by each individual's exercise of that universal reason. It is then authorized in each person's individual narrative, but in a way that still preserves a community. To return to Taylor's (1989) language, the universal exercise of reason safeguards the webs of interlocution which give a self its orientation.

Kant's safeguarding of both the individual and the collective, both narrative and metanarrative, is to be achieved through the categorical imperative—that moral law to which any reasonable person would subscribe if he or she exercised his or her reason. These are not, then, rules as such; their "authority and objectivity . . . is precisely that authority and objectivity which belongs to the exercise of reason" (MacIntyre, 1984, p. 65). These rules have no claim on the individual which is external to that person; they are really just an extension of the person's autonomy.

The categorical imperative is a procedural principle. It is a proposal to undo the Gordian knot by claiming that there are rules, but that they have no necessary content, only form; it is a metanarrative that specifies only *how* each author tells his or her story, and not what that narrative necessarily consists of. We are to follow the dictates of reason, which, as the universal principle that makes webs of interlocution possible in the first place, is to be trusted to discover the principles that will safeguard those conversations. The individual, by virtue of his or her having reason, can enact the universal, can participate in a shared understanding of the Good without losing autonomy. We can be better than

Othello, because we can detach from the lived world and think about our involvements in it in order to enter the narrative space in which we can carry them out both well and wisely. And we can be better than Iago because when we exercise our reason, and thus tell our own story in a way that can be taken up by a community, we cannot help but find our way into a conversation with other people who are doing the same thing.

The emptiness I am here calling nihilism is not to be filled with lists of rules or rights or any other content. But, in an important way, this still leaves a void at the heart of our conversations, one that continues to raise the spectre of a world of Iagos. An example of the problems such a solution raises might be found in the current controversy in this country about abortion. We can perhaps all agree that murder is wrong, that it violates the categorical imperative by failing to treat others as ends, but we cannot agree about whether, for instance, a fetus is human and therefore whether it must be treated as an end in itself. More important, there is no agreement about the means by which we are to determine the standing of the fetus. Some, like Dworkin (1989), argue that the fetus, its other attributes notwithstanding, is not a *constitutional* person, and therefore is not protected by the laws enabled by the U.S. Constitution. Others would ground their notion of moral action with respect to fetuses in religious traditions that proscribe abortion. For some the fetus is entitled to a protected status simply by virtue of its biological existence; it is human and may not be murdered any more than any human may. For others, human life has to do with independence and autonomy, with so-called "quality of life" issues, and the mother, by this definition, clearly has priority for protection over the fetus. Her freedom to control her body must not be compromised by the presence of a fetus within her.

The divergence between these views (and among other interpretations of the abortion question) is a difference between competing ontologies. The "moral reactions" of the various commentators are, as Taylor (1989) would have it, affirmations of divergent understandings of being human. But they are incommensurate understandings. As a result, their proponents are incapable of meaningful conversation with one another because they are, in effect, speaking different languages. Unlike Iago, the participants in this debate do not refuse to "speak word," but the ability of these words to cohere into a debate that would shed light on the problem at hand is questionable, and seems no more satisfying than the "dialogue" between Othello and Iago. As MacIntyre (1984) says, "because there is in our society no established way of deciding between these claims . . . moral argument appears to be necessarily interminable" (p. 8). Even when people are willing and able to make their narratives explicit and rational, there is no guarantee that they can be placed in meaningful debate.

If the individual is free to figure things out for him or herself, and there is no constraint on this freedom other than that it must be exercised rationally, then the arising of competing ontologies such as appears in the abortion controversy is inevitable, and no ability to apply a universal procedural principle will resolve it. The ability to construct our own story—what we might call a "world-view"—based on the authority of one's own cogitations cannot help but lead to a breakdown in conversation, to what MacIntyre (1984) calls "incommensurability." He traces this breakdown to an incommensurability at the heart of the concept of the individual self. As he puts it, philosophers who would undo the Gordian knot

> engaged in what was an inevitably unsuccessful project; for they did indeed attempt to find a rational basis for their moral beliefs in a particular understanding of human nature, while inheriting a set of moral injunctions on the one hand and a conception of human nature on the other which had been expressly designed to be discrepant with one another. (p. 55)

Old wine, MacIntyre seems to be saying, cannot be poured into a new skin. *Either* human beings are sovereign and complete individuals, in need of nothing but their own reason, bound to no particular metanarrative, no tradition or community that might adjudicate among the resulting "world-views," *or* they are imperfect and incomplete members of a community that must shape each individual's story toward some telos. It is incoherent, in this view, to try to make these two possibilities commensurate, because they are "expressly discrepant." As a result of this "design," MacIntyre argues, a fault line opens up between disputants holding to different ontologies, and attempts at conversation fall into the resulting abyss. A person who believes that "biology" constitutes human life cannot "speak word" with someone who understands human life in terms of autonomy and other considerations of "quality." Both parties to the "debate" simply know what they know, and have nothing to say to one another. Conversation across the divide is mere gainsaying and political manipulation; conversation on one side or the other is preaching to the converted. So long as both narratives are coherent, even logic and rationality cannot reach across the abyss.

The sole author may be, as Taylor (1989) says it is, necessarily entangled in webs of interlocution. But the very movement by which we are capable of detaching ourselves from those webs in order to tell our own stories about them seems to make it difficult, if not impossible, to place ourselves back in them in a meaningful way. An interesting irony, one of crucial import for this inquiry, arises here. Projects undertaken intentionally to ward off the spectre of nihilism raised by the cutting loose of the individual from a given "providential order" cannot succeed; given MacIntyre's (1984) analysis, they can only deepen the abyss by becoming further instances of incommensurability. If, as the codependence literature would have it, everyone is "free to be who he or she is," then one strong evaluation is as "good" as another; while they may be widely divergent in content, there is no possibility of a conversation that can establish a hierarchy of those discrepancies. And any possible hierarchy, as MacIntyre points out, can be seen to "offer a rhetoric which serves to conceal behind the masks of morality what are in fact the preferences of arbitrary will and desire" (p. 71). (This is perhaps why the codependence literature conceals its authority so deeply: to reassure the reader that its teachings are not simply arbitrary preferences of a particular agent.) Moral conversation—the attempt to determine, validly and nonarbitrarily, the value of one story over another—becomes endless unmasking, and a search for meaningful difference gives way to a leveling of all difference, that is, to nihilism.

Iago refuses to speak, refuses to make his differences clear, but for Shakespeare, the telos of Elizabethan England (read into sixteenth-century Venice) still holds sway, and Iago's silence shouts out his depravity. Without that telos, that shared understanding of being, however, Iago's silence might just as well be a lengthy monologue about the early childhood trauma that led him to his crime, delivered to a person who is outside any web of interlocution like the codependence literature. There would be no background against which his actions could be viewed as better or worse than anyone else's. The difference between Iago and a twentieth-century conspirator like Oliver North is that the latter can speak volumes of words about his crimes to people who do not understand them as crimes, and earn their adulation in the process, while Iago's criminality is clear whether or not he speaks one word. For one, webs of interlocution have no necessary content, and crimes are, as a result, not necessarily crimes. For the other, stepping outside the conversation is inescapably criminal. The difference can be found in the different moral backgrounds of the two conspirators—the one in which there are shared understandings that are binding, the other in which those understandings are absent, and any coherent narrative is as good as any other.

The story comprised by these ongoing attempts to render a metaphysical ethics takes place against a background largely constituted by that absence. The invention of the individual as a sole author has "wiped away the horizon." The only shared understanding that remains is that there can be no shared understanding, that it is all a matter of one's point of view or one's authorial perspective. Ironically, this empty shared understanding, in its turn, seems to emerge from a concern to safeguard a realm of meaning and seriousness from the kind of emptiness that Othello embodies. Instead of the possibility of a world of Othellos, whose entanglement in webs of interlocution cannot hold against the unpredictability of political life, we are faced with the prospect of a world of Iagos, whose absolute detachment from those webs brings about an incommensurability that makes moral discourse incoherent. In such a world, there are only sole authors and their stories, whose basis is, perhaps, a "feeling good" that is entirely private and cannot be fully and rationally explained to any other person. There may be no agony of entanglement, but neither is there any shared understanding of what the Good is. There is only the agony of fragmentation.

"THE TRIUMPH OF THE THERAPEUTIC"

Something about this lost horizon has not yet been illuminated, and it can help to explain the failure of these discourses to give us a way to overcome this modern agony by placing our stories into meaningful human relationship. Heidegger's account of the "essence" of nihilism will provide this illumination. But before taking up that argument, it is important to point out a significant difference between the kinds of moral discourse constituted by "metaphysical ethics" on the one hand and the codependence literature on the other. The former are intentional searches for a universal basis of narrative, for a public shared understanding of the Good. And the latter, in its attempt to overcome the agony of entanglement, is content to take incommensurability as given, to say that the good life is attained simply by aspiring to free individual narratives from any influence "outside the person." There is, according to the codependence literature, no reason to fear that the loss of a shared horizon necessarily leads to a world of Iagos. It is far more important to safeguard against a world of Othellos, of people with insufficient "boundaries" separating them from others. The public world, it seems, will take care of itself, without benefit of anything like a categorical imperative: the "internal moral code" will simply emerge as we "recover." So we are not to strive to attain the moral thinking which is Kant's "the guide and supreme norm" for our relatedness. Rather, we are just to do what "feels good," and the rest will follow as a matter of course.

But how can we understand a guarantee like this, which seems to pivot on the assumption that conversation will be restored only when all "supreme norms" are eschewed, when the conditions which seem to make for incommensurability are themselves affirmed and enhanced? If this is not to be dismissed as an outright impossibility, an absurdity in the codependence literature's position that "recovery is about learning to be in relationships," then it is crucial to understand how such a discourse substantiates that "guarantee," how it proposes that conversation will be restored. The codependence literature itself, as we have seen, cannot be trusted to answer this question, relying as it does on an understanding of others' narratives which is really a concealing of them. But, just as this genre does not originate the concern with finding a way to bind the individual back to a community, neither is its attempt to do so by openly eschewing the public realm constructed out of whole cloth.

There is a body of thought, which some critics have identified as the "therapeutic" (see, e.g., Bellah et al., 1985; MacIntyre, 1984). At least one of these works (Rieff, 1966) takes up in a more sophisticated and less concealing way the questions about the possibility of conversation that arise in the understanding of the good life as the life lived in front of no necessary horizon. I would like to turn now to this perspective as it is elucidated by Rieff in order to see how these questions are answered. It will be clear in the course of this analysis that Rieff's argument is, in many respects, congruous with what we have already seen in the codependence literature; but he offers a much clearer account of relatedness than those books. This section will be concerned to show how this understanding of the restoration of conversation still fails to find a way across the "abyss." Showing this will help to highlight the way in which nihilism haunts an understanding of relatedness, like the codependence literature's, which takes a loss of horizon for granted.

Rieff (1966) is a fitting source for this discussion, as he openly proclaims the "triumph of the therapeutic."[3] In his view, the leveling of moral distinction is a "cultural revolution," one in which the "sacred becomes symptom" (p. 77). The wiping away of the horizon of common shared understandings—what Rieff calls "positive communities"—is thought to be Freud's gift to humankind, for it replaces a superstitious and enslaved "religious man" with a new paradigm: "psychological man," enlightened by therapeutically gained self-knowledge and chained to no one but himself. This shift is precisely the triumph of the therapeutic, and Rieff argues that it signals not the end of conversation, but its beginning as a psychologically healthy, authentic practice. In the postrevolutionary world,

> [a]ll binding engagements to communal purpose may be considered, in
> the wisdom of therapeutic doctrines, too extreme. Precisely this and no
> other extreme position is stigmatized as a neurotic approach to paroxysms
> of demand for a more fundamental revolutionary dogma. . . . The [cul-
> tural revolution] is a calm and profoundly reasonable revolt of the private
> man against all doctrinal traditions urging the salvation of self through
> identification with the purposes of community. (p. 242)

Stories like Othello's bear witness to the dangers of "binding engagements," and must give way to stories based on a binding engagement to
the the private self, a commitment to narratives legitimized only by their
ability to bring about their authors' well-being. "'I believe,' the cry of the
ascetic, los[es] precedence to 'one feels,' the caveat of the therapeutic."
The quest is now for one's "feelings," for the articulation of the distinctions which they disclose about one's well-being. This articulation
becomes the only valuable guide to action, the source of meaningful
distinctions. The emptiness resulting from the loss of horizon is to be
filled by a discovery and enactment of one's "inner values." This can be
understood as the theoretical basis for statements like Beattie's that
one's "moral code" cannot help but show up in the course of "recovery."

The significant web of interlocution becomes a self's conversation
with itself. If the only understanding we can share is that we cannot
share any understanding which is imposed from without, then we must
develop the capacity to find and to articulate our values. MacIntyre
(1984) has called this move "emotivism" (pp. 16-35), Taylor (1989) calls
it "expressivism" (pp. 369-90), and Bellah et al. (1985) refer to it as
"expressive individualism" (pp. 46-47, 138-40). For all these writers, the
source of important distinctions, and thus of meaning, becomes the
"heart" of the individual. Bellah et al. put it this way.

> A healthy person moves from discovering feelings to defining values,
> from setting priorities among values to generating alternative strategies to
> realize a priority, from selecting one such strategy to following through on
> it: these steps provide a checklist for strategic action aimed at self-fulfill-
> ment. This is how a healthy person lives, and so by implication how we
> ought to live. (p. 128)

Here Bellah et al. clearly draw the connection between "health" and
morality, between the kind of "ought" that refers to weak evaluation, and
the kind that is embedded in an understanding of the good life. "Mental
health," in their reading of the "therapeutic", *is* the good life, and, as
such, its attainment is a moral imperative, a practice that will secure a
realm of meaning even in the absence of a commitment to a "positive

community." We have already seen the echoes of this argument in contentions like Schaef's that "external referenting" is "dishonest."

The view that conversation can be restored through proficient—and "honest"—self-conversation is not peculiar to Rieff's (1966) reading of Freud. Indeed, many writers have noted that this idea dominates American psychology (see, e.g., Thompson, 1986; Baumeister, 1987; Sampson, 1985; Cushman, 1990). The idea of the "self-contained individual" is, according to Sampson (1985), the "indigenous psychology" of Western culture; and, of course, it underlies the codependence literature's suspicion of anything "outside the person." This idea takes as given a radical separation between agency and community, a separation that is to be overcome by strengthening the container that holds the individual. As Sampson says, in this model,

> there exists a region intrinsic to the person and a region of the "other." Proponents of this view hold that maintaining boundaries and sharp distinctions is central to good health and societal functioning. (p. 15)

Failure to maintain sharp boundaries is thought to be the predominant contemporary psychological problem, replacing the classical conversion neuroses which gave rise to psychoanalytic theory with disorders of a fragmented self (see Lasch, 1979, pp. 71-100; see also Taylor, 1989, pp. 18-19; and Cushman, 1990). This failure is understood not only as a cause of subjective misery, but also of interpersonal distress, what Rieff might call "societal dysfunction." To "fill up" a self in this fashion is to make it into something that can engage successfully with a community by virtue of its boundary strength and the ensuing proficiency of the self at determining its own heart and its own values, at telling its own story.

A danger arises here that the inner life will be poorly understood and articulated, that the discovery of values will therefore be flawed, and that the social order will founder. The narrative constituted by a self's conversation with itself has, as Taylor (1989) points out, the "capacity to confer meaning and substance on people's lives." But, he continues,

> the act by which their pronouncing releases force can be rhetorically imitated, either to feed our self-conceit or for even more sinister purposes, such as the defence of a discreditable status quo. Trite formulae may combine with the historical sham to weave a cocoon of moral assurance which actually insulates us from the energy of true moral sources. . . . Without any articulation at all, we would lose all contact with the good, however conceived. We would cease to be human. (p. 97)

A self must be so proficient at its conversation with itself that it can recognize when its language turns into a rhetoric emptied of meaning by its unacknowledged and invisible distortions. But the danger that Taylor raises can, according to the therapeutic discourse, be addressed without any necessary appeal to "communal purpose." The way to avoid the emptiness of rhetorical imitation is to become expert self-conversants, master storytellers. This requires skills, and particularly those skills that are attained through the apprenticeship of psychotherapy (or, perhaps, the reading of codependence books). As Rieff (1966) says, "if the therapeutic is to win out, then surely the psychotherapist will be [psychological man's] spiritual guide" (p. 25).

Seriousness and meaning are to be found not in a transcendent realm of universal and impartial benevolence (which may, in any event, now be impossible), but in the radically immanent realm of one's self. By becoming proficient in the skills of self-conversation, our lives are to become a narrative quest for meaning, a journey whose purpose is to discover and to articulate our "values" well, and, therefore, wisely. We can, and must, restore contact with that "deep important part of ourselves that feels appropriate feelings, senses truth . . ." (CNM, p. 95). Through a "therapeutically" guided quest for this value-making "part," the problem of how to bind the individual back to the social world is "solved" not by restoring the now-obliterated distinctions which have to do with transcendent understandings of right and wrong, but rather by accepting that leveling and then turning toward the distinctions made by a private self on the basis of its "inner feelings." Moral action becomes a matter of managing those feelings skillfully enough to establish our own values; achieving the good life becomes a matter of technical expertise, without any appeal to universal standards. Indeed, this proficiency is to be a purely procedural, content-free guarantor of universal and impartial benevolence, without even the categorical imperative's reliance on "reason" as that which best safeguards our conversations. We all, after all, have emotions, just as surely as we have reason; we can all, it would seem, avail ourselves of a secular spiritual guide who can help us to manage them effectively, to discover what is of value to us in our own life stories.

If the dangers of inarticulacy can be addressed by psychotherapy, still Taylor's (1989) warning raises questions that "skills enhancement" might not sufficiently address. If the primary web of interlocution is to be understood as the individual's "inner self," then it is clear that technologies like psychotherapy can bring about a full conversation in someone experiencing the impoverishment of psychological distress. The patient learns to talk to and about him or herself. But how is the value of each person's quest for value, and, more importantly, its outcome, to be determined? If the horizon of communal engagement is to be restored by paying attention only to the private horizon (and thus finding community through becoming an individual even stronger in his or her self-containment), then what is to assure us that that "articulacy," no matter how proficient, is not only a mask for "trite formulae in defense of a discreditable status quo"? There are, after all, to be no webs of interlocution that are "outside the person," and which grant meaning to him or her; so there can be no background against which such formulae can emerge sufficiently to be unmasked. And, according to Rieff, this is a problem hardly worth notice.

> [P]sychological man is likely to be indifferent to the ancient question of legitimate authority, of sharing in government, so long as the powers that be preserve social order and manage an economy of abundance. (Rieff, 1966, p. 26)

No status quo that provides sufficient order to allow for psychological man's self-development, which grants, for example, the freedom of assembly to Twelve-Step groups, is discreditable; conversely, only the failure to provide this would be occasion for a response other than indifference.

Clearly, the possibility that this understanding of the individual will give rise to such indifference is not new with Rieff (1966). Tocqueville (1840/1990) raised it in 1840, but was far less sanguine about it. He worried that a

> nation that asks nothing of its government but the maintenance of order is already a slave at heart, the slave of its own well-being, awaiting only the hand that will bind it. (p. 142)

If all meaningful distinctions can be reduced to private concerns, as Rieff (like the codependence authors) argues that they can, then problems like those Taylor (1989) identifies will not even emerge as problems. The "slavery" Tocqueville is concerned with is of a particularly pernicious variety. For it is slavery by assent, ensured and strengthened by the well-being that the maintenance of order secures. There is no apparent master to appear as a malignant tyrant who must be overthrown; rather, there is just a social order which appears to be benign, whose otherness, insofar as it might show up as an oppressive authoritarianism, remains concealed.

Foucault (1983) argues strenuously against this understanding of the individual for just this reason: it enslaves people by eliminating the horizon against which their enslavement might appear as such. A social order that is a matter of indifference, that can be taken as given, engages in the most deceptive of deceptions: it appears to be neutral, so its atrocities remain invisible.

> It seems to me that the real political task in a society such as ours is to crit-
> icize the workings of institutions which appear to be both neutral and
> independent; to criticize them in such a manner that the political vio-
> lence which has always exercised itself obscurely through them will be
> unmasked, so that one can fight them. (Foucault, cited in Rabinow, 1984,
> p. 6)

The codependence literature, of course, with its various concealments of its own authority, is just such an "institution," and here we
can see clearly the kinds of dangers that it holds out. The individual,
understood as a sole author dedicated to its own well-being, is self-contained only insofar as he or she is held to be outside of any necessary
webs of interlocution. But for Foucault and other allied critics of individualism's entanglement with psychotherapy like Sampson (1981, 1985),
Cushman (1990), and Rose (1990), self-containment is a dangerous illusion. The self that makes its own values based on its subjective sense of
well-being cannot see that in turning itself into a subject, it is also objectified (see Rabinow, 1984, p. 11). Such a self cannot take account of
the way it becomes what Rose (1990) calls "a vital element in the net-
works of power that traverse modern societies" (p. 213). Rose goes on to
describe the entanglement that might result from Rieff's indifference in
this way:

> The regulatory apparatus of the modern state is not something imposed
> from outside upon individuals who have remained essentially untouched
> by it. Incorporating, shaping, channeling, and enhancing subjectivity have
> been intrinsic to the operations of government. But while governing soci-
> ety has come to require governing subjectivity, this has not been achieved
> through the growth of an omnipotent and omniscient central state whose
> agents institute a perpetual surveillance and control over all its subjects.
> Rather, government of subjectivity has taken shape through the prolifer-
> ation of a complex and heterogeneous assemblage of technologies. These
> have acted as relays, bringing the varied ambitions of . . . authorities into
> alignment with the ideals and aspirations of individuals, with the selves
> each of us want to be. (p. 213)

A self in search of well-being, in a society which holds that "well-being" as
its only common understanding of the good, cannot be distinguished

from its background. Its conversation with that background is hampered by the concealment of the horizon's otherness.

Such a self *thinks* it is free, but it is only "free" against the backdrop of a social world that has already defined freedom as a certain set of priorities. "Recovery" may be the freedom to buy and proudly drive a Mercedes, but this understanding of freedom is always already constituted by some ontology. This understanding, which may be thoroughly concealed, gives its subjects the sense that having a Mercedes is intrinsic to the good life, that they ought to want to be the kind of person who can buy one. This in turn might make that person hold the concern with getting the car as a priority over, for instance, a concern with how the money is made to do so, with what societal practices and/or institutions are perpetuated by this pursuit. "Psychological man" can thus be "governed" through the very technologies and bureaucracies that promise to secure his well being.

The "therapeutic," as Rieff (1966) describes it, takes its place among those technologies, claiming that its ability to help a person clarify his or her private values is the most important safeguard of the public world. The establishing of values is not to be understood as a moral practice, but a technique which, at least to Bellah et al. (1985, p. 128), sounds "not altogether different from a textbook description of decision making in a school of management." But a technology, as Ihde (1979) reminds us, can never be value-neutral. It must always emerge from a particular understanding of being against which its practices make sense (p. xii). Clearly, that understanding makes of subjective well-being a high priority, and the ontology of this evaluation, as we will soon see, is inescapably nihilistic.

For now, it is important to notice that the conceit that "values" are best clarified privately, while it might seem the "best" way to fill the public world with meaning, remains empty in a crucial sense. In its pretense toward value-neutrality, it fails to specify the ends toward which we are managing ourselves. This emptiness might make us unwitting stooges of corporate and government interests, or compulsive consumers who believe that our well-being depends upon the obtaining of certain commodities, or well-meaning characters who cannot articulate our values outside of the language of management school textbooks. In these and other interpretations, the turn toward the private can be seen as further obscuring the horizon against which anything other than considerations of private well-being might show up. In the triumph of the therapeutic, the public world is left to its own devices; the status quo remains unchallenged, so long as well-being remains safeguarded.

When psychological effectiveness and technique replace ethical reasoning and striving as a mode of establishing and maintaining value, then there is no check on corporate power, whether in the form of a state or a less formal affiliation of interests. "Social order" and an "economy of abundance" of the kind that allows for a proliferation of Twelve-Step programs might be provided by many kinds of "regulatory apparatus." And the emphasis on well-being, as opposed to a particular public understanding of what the good life consists of, leaves open the possibility of, for example, a National Socialist government whose genocidal practices would presumably be tolerated so long as that order and abundance were preserved, so long as everyone could be working toward "recovery." A self understood as the seat of all valuing cannot safeguard values that might go beyond self-interest. If the conditions of our world are such that well-being depends on our performing our job in the concentration camp—or, for that matter, on our unambiguous "feeling good" about a morally ambiguous war in the Persian Gulf—then there is no reason to lose our well-being by questioning the morality of that genocide or that war. This is the contention of Arendt's (1965) account of Adolf Eichmann, which shows him to be a man more concerned with well-being, understood as functioning effectively, than with questions of right and wrong. The distinctions that were meaningful to him were not about the morality of his strong evaluations. It may at least be imagined that events like the Holocaust are made possible by the laissez-faire attitude toward "the powers that be" that Rieff singles out as integral to the "triumph of the therapeutic."

Rieff (1966), of course, is not oblivious to the problems raised by the Nazi Holocaust for a theory espousing an enlightened indifference to the social world. Indeed, he is writing in the shadow of the concentration camps, and he sees that disaster as further support for his position. "This temper against moralizing," he argues, "has its justifications. The Germans recently manipulated all corporate identities and communal purposes with a thoroughness against which the analytic attitude may be our surest protection" (p. 24). Precisely by establishing transcendent moral values, Rieff claims, the Nazis controlled their subjects; the "average German's" ability to base his or her values on self-knowledge was lost in the identification with a "positive community." The disaster of Auschwitz can, according to Rieff, be understood as further evidence *against* the wisdom of anchoring morality in a communal purpose. Eichmann need not be understood in moral terms; he was simply a neurotic in need of analysis.

Psychotherapy, in its ability to guide us to an understanding of emotion which will allow us to clarify our values, is to become the prophylaxis that will guard against the unwarranted dominion of individual desire and will. The way to preserve and enhance the social world is to preserve and enhance the individual world, to keep it empty of considerations of the public. In the language of the codependence literature, it is to minimize the possibility that considerations of public understandings of the good will undermine my self-esteem. Instead, I ought to enter a Twelve-Step program, a narrative space in which it appears that to safeguard my own well-being is to safeguard that of everyone else.

In the "therapeutic" turn, then, the Gordian knot is undone by a sleight of hand in which the public world becomes a matter of indifference. Indeed, strong evaluations that emanate from communal purpose are themselves the source of corruption: the individual *must* be left to his or her own devices, lest he or she be "manipulated," or lose "self-esteem," or become codependent. The public world is to be comprised of mentally healthy people who share, more than anything else, a suspicion of the ability of communal values to bring about their well-being. This move pivots on the assumption that obligatory shared understandings interfere with the "natural" development of the individual, and therefore with the well-being of all. In this view, the leveling of moral discourse is a good thing; Iago and Othello are seen as guilty of the same trespass: both fail to know themselves adequately. Iago's refusal to confess can be seen as bearing witness to his own not knowing why he committed his villainy, which in turn might give us a clue to the "neurosis" that makes him so jealous. Othello's murder of Desdemona can be seen as the result of his failure to look within and clarify the relative value of honor and preserving someone else's life. The hierarchy that makes one the tragic hero and the other the villain can disappear in the realm of the therapeutic. From the standpoint of the imperative to find value within, they are the same. And it is conceivable that Iago's confession of his psychological state might arouse our sympathy even as we scoff at the simple-minded (and unanalyzed) murderer Othello.

A recent scholarly article (Omer and da Verona, 1991), which examines "Doctor Iago's treatment of Othello," is worth mentioning here. In it, the authors attempt to account in therapeutic terms for Iago's ability to persuade Othello to kill his wife. Iago is "Hell's master therapist," able to lead Othello "from a sense of highest personal and professional self-assurance, control, and satisfaction to a pit of insecurity, hatred and recklessness" (pp. 99-100). This is obviously the inverse of what a good therapist would do, but, the authors argue, Iago's "craftsmanship resembles . . . that of many of today's illustrious therapists" (p. 99). We can, it would seem, cast aside his values and motives in order to understand Iago as an exemplar of psychotherapeutic practice.

It is just this kind of distinction, however, that is troublesome. How, after all, are we to know that Iago is a therapist from Hell? By what standard is he to be judged? According to Omer and da Verona, it is that he leads Othello to certain psychological states which work against the Moor's ultimate well-being: he "makes use of the hero's basic insecurity on account of his blackness" (p. 112). To learn from Iago, all we need to do is to adopt his techniques in service of the well-being, rather than the destruction, of the patient. This opens the possibility that if Iago had made Othello feel "better," and that if, in his increased self-esteem (and perhaps his recognition of his anger about being made to feel insecure about his blackness) he had slain Desdemona, Iago's proficiency might not be so hellish. Indeed, to indulge for a moment in anachronism, if he had used his "techniques" to enhance Othello's self-esteem such that he and Desdemona could drive out of Venice in a Mercedes, then Iago might be imagined a therapist from Heaven. The therapist's skills are value-neutral and can be practiced without any reference to a universal social order. They need not, indeed cannot, be judged by anything other than their success at bringing about the well-being of the individual.

In the "triumph of the therapeutic," the project to bind the individual back to a social world culminates in the abandonment of that "world" in favor of an exclusive focus on the private. Only the distinctions arising from the latter are meaningful, and morality becomes a matter of psychology: the therapist is to be our guide to well-being, and well-being is the key to achieving a just public world. All that we need to restore a basis for conversation is an end to attempts to establish that basis through religions or categorical imperatives or accounts of virtue, or any other binding commitment, and a replacing of those distinctions with "therapeutic" ones. All that is needed is a thorough emptying of the public realm.

Clearly, critics like Rose (1990) and Bellah et al. (1985) are suspicious of this resolution, particularly of what Bellah et al. call its hyperindividualism. The critique of the therapeutic triumph points out that the distinction between private and public is not so thoroughgoing as Rieff (1966) might think: in the private discovery of value can be found traces of a public world, whose concealment is made possible by the privacy of that discovery. And then a self which finds its values based on well-being can easily, if unwittingly, become a part of a world whose atrocities are not so florid as those of the Nazis, but nonetheless remain atrocious. Moreover, because of the alignment of interests described above by Rose, a person's participation in these atrocities is easily concealed.

The entire question of a shared understanding of the Good is rendered moot by the therapeutic "triumph" described here, and this raises disquieting possibilities. When the only understanding shared by value-positing private selves is that there is no necessity—and, perhaps, no possibility—of universally binding shared understandings, we are free to bond with others whose hearts, and therefore whose values, are kindred with our own. Given this foreclosure of the public world, webs of interlocution are reduced to what Bellah et al. (1985) call "lifestyle enclaves" (pp. 71-75). The binding we experience in these groups need not go beyond the boundaries of that enclave. If it happens to be Jonestown or a country club that excludes black people or a National Socialist party or a Twelve-Step group or a "Save the Rainforest" coalition in which we find kinship, there is no way to distinguish the relative merits of the values of any particular group.

If there is no shared understanding, nothing truly Other, and if all attempts to find one are to be understood as ultimately inimical to the achievement of universal benevolence, then the problem of how to bind an individual back to the social world is not really solved. It is simply declared irrelevant; all that is needed is to bind a person securely to him or herself, which, given the analysis of the previous chapter, is to conceal otherness entirely. But then by what criteria can we say that an event like the Nazi Holocaust is a bad thing? Rieff says it is, and is evidently appalled by the extermination camps. But his diagnosis of that atrocity as a manifestation of a neurotic failure to exercise self-determination founders both theoretically and empirically. Arendt's (1965) analysis of Eichmann as an essentially well-adjusted, even bland, bureaucrat who lived in pursuit of well-being seems to hoist Rieff on his own petard. Rieff's account also overlooks the flourishing, documented by Cocks (1985), of psychoanalysis during the Nazi era. If well-being is to replace more traditional standards as the grounding of important distinctions, then what is the basis of Rieff's contention that there is something wrong with the Holocaust?

Less dramatic examples can make the same point. If jobs building nuclear weapons are essential to the well-being of both the arms-builder and the overall economy, then what allows us to assess that building as a bad (or a good) thing? If driving ourselves from place to place in automobiles ensures our well-being even as it threatens that of future generations, then how are we to judge (and manage) that practice? If our only obligation is to know and express our "feelings" and to base our values, and subsequently our actions, on them, then how are we to understand the actions of a Iago or a Stalin or a Charles Manson or anyone else who, while marching to the beat of his or her own heart, stills the hearts of others?

Of course, it is possible simply to say that these questions disclose yet another location of incommensurability, that they arise out of an ontology in which the sovereignty of the individual is not simply to be trusted to bring about a just world. What one discourse understands as nihilism—the leveling of moral distinctions—the other understands as salvation. But it is important to notice that that lack of meaningful distinction haunts an individualist ontology as well. As MacIntyre (1984, p. 31) points out, without some universal standard, "Everything may be criticized from whatever standpoint the self has adopted, including the self's choice of standpoint to adopt." This is not just true of critiques from outside the individualist perspective, like that of Rose cited above. *All* first principles can be unmasked, even the one by which we understand our own viewpoint to be sovereign. If we subscribe to the view that there can be no universal and transcendent realm of benevolence, we are consigned to what Sloterdijk (1983/1987) has called "enlightened false consciousness" (pp. 5-6): we are always already unmasked; we know (because it is part of our empty shared understanding to be suspicious of all shared understandings) that wherever we stand is not above suspicion, and may be undermined at any time. If no tradition or community is binding, then no understanding of being is safe from cynicism, except perhaps the cynical understanding which undermines all meaningful difference, and leaves only what Cushman (1990) calls the "empty self."

These issues might not be problematic if the therapeutic turn simply signaled an end to the project of binding the individual back to the social world, and an affirmation of a concept like Nietzsche's *Übermensch*. But Rieff's (1966) work, like that of the codependence authors, is decidedly utopian. The codependence writers have in mind no less than "healing the human condition" (Whitfield, 1991). These technologies do not hold themselves out as simply enhancing the will to power; rather, they announce themselves as practices that will usher in an age in which the "arts of psychiatric management enhanced and perfected, men will come to know one another in ways that could facilitate total socialization" (Rieff, 1966, p. 21). They promise that there will be no more holocausts, either on the scale of Auschwitz, or in our private relationships. The turn inward is still seeking, through therapeutic technologies, a basis for relatedness. The location of metaphysical certainty has simply shifted from "out there" to "in here," from the categorical imperative to the "Inner Child." But the project remains the same: to fill in the abyss of meaning that opens up with the invention of the modern self, to find a way to make our differences commensurable. And the result of this project is a plethora of individual, intrapsychic distinctions which still fail to give a basis for public, intersubjective distinctions. We are perhaps proficient at understanding our differences, but still at a loss to account for what those differences mean, to know how to bring our narratives into conversation with those of others. Othello and Iago are reduced to the same.

"THE EYES OF THE WORLD"

Both traditional attempts, like Kant's, to establish a realm of universal and impartial moral law and the attempts to find that understanding of the good in radical inwardness remain nihilistic in the sense that they fail to give us a basis for a grounding by which strong evaluations can emerge as different from, but still related to, one another. Difference remains, but meaningful difference disappears, and attempts to bring it back, either by reforming the public sphere or managing the private, seem inevitably to fall into the abyss. Under this interpretation, the sovereignty of the individual can trump any metaphysics which threatens to turn us into Othellos; the spectre of a world of Iagos, whose crimes may not even be understood as such, in turn trumps the possibility of turning away from the endeavor to find first principles in a transcendent realm.

By now, it should be clear that efforts to unravel that knot point toward a background in which shared understandings, and with them the conversations which disclose meaningful differences between autonomous individuals, have been shattered, but in which the yearning to establish a basis for those conversations seems to continue. The search for first principles—whether categorical imperatives or mental health—bears witness to some ongoing dream of ending fragmentation, and, at the same time, to the elusiveness of such an achievement. Attempts to restore wholeness seem inevitably to be shipwrecked by the apparently incommensurable gap that opens between a person and the world of others in the understanding of the individual as a sole author. Neither traditional metaphysics like those described by Taylor (1989) and MacIntyre (1984) nor therapeutic technologies like the code-pendence literature will abandon either the individual or the community, but thus far, it seems, neither can move beyond the nihilism constituted by the abyss that has opened between them.

The apparent inescapability of nihilism, however, points to something that offers some hope. This abyss still appears to be a problem, still seems to call forth efforts to reach across it. We already have seen that the shared understanding of being that makes phenomena like the code-pendence literature possible is that there is no shared understanding, that this fragmentation is inherent in the notion of the individual as it has been described here, and that technologies that take the sole author/self for granted only seem to worsen it. But another aspect of that ontology is what I just called a yearning for wholeness: some wish to undo the fragmentation. We are apparently not content to be separate selves, but neither are we willing to give up our autonomy. The codependence literature does not turn its back on the possibility of conversation; it just goes about restoring it in a way that is highly problematic, that in its zeal to help its readers "break free" leaves them with no basis for entanglements with others.

Nihilism as the absence of a basis for meaningful relationships remains a spectre which, as a culture, we seem to continue to seek to overcome. But perhaps we do not yet understand this nihilism well enough. Perhaps the practices that disclose both the yearning for meaningful conversation and the apparent impossibility of its satisfaction themselves bear witness to a background that remains to be illuminated. Heidegger (1952/1977a) warns us that

> Because we do not experience nihilism as a historical movement that has already long endured . . . we succumb to the ruinous passion for holding phenomena that are already and simply consequences of nihilism for the latter itself. We set forth the consequences and effect as the causes of nihilism. (p. 65)

Perhaps it is not the individual understood as a separate entity that gives rise to the loss of meaning I am describing here. Perhaps instead it is an already nihilistic understanding of being that gives rise to the individual in the first place, and thus haunts any effort to overcome the radical isolation of the sole author which takes that understanding for granted.

MacIntyre (1984) and Rieff (1966), although they each value it differently, both take incommensurability as a given implication of the Enlightenment invention of the individual as a sole author. But how did such a problematic arise in the first place? Against what background does the individual appear, and what are the characteristics of that horizon which determine our predicament? What is the shared understanding of being which gives rise, on the one hand, to a notion of human being in which all difference becomes the same, and meaning disappears, and, on the other, to ongoing attempts to establish a meaning in which those differences are truly different? It is not enough to say that the Enlightenment established the individual but refused to abolish the universal, and therefore left us with both the yearning for and the impossibility of commensurability. Before we can understand the code-pendence literature's attempt to reconcile the individual with a world of others, we must understand the groundwork of the sundering which makes that reconciliation both necessary and (apparently) impossible. In the ontology of nihilism will be found the wellsprings of these prob-lems; moreover, it will give us a way to assess the codependence litera-ture's understanding of the good life as a concealing of the otherness of the Other.

Heidegger (1952/1977a; 1952/1977b; 1954/1977) would not dis-agree with MacIntyre's (1984) assertion that moral conversation has broken down, and that metaphysics has failed to restore it. But he under-stands this breakdown quite differently. MacIntyre traces the problem of nihilism to a specific historical moment. In the turmoil of the seven-teenth and eighteenth centuries, he argues, the gap opened between two understandings of being human: the tradition-bound person in need of shaping by a community and the enlightened self in need of nothing but his or her own reason. This in turn created an apparently irreconcilable breach between the individual and his or her commu-nity. Attempts to overcome this gap inevitably fail because the individual has been defined as that which has no necessary connection to the col-lective, and the collective as that which holds the person so tightly that individuality cannot emerge. As a result, both realms—agency and com-munity—bear an emptiness that appears to be inescapable. In MacIntyre's reading, it is as if in "expressly designing" its understanding of human being, the Enlightenment's philosophers simply committed an important logical error, namely, that they left intact two incommensu-rable understandings of the good.

One final note before we take up Heidegger's understanding of this "error." In the following pages, I have tried to minimize the impact of Heidegger's torturing of language, which is reported to have moved some wit to say that Heidegger cannot even be translated into German. No doubt he was to some extent intentionally obscurantist. This is per-haps a reflection of his absolute antimodernism, of his refusal to take even language on its own terms, and its stirring in him an attempt to cre-ate his own language. I turn to Heidegger simply because he has cap-tured the ontology of nihilism as well as any thinker I am aware of, so I ask the reader's patience here. I suggest that you think of a Heideggerian sentence as a clue in a cryptic crossword puzzle. The meaning is not pointed to as in a standard clue; rather it is embedded in the interstices of the sentence.

For Heidegger, the human agent is called Dasein, which literally means being-there. And he bases his understanding of nihilism on the insight that, in the modern age, Dasein is a ruptured entity, a being torn loose from any particular "there." Thus opens the gap in which MacIntyre's incommensurability takes form, in which the seemingly unanswerable question of how we are to be related to others arises. As Caputo (1989) says

> . . . the moral is a post-Cartesian notion that arises only if one conceives of Dasein as a worldless and solitary ego and then poses the problem of how to bind Dasein back to the world and other persons. (p. 55)

But the question arises: how does such a split occur in the first place? Certainly, to us moderns, it seems a matter of common sense that we stand back from and reflect upon the world, cogitating our way, by means of our subjective experience, to certainty. MacIntyre, as we have just seen, is aware of the historicity of this "common sense." He presents a challenge to it, tracing it to a moment in the Enlightenment. This may be as much a rhetorical device as anything else, but he makes the worldlessness of Dasein sound like a design flaw, not unlike the kind that sometimes arises in a new model of automobile. In the interesting and exciting ferment out of which the sole author/self emerges, he seems to say, someone overlooked an important question, and the subsequent blueprint held a major flaw, which manifests itself in an ability to resolve moral disputes. What is needed, then, is to go back to that design flaw and repair it, which MacIntyre thinks is to be done by the restoration and revitalization of certain practices and traditions. But what if the moment MacIntyre wants to revisit is not so originary as he thinks? What if the tradition he would draw upon is itself already an instance of the same nihilism he seeks to overcome?

That this is the case, of course, is Heidegger's position. The question of how the autonomous agent is to be related to other sole authors only arises after a sundering has already taken place.

> The essence of the modern age can be seen in the fact that man frees himself from the bonds of the middle ages in freeing himself to himself. . . . Certainly the modern age has, as a consequence of the liberation of man, introduced subjectivism and individualism. But it remains just as certain that no age before this one has produced a comparable objectivism and that in no age before this has the non-individual, in the form of the collective, come to acceptance as having worth. Essential here is the necessary interplay between subjectivism and objectivism. It is precisely this reciprocal conditioning of one by the other that points back to events more profound. (Heidegger, 1952/1977a, p. 127)

At the beginning of this chapter, I raised the question of what ontology is disclosed by ongoing attempts to find moral first principles and thus bind individual subject to a collective of such subjects. Heidegger would answer that question by seeking out the origin and implications of the distinction which makes that endeavor both necessary and possible in the first place, by taking that distinction as the finger "that points back to events more profound." His account of those events, which places the origins of the problems of the modern self much earlier than the Enlightenment, goes a long way to explaining why the codependence literature's attempt to "heal the human condition" seems only to reproduce some of the most troubling aspects of that condition.

Whitehead (cited in Cuming, 1956, p. vii) claims that "the safest general characterization of the European philosophical tradition is that it consists of a series of footnotes to Plato." Heidegger would agree with this assessment, but would argue that the text emended by those footnotes is itself severely flawed. Dreyfus (1981), in explaining Heidegger's critique of Plato, reminds us that the poets were thrown out of the Republic, because, as Socrates says in the *Apology*, "'they understand nothing of what they say.' The trouble with poets," Dreyfus explains, "is that they cannot make explicit and justify the 'principles' expressed in their poetry" (p. 511). In articulating this prejudice as an epistemological principle, Plato set Western philosophy to the task of explicit understanding through *theoria*. This, in Heidegger's reading, established the foundation upon which the empty self in an empty social world is erected.

For Heidegger, the course to this shipwreck is set when Plato overturns the teachings of the Greek philosophers before him. In particular, Plato forgets (or misunderstands) that, as Parmenides put it, "thought and being are the same" (in Heidegger, 1952/1977a, p. 130). Far from reading this as a precursor to Descartes' cogito ergo sum, Heidegger understands Parmenides to mean that being and thought share the same ground. That which exists is not brought into being or constituted by thought. Rather, thought arises from being. Where Descartes insists that "I think, therefore I am," Parmenides (at least in Heidegger's reading) claims only that "I am given the capability for thought, which comes from Being, and therefore I am able to tell the story in which I am."

This identity means that thought is not the disengaged reasoning which came to be celebrated by Descartes, and certainly not the free-wheeling storytelling advocated by the codependence literature, but rather a concerned involvement of Dasein with the world which gives it thought; it is an apprehending rather than a representing of Being. This kind of thinking never gives the thinker priority over that which is thought, or the author over the story itself. Understood in this way, thinking can only arise out of the call of Being, in a "clearing" which is open to being thought about. As such, thinking remains under the sway of Being.

> The apprehending of whatever is belongs to Being because it is demanded and determined by Being. That which is, is that which arises and opens itself, which, as what presences, comes upon man as the one who presences, i.e., comes upon the one who himself opens himself to what presences in that he apprehends it. (Heidegger, 1952/1977a, p. 131)

Here Heidegger is claiming that thought, in the sense of apprehending, is a joining of openings: "man" opens to Being by "presencing" it; Being opens to "man" by being already present, already open to the one who opens himself. "Being" might be understood as the space that awaits the storyteller, but always already holds sway over the narrative—determines the shape and manner of story that can be told—by virtue of its being the space that requires narration, and in which all narratives must occur.

In Parmenides's thought-that-is-the-same-as-being, then, there is no worldless and solitary author seeking his or her way back into the webs of interlocution that constitute him or her. There is no possibility of the self that reads codependence books to find out how to go about being-with-others. Rather, there is a thinker inextricably immersed in those webs, who knows that disengagement from them is really the end of thinking. This "thinker" understands that a coherent story can never be told by a person who holds himself or herself up as sole author, who seeks extrication from entanglement in order to maintain relationships. For such a thinker,

> [t]hat which is does not come into being at all through the fact that man first looks upon it, in the sense of a representing that has the character of subjective perception. Rather, man is the one who is looked upon by that which is; he is the one who is—in company with itself—gathered toward presencing, by that which opens itself. (Heidegger, 1952/1977a, p. 131)

The thinker in what Heidegger calls the "great age of the Greeks" never forgets that his perception of what is cannot be the same as the Being of what is. He never forgets that his very thinking is itself the sign of the world's already looking upon him, gathering him toward presencing. Being is always already there, but out of it issues a summons, a demand to apprehend or think or narrate the world. The Greek thinker cannot forget his "needed belonging to revealing" (Heidegger, 1954/1977, p.

26), but must never stake a claim to the story that is thus revealed as his own. He forsakes control, but never responsibility, for his involvement. This kind of thinking does not originate in the thinker, but in the world that demands the response of thought when it looks upon him. Neither is that looking upon complete without Dasein answering the summons. So when Dasein looks back, its eyes are also the eyes of the world—not in the sense that looking somehow creates a world, but rather that the world is the basis of looking. My eyes become the world's eyes when they are inhabited by the Other.

This mutual looking, then, holds both an asymmetry and a reciprocity. "That which is" is always already there, but it requires the eyes of Dasein to light it up. When Dasein sees, the world that is already there inhabits its eyes. This back and forth has the reciprocal structure of a conversation, but the webs of interlocution must be understood as arising out of Being, and not out of Dasein. Being always exceeds its thinker; it stands as an Other who is irreducibly beyond him, even as it requires him to think it. Because of this exceeding, "that which is" necessarily eludes an exhaustive elucidation, and always gives us something more to talk about, another story to tell.

This surplus is not a matter of quantity, to be eliminated by means of some better form of thinking; rather, it is an ontological condition. That there is some Other "out there" demanding response, that we are thrown into webs of interlocution, or called into narrative, in the first place, means that those webs must remain in an essential way beyond us. They must remain Other.

The thinking that is the same as Being, then, safeguards the surplus that makes possible the conversation that lights up the world, but only at the expense of certainty. Heidegger (1952/1977a) reminds us that there must always be a kind of agony in our entanglements:

> [t]o be beheld by what is, to be included and maintained within its openness and in that way to be borne along by it, to be driven about by its oppositions and marked by its discord—that is the essence of man in the great age of the Greeks. Therefore, in order to fulfill his essence, Greek man must gather and save, catch up and preserve, what opens itself in its openness and he must remain exposed to all its sundering confusions. (p. 131)

The conversation that is thinking can only arise in the dialectical tension between Da and Sein, between that which is and the human being who lights it up with a particular thought. But because that dialectic remains under the sway of Being, such conversation can never fully become a "being-here," can never achieve complete clarity without closing the clearing in which that illumination is necessary and possible in the first place. Without the vulnerability to discord and confusion that Heidegger attributes to the Greek thinker, thinking threatens to conceal the opening in which it arises and thus to end the conversation.

But Plato would like to do away with this agony of entanglement. So he insists on clarity, explicitness, and objectivity (Dreyfus, 1981, pp. 509-11). If, for instance, we are going to think about our binding to the world of others, it is not enough to be able to give examples of those involvements; rather we must be able to elucidate the rules that hold in all like cases of a particular mode of engagement. If our stories are only thorough descriptions of the lived experience of our conversations, then we are, like the poets, guilty of not knowing what we are talking about. That which is for Heidegger the safeguard of an ongoing conversation—openness to the "sundering confusions" of the Other's otherness—is for Plato the greatest danger. Eschewing the ambiguity of the poets for the clarity of reason, he proposes taking a theoretical stance, seeking the general principles that make our everyday involvements coherent.

This project of eliminating uncertainty by taking a step back from the murkiness of concerned involvement in the world reaches its apotheosis (at least according to Heidegger) in the "footnote to Plato" offered by Descartes, for whom "what it is to be is . . . defined as the objectiveness of representing, and truth is . . . defined as the certainty of representing" (Heidegger, 1952/1977b, p. 127). Through disengaged reason, and its cleaving of the world into subject and object, objects can be lit up in such a way that they stay illuminated, and Dasein becomes a subject that no longer needs to concern itself with the ongoing labor of revealing that which is by apprehending it in conversation. Instead, it seeks to end the agony known subjectively as doubt by achieving the certainty of the object. A representation settles things once and for all by rendering them "unconditionally indubitable" (Heidegger, 1952/1977a, p. 82), and thus gives us a revealing which makes revealing itself no longer necessary. Once the Other has become an object, its sundering confusions no longer need be encountered. Indeed, the Other is no longer other, but simply a product of my own subjectivity.

For Heidegger, the transformation of that which is thought about into object and of the goal of thought into certainty is a scandalous corruption of thinking. It discloses a failure to understand that "reason . . . is the most stiff-necked adversary of thought" (Heidegger, 1952/1977a, p. 112). To the extent that the world is understood as that which is capable of being made certain, it is no longer that which demands authentic response from me. Conversation thus loses its essence, which is to light up precisely that uncertainty which is concealed by representation. When the sundering confusions that can "snag" me are put to rest by the relentless illumination of representation, conversation becomes

> idle talk. And when it does so, it serves not so much to keep being-in-the-world open for us . . . as rather to close it off, and cover up entities within the world. (Heidegger, 1926/1962, p. 213)

Certainty is purchased only at the expense of the opening that makes all projects of thinking (including the endeavor to attain certainty) possible. Thought, freed from the agony of doubt, becomes a concealing of otherness dangerously disguised as a revealing.

This corruption of thinking renders the fluid and discordant opening constituted by "that which is" into what Heidegger (1952/1977b) calls a "world picture," and which we must understand as the story told by a sole author. It is important to see that although this is an epistemological problem, in which the known is understood to be only the certain, it is also, and more disastrously, an ontological problem. What Heidegger calls the "age of the world picture" is not to be understood as a time dominated by a particular representation of the world, but rather as a time in which "the world [is] conceived and grasped as picture" (p. 129). The very idea that the world might be represented and rendered into a static world-view or story underlies and determines any particular world-view or story that might arise. So when we find ourselves beset with competing ontologies that lead to interminable moral argument, the problem is not that one story is just as good as another, but that all such stories are similarly flawed. None can emerge as the best, because all are truly the worst. They all bear the burden of being a representation of a world whose truth is lost in being represented in this fashion in the first place. They are all stories in which the otherness of the Other is concealed behind the storyteller's placid mask, behind his or her pretensions to certainty.

The rendering of the world into "picture" is the oblivion of the concerned involvement that Heidegger understands as crucial to the revealing of truth, for it is a revealing that puts revealing as such out of play. By making that "picture" only an instrumentality of the one who fashions it, it obliterates the otherness of the Other which is "revealed." This obliteration of the world as the location of an ongoing revealing has implications for both the world that is revealed once and for all and for the human beings who live in that world, for both the subjects and the objects which arise against the horizon of representation.

Objects that do not expose us to discord are no longer others whose otherness is always already beyond us. Instead, they are a collection of things that are "ordered to stand by, to be immediately at hand, indeed to stand there just so that [they] may be on call for a further ordering" (Heidegger, 1954/1977, p. 17). If objects exceed us, their excessiveness is only conditional: I may experience, for instance, a tree as "out there," but when I think of it as something to be pictured, its otherness is concealed. The tree is no longer an Other which inhabits my eyes before I see it, an "environment" that "snags" me by arising in front of me and demanding response from me. Instead, it is rendered by the ontology of the calculable as that which waits for me to bring it into focus as something I can use. I command the tree to stand by until I can bring it under my authorial sway as it fits into that story: as, for instance, paper pulp or lumber, a resource to be managed or a location of recreation. Understood in this fashion, the tree shows itself not as an Other to be apprehended, but "only as the object of an assault . . . that establishes itself as an unconditional objectification" (Heidegger, 1952/1977a, p. 100). Reason's arrow may penetrate to some objective heart of the things of the world, and successfully bring them to a standstill so that they might be pictured as objects of my calculations toward certainty. But it does so only by killing them as the others with which I converse. More important, it is not reason itself that is the problem; rather, the extrication of the subject from the agony of entanglement, its mutinous uprising into the sole authorship that must conceal the Other (of which reason is a mere instrument) makes the self-positing subject a nihilist. Reason in the hands of a nihilist is a weapon; according to Heidegger, this is so no matter what his or her intentions.

With the annihilation of the otherness of others arises the possibility of atrocities like Iago's manipulation of Othello. Othello is only a discordant object in Iago's world picture, and not an Other whose very discord is the occasion of the world-safeguarding conversation that Heidegger singles out as the essence of being-in-the-world. Othello becomes an object to be assaulted and eliminated. But manipulation and murder are not the kinds of assault with which Heidegger is most concerned (and we must, in the face of his own position in the Third Reich [see Farias, 1989], condemn this aloofness). Rather, a manipulation like Iago's is only a florid example of what *must* happen when conversation gives way to "assault." In the world understood as picture, as the location of the unfolding of the individual's own story, even well-meaning efforts to bind Dasein back to the world of others, like the codependence literature, are doomed. For they arise against a background in which that binding has been eliminated through the pursuit of sole authorship, through the annihilation of the excessiveness which alone can command us to a true conversation with the Other. Such efforts, precisely because they pivot on the subject's authorial "power," on his or her extricating him or herself from agony by holding sway over the narrative and all others in it, still constitute an assault.

Rather than looking at examples of people at their most atrocious, then, Heidegger finds it possible to glimpse the annihilation of the Other even in the attempt to achieve the good. We have seen that for thinkers like MacIntyre (1984), the establishing of values as the medium that is to orient us to our webs of interlocution does not succeed in providing a prophylaxis against nihilism: the distinctions made by an individual's valuing turn out to be bereft of any final significance because they arise out of discourses which, like the codependence literature, explicitly hold no place for ultimate judgment. For Heidegger, however, the problem is not that there is no longer the possibility of coherence for our value judgments, but rather that we continue to seek after the authority which can ground certainty, of which "value" is an example, at all.

> If God in the sense of the Christian god has disappeared from his author-
> itative position . . . this authoritative place is still always preserved, even
> though as that which has become empty. . . . The empty place demands to
> be occupied anew, and to have the god now vanished from it replaced by
> something else. New ideals are set up. (Heidegger, 1952/1977a, p. 69)

These new ideals are, of course, values, and are discovered by the person living the good life in which he or she occupies that authoritative place. Determined in this fashion, such "values" cannot but fill the emptiness with more emptiness. The horizon was wiped away in the first place by attempting to bring things to a standstill (of which Heidegger also under- stands the "Christian god" to be an example). And "values" are simply another manifestation of that attempt.

> Value is value inasmuch as it counts. It counts inasmuch as it is posited as
> that which matters. It is so posited through an aiming at and a looking
> toward that which has to be reckoned upon. Aim, view, field of vision,
> mean here both the sight beheld and seeing, in a sense that is determined
> from out of Greek thought, but that has undergone the change of *idea*
> from *eidos* to *perceptio*. (Heidegger, 1952/1977b, p. 72)

Insofar as they "count," values just disclose another location of the ontol- ogy of the calculable, and thus contradict themselves in their attempt to establish a basis for relationship.

The endeavor to find "value" in an "inner child" must shipwreck because it counts on a world from which we are already extricated rather than one that insists upon our entanglement in the work of its immediate apprehension. Pictures are just "pictures": they are an environment which cannot "snag" the one who makes them. The person who is understood as another country, with whom I am only to conduct adequate foreign relations based on my own understanding of value (my "self-esteem," who I "really am," how I "feel"), can certainly not command my "patriotism." That person is nothing worth agonizing over or dying for, nothing with which entanglement is even a possibility. The world that is only the story I tell myself about it, based on my own inner sense of "value," is always already devalued, and no project of valuing, like "replenishing" my "supply of self-esteem" and thus becoming a "powerful" sole author, can rehabilitate it. Any such project is always already an "extrication" from concerned involvement, and this extrication is, in Heidegger's view, always the first step on the slippery slope to nihilism.

In calculations of value can be seen the problematic that shows up both in Iago's failure to value Othello and in the codependence literature's failure to find a way to bind the reader to others without obliterating those others. Both are instances of the concealing of the otherness of the Other, of that which alone can call a human being into genuine conversation. This conversation, in turn, is genuine only to the extent that it safeguards the Other who demands response, that it starts with the understanding that I *cannot* ever be a sole author, and that in some important respect the story is always telling me. What is nihilistic about our failure to find that which is valuable, then, is not the absence of any standard, but the concealing of the excessiveness of the Other that allows it to demand response from me.

Followed to its ontological ground, the quest for sole authorship leads us here: the Other demands response, but in this demand is the agony of sundering confusion. The modern self responds by doing away with the demand, subjecting the Other whence it arises to his or her own sole authorship, concealing the otherness of the Other. This is why Heidegger (1952/1977a, p. 108) says, "thinking in terms of values is radical killing. It not only strikes down that which is as such . . . but it does away utterly with Being." Such standards belong only to the world already understood as a "picture," which is always already a world misunderstood as that which is under the purview of the sole author/subject, and which is not necessarily an ongoing source of agony. No longer is Being that which demands thought, that which gathers Dasein into relationship. Rather,

[m]an becomes that being upon which all that is, is grounded as regards the manner of its Being and its truth. Man becomes the relational center of that which is as such. (Heidegger, 1952/1977b, p. 128)

This is the codependence literature's understanding of "man" at his best, living the good life of "recovery." This understanding places that "man" inside his own fences, where he can best "own his own reality," and remain extricated from the "agony of entanglement," from the Other's ongoing demand for response.

If attempts to safeguard the world against Iago by the establishing of values against which he might be judged are really acts of annihilation, then an important question arises: who is perpetrating these atrocities? What kind of person makes the negotiations and calculations of valuing? Heidegger would not be surprised at the codependence literature's claim that 96 percent of us are "diseased." He would simply locate the "illness" in the existential-hermeneutic realm, as the inscription of modernity on all of us. We are thrown into the hubris of the modern self-understanding, into a world that Heidegger describes in these apocalyptic terms.

The earth, as the abode of man, is unchained from its sun. The realm that constitutes the suprasensory, which as such, is in itself, no longer stands over man as the authoritative light. The whole field of vision has been wiped away. The whole of that which is as such, as the sea, has been drunk up by man. For man has risen up into the I-ness of the *ego cogito*. Through this uprising, all that is, is transformed into object. That which is, as the objective, is swallowed up into the immanence of subjectivity. The horizon no longer emits light of itself. It is now nothing but the point-of-view posited in the value-positing of the will to power. (Heidegger, 1952/1977a, p. 107)

The subject uprising into sole authorship does not see with the eyes of the world. Rather, its seeing is a point of view, a "subjectness" from which it looks with Prufrock's "eyes that fix you with a formulated phrase" (Eliot, 1936/1964, p. 5). The horizon against which others show up is no longer "out there"; rather, it is "from here," constituted by the authorial "power" of which the codependence literature makes a virtue. As Eliot has Prufrock say, it is "as if a magic lantern cast the nerves in patterns on a screen" (p. 6). The light emanating from that screen is only a reflection, and its authority is only that which is given to it by appearing within a subject's narrative. It is not anything necessarily beyond the storyteller, but rather only that which appears as an instrumentality of the subject's sole authorship.

The sole author cannot be bound back to the world of others because, strictly speaking, there is for him or her no such world; its otherness has already been concealed. The "out there" has been reduced to a collection of "yous" fixed "in here" according to our own narrative authority. When we step back from our concerned involvements, and try to bring others into our stories in a way that prevents them from "affecting" us, we cannot but annihilate them as others. When, as one of the codependence texts' titles claims, "love is a choice" (Meier, Minirth, Hemfelt, and Hawkins, 1989), we are no longer humans mutually involved in the work of "gathering of presencing," but objects of each other's subjective gazes, Othellos of each other's Iagos, Soviet Unions of each other's United States, no matter what our intentions. We are individual storytellers whose narratives go on in front of no horizon which itself has set the stories in motion, and thus might hold us together in a meaningful way. Even if you appear to me to be a character worthy of inclusion in my story, still I am only "choosing" to allow you past my boundaries, and you are only another pattern cast on the screen by the same magic lantern, by my authorial power. And I may "choose" to extinguish that light at any time. I am still the sole author who

> contends for the position in which he can be that particular being who gives the measure and draws up the guidelines for everything that is. Because this position secures, organizes, and articulates itself as a worldview, the modern relationship to that which is, is one that becomes, in its decisive unfolding, a confrontation of world views; and indeed not of random world-views, but only of those that have already taken up the fundamental position of man that is most extreme. (Heidegger, 1952/1977b, p. 134)

The central thread of modernity under consideration here, the invention of an individual self cut loose from its moorings in a social world, is problematic not only because, as MacIntyre (1984) would have it, it signals the end to necessary obligations to certain rules; moreover, that individual already occupies the world that is pictured, the world which does not necessarily exceed me and leave me vulnerable to discord, but is rather whatever story I tell myself about it. And whether or not that story includes virtues or other kinds of values, in being authorized only by me, it bears the traces of the annihilation of the Other which makes genuine conversation impossible. The good life inscribed in the narrative space of the codependence literature is one achieved by striving for a "better" way of telling my own story, for a more complete sole authorship. It overlooks and conceals what Heidegger (1952/1977b) makes so clear: that sole authorship is only possible when a person "rises up into the subjectivity of his essence [and] enters into insurrection" (p. 100). For such a person there is really no Other for whom to act morally, with whom to suffer the agony of entanglement; extrication is annihilation. The "recovering" person "recovers" precisely by deepening the wellsprings of the nihilism of our times, by cultivating a technique for "rising up into the subjectivity of his essence." Given Heidegger's understanding of this uprising as a dangerous mutiny, attempts to restore conversation that take sole authorship for granted, or, as is the case with the codependence literature, that glorify it and seek to make it the basis of the good life, must drift aimlessly or shipwreck.

8

Conclusion:
A Reconstitution
of Codependence

Look into any eyes
You find by you, you can see
clear through to another day.

—Robert Hunter, "Box of Rain"

INTRODUCTION: THE "HEIDEGGER PROBLEM"

The wellsprings of the leveling of all meaningful difference, which I
have called nihilism, turn out to be the concealing of the excessiveness
which makes the Other an other in the first place. Being closed off to the
Other is not simply an effect of nihilism; rather, it is its moral ground,
and discourses that attempt to limn a good life but which take that
grounding as given cannot help but become further instances of
nihilism. We have seen that the codependence literature is just such a
discourse. In its emphasis on sole authorship, its insistence that my obligations to others cannot exceed my narrative authority and must proceed from my own making of "value," its proposal of a horizon which is
legitimate only because it cannot hold sway over my story, these books
appear to be profoundly nihilistic, even as they present themselves as
guides to a meaningful life.

Despite their various concealments and denials that there is any-thing binding upon or necessarily exceeding the individual's authorial power, the books themselves constitute a culture that shapes its readers even as it tells them they are merely being provided with a mirror. And in this "mirror" the reader finds that she can live the good life only when she extricates herself from painful entanglement with others, an extrication which takes place by denying the otherness of the Other. This proposed good life is not a new invention; rather, it is a deepening of what is already understood as the best way to be a "self" in modern Western culture: to be a sole author, extricated from agonizing entan-glement. Because this proposal fails to uncover its own prejudices, it founders on the shoals of nihilism.

I stated at the outset that hermeneutics is a method that places prejudice squarely on the table, rejecting the pretense of "objectivity" and "value freedom," and replacing it with an endeavor to uncover the (inescapably prejudiced) grounding of the phenomenon under study. I believe this method has brought to light many of the important preju-dices of the codependence literature, and placed those prejudices in their proper context. But the reliability of a hermeneutic account is to some extent contingent on its ability to uncover as many of its own prej-udices as is possible. It is fitting, therefore, for my conclusion to reflect upon some of the prejudices of this study, to acknowledge and to address the limitations that they create.

One prejudice stands in a dangerous juxtaposition to the problems that I have already discussed regarding my use of Heidegger's thought. I have assumed that the Nazi Holocaust stands as a central, and disastrous, instance of modern nihilism. In effect, I have implied that unless a psy-chological discourse like the codependence literature can tell us how it safeguards the world from such an atrocity, we must be suspicious of its ability to bring about a good life that is truly good. I don't think that it can be credibly argued that the Nazi extermination program was *not* an atrocity, or that it did *not* hinge on a concealing of the otherness of the Other (see Wyschogrod, 1985). I am comfortable with this particular prejudice. But I am not so comfortable with allowing Heidegger to have the last word on this matter, as he, alone among all the authors whose work I have discussed, was a Nazi. And he did not join the party out of some pragmatism regarding his job or his university, but rather out of belief in and commitment to the Nazi cause, out of a conviction inherent in his philosophy, that the arising of the German *Volk* would be the way out of the bind of Western metaphysics (see Wolin, 1990, pp. 16-66).

One way to understand the "Heidegger problem" is to say that Heidegger failed to provide a way to make useful pragmatic distinctions. This is, as I said earlier, a danger of ontological hermeneutics: there are no parameters placed around interpretation, no ideal like freedom from domination against which interpretation must be made and toward which it should lead. Heidegger's critique cuts to the heart of Western modernity, and yet its reliance on "an evocative linguistic magic leads to a mimesis of fate rather than to an analysis of concrete social causes of the feeling of crisis" (Sollner, cited in Wolin, 1990, p. 19). Heidegger can thus tell us much about what is wrong with our Cartesian self-understanding, about how the uprising into subjecthood is deeply problematic. But perhaps because he eschews all pragmatic questions as hopelessly entangled with a nihilistic ontology, he leaves us with an analysis of the everyday which fails to situate the subject in a particular social history. Because he cannot reveal the web of concrete social relations in which a given phenomenon is embedded, he cannot answer the pragmatic question of what is to be done about those relations. The answers he provides are most unsatisfactory, ranging from his own (never-recanted) Nazism to his nostalgic preoccupation with an idealized ancient Greece, to his quasi-mystical ramblings about the "fourfold," to his posthumously published warning that "only a god can save us now." Such answers cannot tell us what we might do about the real human suffering that the codependence texts have so poorly understood, nor help us to shape a notion of the good life that is truly good.

I share Heidegger's suspicion of the pragmatic; indeed, an assumption of this book is that it is not sufficient to observe that the codependence literature "works," that is, that it helps people to feel better, without taking stock of what it works toward. At the same time, the conclusion that the codependence literature works toward the nihilism of the modern self may leave us too far from the pragmatic to be useful in answering the question of what is to be done. But I think there is practical value in stopping to look at the prejudices of a popular phenomenon, and that it is to be found in the space of questions opened up by the interpretation at hand.

The rest of this chapter will take up some of the uses of my analysis. First, I will present a recapitulation of my argument so far. Then I will offer a reconstitution of the notions of codependence and "recovery" that does not leave their ontological background hidden. I will use this reconstruction to point to the kinds of questions that clinicians and researchers can be asking in order to address the pragmatic that my interpretation raises. For in the end, if this book has any utility at all, it is to help to lay the groundwork for answering the question of what is to be done about the difficulties we face in knowing how to be with one another.

CODA: A BRIEF SUMMARY OF THE ARGUMENT

Before discussing some of the questions this book has opened up (but not addressed), it might be wise to recapitulate those I claim to have answered. We have found that the codependence literature, a highly popular group of mass-market self-help books, presents itself as a homogeneous body purporting to describe a "disease" encountered by the self in its relationships. The books claim that virtually all of us encounter "agony" in our entanglements with others, and can end that agony by "recovering," that is, by taking up the understanding of being-with-others offered in these books as the "healthy" one.

I have brought certain ideas to bear on this claim. First, I have argued that the "self" is not a transhistorical, universal entity, but rather the concept or set of concepts about the individual human being that holds sway in a given culture. Next, following MacIntyre (1984), I have argued that an important feature of the self-understanding which prevails in our culture is that the self is constructed through narratives. And, following Taylor (1989), I have argued that these narratives serve to give the person an orientation in "moral space," that is, they are stories about the kind of life to which a person ought to aspire.

Thus, I have argued, the codependence literature can be understood as a moral discourse, that is, a narrative space in which readers encounter not so much a story about "disease" and "health" as an account of "bad" and "good," or an account of what the good life is, and how they have failed to attain it. In this view, the codependence literature turns out to be a narrative space that urges those who enter it to become the sole authors of their own stories and thus to attain a good life. This achievement is contingent upon the purging from that story of all possible coauthors, and, indeed, upon what I have called a concealing of otherness. I have described this concealing as an ontological problem that reaches into our most everyday life, always already present in many troublesome and widespread social practices.

I have then taken this account of the good life and placed it inside a larger story, namely the story comprised by various accounts of how the modern self is to be bound back to a world of other modern selves. I have argued that this larger story is fit to provide a gloss on that of the codependence literature because both stories share a concern with the problem of being-with-others. The larger story, I have claimed, is one of frustrated attempts to find a way between the agony of the self's fragmentation and isolation on the one hand, and the agony of the self's being entirely subordinated to a tradition on the other. I have shown that these various attempts fail to secure a means for the cogito to find the good life through entanglements with others.

I have called this failure a problem of nihilism, because the loss of moorings constituted by this modern understanding of self, a loss which these attempts seek to overcome, discloses the disappearance of a horizon against which certain distinctions can show up as more or less valuable than certain others. And I have shown that understanding the self as the seat of all valuing cannot overcome this nihilism. Indeed, it has turned out, such an endeavor, which has its roots in certain modern understandings of autonomy, and of which the codependence literature is a paradigmatic case, cannot help but reinforce this loss of meaningful distinctions. The project fails, I have argued, because it takes for granted the radical separation of self and world which is the wellspring of that nihilism in the first place. That separation in turn hinges upon the erasure of the Other as an other, and the codependence literature turns out to provide a technique for achieving that erasure. To the extent that it thus seeks to strengthen the "metaphysical pillar" of our age, to make it the cornerstone of the good life without taking account of the crucial problems such a pillar presents for the building it supports, the texts under scrutiny here make a virtue of what might be better understood as vicious. The codependence literature, because it amounts to a nihilistic technique of the self, must therefore be understood as a force which contributes to the problems that arise in the culture which inhabits that building.

A RECONSTITUTION OF CODEPENDENCE

The central problem captured in the word "codependence" is that some people put the needs of others before their own, and experience subjective distress as a result. We might say that the Other's otherness looms too large for the codependent, so that she is, in Beattie's unfortunate phrase, "snagged by the environment." The codependent redeems herself by redirecting her focus toward her own story, by becoming a sovereign sole author on a private narrative quest. The codependent loves others too much; "recovery" is the recovering of that love for oneself.

So long as we understand the agony of entanglement as a "psychological" problem, this analysis, simplistic though it might be, is hard to gainsay. Every psychotherapist has encountered many people (mostly women) who are suffering from their seemingly compulsive tendency to put others first. The lack of self-worth experienced by these people is palpable, and shows up in all aspects of therapy. A person whom the literature would call a codependent is often a patient who quickly enslaves herself to the therapist, and is usually made uneasy when the therapist shows himself or herself to be someone who doesn't want to be a slave-master. The pragmatist's temptation is to stick with the useful, if philosophically impoverished, account of codependence, and to work with the patient to help him or her stop being for the sake of others and to start putting him or herself first.

But let us look again at the idea that it is a problem to put the Other first. At this point, we can say unequivocally that the "agony" this entails is not simply the result of the disruption of the machine's smooth functioning. Neither is it the loss of some pristine state of psychic balance which, had it not been disrupted by bad parenting, would facilitate entanglements that are not agonizing. Instead, my interpretation indicates that Beattie's agony must be understood as a result of a deficiency in the understanding of self into which we are all thrown. That the Other arises in a way that creates such difficulty points to the rupture between self and Other constituted by the given understanding of the self as a sole author. And one consequence of this rupture (the consequence that shows up in the texts as a "disease") is that we modern selves who understand ourselves as sovereign entities must find it difficult to understand and to live with the experience of being commanded by another. If we are, as so much in our political and cultural worlds tell us we are, to be self-contained, self-sufficient, self-loving, independent, and so on, then any experience which makes us feel otherwise may well be agonizing. It will certainly be confusing when we find ourselves confronted with an Other whose very presence seems to command us to abandon our own authorship—not because this being commanded is inherently pathological, but because there is little or nothing in our history of self-understanding that prepares us for it. Codependence thus signifies the ontological breakdown that occurs when the sole author is confronted with a possible narrative authority other than him- or herself.

This last remark might help us to address a feature of the codependence literature (one which it shares with most of psychotherapeutic theory and practice) that I have thus far left mostly unexamined: the notion that the family is the crucible of psychopathology. This claim seems to be valid as far as it goes; no therapist can reasonably deny that the self bears the inscription of its family history, that many pathologies (as well as many nonpathological characteristics) can be "read" as the palimpsests of a family's hidden life. But let us take this notion one step further, and ask if it might point the way to something else, to something that might help us in our reconstitution of codependence.

It is safe to say that the codependence literature's account of family history as that which is to be "recovered" from comes ultimately from Freud, who turned his attention to traumatic infantile experience as the source of adult suffering.[1] Schorske (1981) has argued that this focus must be held in suspicion insofar as it constitutes a reduction of politics "to an epiphenomenal manifestation of psychic forces" (p. 183). Schorske's argument, in brief, is that Freud abandoned politics for the psyche out of frustration at his own powerlessness: his childhood aspirations to law and government had been thwarted; his career as a professor was, at the time he wrote *The Interpretation of Dreams*, foundering. This was due in part to a resurgent anti-Semitism that accompanied the waning of liberalism in turn-of-the-century Vienna. According to Schorske, Freud thus overlooked the political status of his own dreams' characters as he worked out his theories of dream interpretation and unconscious processes. Many of these characters were politicians, or people with political power, but in Freud's interpretation they lost their social and political context and meaning. He understood them psychologistically, so they became representatives of the timeless notion of authority that Freud ascribed to fathers in general. He thus interpreted his dreams as witness to his struggle to throw off the shackles of his father's influence, to lay his ghost to rest, and *not* to avenge the loss of the tolerance and liberalism that Jakob Freud had espoused.

Freud, Schorske (1981) argues, encoded this personal struggle in his novel interpretation of the Oedipus myth, which became not a story of "a regal hero motivated by political obligation . . . to remove the plague from Thebes" (p. 199), but of a man laid waste by guilt over his own past. Thus,

> Freud's Oedipus is not *Rex*, but a thinker searching for his identity and its meaning. By resolving politics into personal psychological categories, he restores personal order, but not public order. (p. 200)

In this resolution, Freud developed a view of human nature that extricated it from any necessary entanglement in a polis: Freud's dream characters were *not* Viennese politicians; Oedipus was *not* King of Thebes, but rather stood for all men at all times. This, Schorske says, is a

> counterpolitical triumph of the first magnitude. By reducing his own political past and present to an epiphenomenal status in relation to the primal conflict between father and son, Freud gave his fellow liberals an a-historical theory of man and society that could make bearable a political world spun out of orbit and beyond control. (p. 203)

The codependence literature is heir to this resolution. Indeed, it takes Freud's reduction of regicide—political revolution and liberation—to patricide—the individual liberation of liberalism—one more step. In the codependence literature, as we have seen, it is no longer necessary even to take account of what Freud saw as the primal conflict between father and son (or parent and child). The conflicts between parent and child are no longer seen as the inescapable and necessary crucible of psychic development, nor are those conflicts somehow built into "human nature" as they were for Freud. Indeed, to understand the human is not to look to the endless conflicts of psychic forces, which are dependent both for their shape and their resolution on outside forces such as one's family. Rather, the codependence literature offers a turn to the radically private inner child, to a being potentially unencumbered by conflict, whether political or familial in origin. Now the family, to which Freud turned for liberation from a fragmented political world, itself becomes the force from which to be liberated.

The "recovering" person declares him- or herself free from any necessary entanglements, free from even a vestigial history, relieved of the "baggage" that a family's (and a society's) coauthorship constitutes. Like Freud's Oedipus, he or she does this not to restore an intersubjective order, but to seek the order of his or her own subjectivity. But this subjectivity is even more purely private than Freud thought of it as. Redemption is no longer even a matter of coming to terms with one's own parents, and with the limitations posed simply by being the kind of being which bears the inscription of a particular family's history. Instead it is to be found in becoming the parent of one's own inner child, freed from the constraints of history and the "contamination" of external events, and thus erasing even what Freud left behind as a necessary entanglement with the Other.

Schorske (1981) suggests that Freud's transformation of regicide to patricide was in service of comforting himself and "his fellow liberals" (p. 204). One of the limitations of this book is that a full analysis of the ideological dimensions of the codependence literature's analogous turn from patricide to parentlessness is beyond my scope. But the ontological analysis can at least lay bare this part of the background of the "dysfunctional family": the nuclear family is one of the last associations remaining in our society that is not entered into as a matter of choice. As Schorske points out, "childhood experience, whatever universals may govern it, must be lived in a cultural milieu" (p. 188). Our cultural milieu is one that has little space for narratives which claim us, as our family histories do, without our choosing.

Heir to this self-understanding, the nuclear family thus discloses an ontological contradiction: on the one hand, all otherness is to be brought under the purview of a freely choosing subject; on the other hand the family seems inescapably to be an Other, at least a coauthor of our own stories. The child who is conceived as a sole author is also conceived intersubjectively, as inescapably the subject of others'—his or her family's—narratives. As other cultural forms (like codependence books) erase themselves as Others, as other involvements like local communities become increasingly matters of contingency, increasing pressure is brought to bear on the family as coauthor. Perhaps no technology of the self can erase this intrusion on the individual's narrative authority. But as the "cultural milieu" becomes more and more individualistic (aided, undoubtedly, by such phenomena as codependence books), this contradiction deepens, and the family's coauthorship becomes more and more a locus of "sundering confusions," of agonizing entanglements.

The family commands us. Little or nothing that we find out about ourselves tells us what to do with this being commanded, except that we should throw it off. Neither are we prepared to be the commanding Others for other selves, such as our children. Perhaps this claim is only an obscurantist version of the recovery movement's catechism about the "cycle of abuse." But I think not, because it illuminates the background of the family's importance as a pathogen. It is not that there is an unsullied inner child who is intruded upon unfairly by parents who don't know how to leave their children "free to be who they really are," who are ignorant because of their own upbringing by similarly ignorant parents who can perhaps trace their pathologies' lineage to Adam and Eve. Rather, I am suggesting that the particular understanding of ourselves into which we are thrown—the self as sole author—cannot tell us how to be coauthors, and coauthorship seems inescapably to be our lot. Indeed, if we reconstitute codependence this way, then it becomes just as important to investigate the possibilities of coauthorship as those of sole authorship. It is no more ludicrous (or dangerous) to suggest that self-help consists in learning how to cultivate our openness to others than it is to exhort people to help themselves by sealing their "boundaries" and becoming self-contained.

The focus of the codependence literature on the pathogenic family might then point us in two directions at once. First, it helps us to see that what the texts call codependence is the distress that occurs when our understanding of our being is contradicted by the arising of another (suppressed) ontological possibility, a contradiction that is inevitable, given the apparent inescapability of entanglement with others. Second, the fact that the family commands us in a way that disrupts sole author-

ship points to the fact that that possibility has not yet been entirely suppressed. We still might understand ourselves differently: as beings who
can be commanded by the Other, who cannot be selves outside of webs
of interlocution, and who thus must learn how to live with and safeguard the possibility of coauthorship, of being called out of our own narratives and into those of another. This possibility remains even in the
face of all the manipulations of the marketplace, all its encouragement to
be all that we can be by buying all that we can buy, to seal ourselves in a
hermetic autonomy. It persists in works like the codependence literature
as "pathology," as the widespread sense of victimization of "Adult
Children," and as the equally widespread difficulty of unsealing autonomy sufficiently to be an Other for another self.

Despite this difficulty, despite the domination of the ontology of
the sole author, the Other can still arise in front of my horizon, pull me
out of my own narrative, and inhabit my story in a way that cannot help
but change it. The codependence literature bears witness to this possibility; it is the sine qua non of the texts, for if otherness had truly been
obliterated, there would be no need for books offering a technique of
erasure. But, of course, it bears its witness witlessly, pathologizing the
vestigial appearance of a suppressed ontological possibility, urging readers to strengthen their walls against this "disease."

Some, like Rilke (1912/1987), have a different view of this ontological possibility.

> O Lovers, completed in
> one another, I turn
> to ask you of us.
> Is there certainty in your embraces?
> Look at it this way . . .
> my hands sometimes recognize each other
> and offer sanctuary to my weary face.
> This yields some slight sensation.
> But what proof of existence is that?
> You who fan the fires of one another's
> passion till, overcome, you cry
> "No more!"—who, beneath lover's hands,
> swell like purple grapes at harvest;
> who subside, that the other may
> more completely come to be;
> I ask *you* about *us*. (p. 21, ellipses in original)

Rilke finds significance in what the literature dismisses as "disease." To
be "completed in/one another" is anathema to the notion of sole

authorship; it is, according to the codependence literature, the well-spring of "disease," for it opens the way to experiencing oneself as incomplete, in need of the Other for one's own existence. The "us" that is other than "you" and "I" is the greatest danger for the codependence literature, for it opens the way to "abuse." The recognition of one's hands by each other is for Rilke the faintest glimmer of life, but for the codependence literature its strongest showing. The rapture that is for Rilke the "proof of existence" is, in those texts, its negation.

If we recast codependence as the fate of rapture in a world whose moral architecture provides no space for it, then we might come to see codependence—and particularly its apparent universality—as evidence that sole authorship has not yet suppressed the possibility of being for others. That people continue to suffer for love at all bears a spectral witness to the continued presence of the Other's otherness: it has not been entirely eclipsed by the uprising of the subject into sole authorship. The texts identify a real problem in our self-understanding; but they do so in a way that misses the true meaning and import of that problem, and thus prescribes the "pathogen" as the cure. Instead of offering a way to be for and with others, they offer a way to be with oneself, with the imaginary playmate called the Inner Child.

The phantasmic presence of the Other that haunts these texts is also disclosed in an ironic way in the conversation between the authors and the readers of the codependence texts. People buy these books in an attempt to figure out how they are to live with others, and find in the texts a horizon, albeit one whose otherness is concealed and, indeed, in front of which all otherness suppressed. But even if this nihilistic message is what the reader encounters, in encountering anything at all, she is still commanded by an "out there," still seeking confirmation of her existence by an Other. The texts cannot get around this, try as they might: the reader who is told to look only within is still looking beyond herself when she receives this advice.

These entirely unintentional meanings of the texts are obviously not enough to make them reliable sources of self-help; they are, after all, hamstrung by the groundlessness of their assumptions about the self. But let us look at a description of codependence in the light of the ontological possibility articulated by Rilke.

> The codependent is invariably a Good Person. Codependents are devoted to taking care of others within the family system and often beyond; many become professional caregivers (nurses, doctors, counselors). . . . Codependents . . . find meaning in making themselves indispensable to others. . . . They throw themselves into their work. . . .

> Codependents are sufferers—Good Christian Martyrs. Their good-
> ness is directly related to their suffering and the rewards they expect (and
> receive) because they are willing to sacrifice so much. They are always
> putting others first, taking the smallest piece of pie, wearing old clothes.
>   Codependents are servers. They are the volunteers, the people who
> hold the society together, who set aside their own physical, emotional,
> and spiritual needs for the sake of others. They end up overburdened
> and exhausted, and we see them as heroes. (Schaef, 1987, p. 30)

Codependents, in other words, have not taken up the mantle of sole
authorship. At this point, however, we might well wonder what is wrong
with this. In light of the present analysis, it might seem that our society
needs *more* people to hold it together, people for whom sole authorship does not hold the charm that it does for others and who understand
themselves as completed only in relation to an Other. Of course, Schaef
has rejoinder to this suggestion. People who do not take up the prevailing understanding of themselves

> tend to have ulcers, high blood pressure, colitis, back pain, and rheuma-
> toid arthritis; they are at high risk for cancer. Codependents who are chil-
> dren tend to develop allergies, skin problems, asthma, bed wetting, and
> learning disabilities and are frequently accident-prone or suicidal. (p. 30)

The problem with setting aside one's own needs "for the sake of others"
is that it creates suffering, and not only the laundry list of medical problems that Schaef cites. Moreover, as we have seen in the texts, the person
who lives for the sake of others is easily oppressed and exploited.
    But is this suffering a problem in the same way that the suffering
caused by, say, cancer is a problem—that a process interferes with normal
cell reproduction in such a way as to threaten one's health? Or might we
better understand it as the price one pays for being-for-the-sake-of-others
in a world which has largely eclipsed that possibility? Here we might
return to the observations of critics like van Wormer (1989) and Krestan
and Bepko (1990) that codependence is really the pathologization of
the traditional view of women, and speculate that it falls upon the disenfranchised to bear the burden of the suppressed ontological possibility articulated by Rilke. Concrete social relations in our society are medi-
ated by an understanding of ourselves that does not tell us how to be in
relation to others, and particularly how to maintain a sense of self when
an Other arises in front of us in such a way as to rupture our self-con-
structed narratives. Those who have not mastered the techniques of
sole authorship are exploited, oppressed, abused, and otherwise
marginalized, but only if one takes for granted that this ontology is the

best possible understanding of ourselves does the uprising into subject-hood constituted by "recovery" emerge as the best way to overcome this disenfranchisement. Only when the prejudices of that ontology remain concealed does codependence show up as a "disease" rather than as a finger pointing to the deficiencies in our understanding of ourselves as sole authors.

The ontology of sole authorship, as I argued at the end of chapter 5, upholds and is supported by the complex web of practices that constitutes the contemporary social world, at least in the United States. The inherent inequities of free-market capitalism are intolerable for one who finds "proof of existence" only in the "us," and who thus understands one person's prosperity as another person's homelessness, one person's driving a car as another person's oil-fouled fishing grounds. The codependence literature resolves these contradictions by reminding its readers that they are responsible for no one but themselves; to the extent that they suffer, it is because they cannot put brackets around their concern for others. Their suffering will end only, according to the texts, when they learn how to do this, and not when they challenge a social and political world that alienates and penalizes (or pathologizes) the person who does not easily take up the mantle of sole authorship.

I do not mean to glorify codependence or to deny that people suffer unduly when they are for the sake of others. Rather, I mean to point out that this suffering offers us lessons quite different from the codependence literature's claim that "recovery" lies in extrication from entanglement. First, it tells us that we live in an inhuman world, at least to the extent that its social and political structures make being-for-the-sake-of-others an "illness." Second, the presence of that suffering is evidence not so much of the failure of certain people to have purged all coauthors from their stories as of the continuing pull exerted on all of us, no matter how inhuman our world, by the claim of the Other. And third, that "recovery" might be better understood as developing the capacity for immersion in the world of others, and in working toward a world which safeguards such immersion.

The world pictured on Prufrock's screen still commands him, and if the interplay between subject and object points back to events more profound, those events are not only the various turns in the history of philosophy which have brought us to an apparently inescapable nihilism. They are also the genuine conversations which now come to light only as the phantasm of strongly bounded selves striving somehow to be related to others, and experiencing the subjective distress these texts call "codependence" when those others arise in such a way as to shatter the ontological background of sole authorship. Those spectral conversations which

246 THE SELF ON THE SHELF

remain continue to bear witness to the presence, however muted, of the "out there." Even in our most impoverished understanding of them, webs of interlocution still claim us. We are still thrown into them, even if they are diminished by the self-understanding that leaves room for nothing beyond that self and is agonized when it finds itself claimed by the Other.

The Other, it might be said, continues to summon us even as we talk about it in a way destined to make it disappear. But it calls out quietly, and is easily obscured by the concatenations of sole authorship and its search for narrative dominion. We continue to be summoned, and attempts to unravel the Gordian knot like the codependence literature testify to that summoning, even as they further conceal it as a summons. But when the subject answers that call, it risks annihilating the Other from which the summons originates. This, in turn, puts the narratives in which we attempt to orient ourselves in constant danger of breaking down. As Eliot/Prufrock laments,

> And when I am formulated, sprawling on a pin,
> When I am pinned and wriggling on the wall,
> Then how should I begin
> To spit out the butt-ends of my days and ways?
> And how should I presume? (Eliot, 1936/1964, p. 8)

When we start from the horizon of "subjectness," we deny the claim of the Other upon us, and turn our illumination of the horizon into the presumptions of sole authorship. But these efforts also hold out hope in the sense that they start from any horizon at all, and thus preserve, perhaps unwittingly, the vestiges of that claim.

The apparent widespread difficulty of bringing others into one's own narrative can now be reconstituted as the disclosure of an understanding of being which cannot help but make otherness problematic. Of course, the codependence books, embedded as they are in that ontology, can show that problem only as a failure to be a "good enough" sole author. So to read these books is to find that the troubles that plague us are best solved by "going within," by turning away from the entanglements in the social and/or political worlds whence those troubles arise. Hillman (1992) notes that this is

> . . . an idea basic to modern therapeutic practice. How are you going to help the world if you're not in order? You're just going to be acting out; you're going to be out in the street making trouble. First get inside yourself, find out who you are, get yourself straightened out, then go out in the world, then you can be useful. We've held to that view, but I don't think it works. (p. 99)

And Heidegger tells us why it doesn't "work." Getting "inside yourself" is only deepening the "subjectness" that has alienated us from those others, from the social and political structures that are the context of the breakdown addressed in the codependence literature. The codependence literature makes a virtue of this alienation, telling us that the good life is one in which we are free to drive away from a world of dwindling resources, increasing poverty, and a degenerating global environment in a fine new Mercedes.

In openly encouraging this nihilism, in making it the cornerstone of its understanding of the good life, the codependence literature must be considered a dangerous discourse. It only deepens an abyss, whose emptiness is in turn concealed. This concealment shows up as a fullness; for the "recovered" person is one who is so full of himself or herself, so full of narrative authority, that he or she is never pulled out of his or her own story. This kind of "fullness," it would seem, is a problem that haunts the interminable debate I discussed in the previous chapter. Positing a world-view, seeking to make it commensurable with that of others (or, for that matter, abandoning that project altogether in favor of an emphasis on getting "inside yourself") is always already a concealing of the Other's necessary claim on me and the agony inherent in that being claimed. So long as it is a sole author that seeks the bonds with others, that person is bound to fall into the abyss that opens between it and other sole authors. It is bound to be an "empty self," restlessly seeking fulfillments that cannot help but be further instances of the emptiness of nihilism. And, to deepen the paradox, what that empty self most lacks is a lived experience of lacking, an understanding of its being-in-the-world that preserves the claim of the Other as that which is necessary to the conversation which calls us into being.

In attempts to bind the individual back to the world of others, then, much depends upon how those others are understood. Clearly, to the extent that the horizon remains under the sway of the subject, the effort to establish a basis for relationship must shipwreck from its own internal contradictions. The subject remains a monadic self, formulating, manipulating, and controlling, even in the face of a commitment to do otherwise. And the codependence literature, which announces itself as offering a technique by which conversation might be restored, instead discloses a location of the dwindling of meaningful conversation. By seeking to free its readers from any necessary claim of the Other, it offers a "recovery" of conversation which can only threaten conversation. By safeguarding only the "in here," the "power" of sole authorship, it offers only more nihilism, a "recovery" of the self's entanglements with others which is really a "radical killing."

Avenues for Further Research

My attempt at pragmatism is imbued with another prejudice, or set of prejudices, which I should address here. My reconstitution of codependence suggests that true recovery from the agony of entanglement, rather than proceeding from a maximization of the self's sole authorship, might be better seen as the recovery of one's capacity to be open to the Other. Clearly, this hinges on a highly idealistic notion: that one's openness will not be exploited by the Other, and this poses an enormous problem. The exploitation of what the texts call codependents can be seen as a function of the oppressors' failure to know how to be Others for other selves. I would argue that this failure bears witness to the rupture embodied in the codependence literature, namely, that we do not know how to be in relation to one another. Some—primarily those who, due to the contingencies of our social history, have power—exploit the openness of others; and some—the disenfranchised, the powerless—are exploited. The texts speak primarily to the latter, and suggest a technique for becoming immune to (and perhaps more like) the former. And the prejudice I bring to bear on this analysis is that the ontological possibility that both modes of being suppress—that confirmation of existence is found in the "us"—should not remain suppressed. We are, as MacIntyre puts it, "never more and sometimes less than the co-authors of our own stories." We are called into being by the Other, and preserving the Other's claim on the self is also an act of self-preservation. Moreover, preserving an openness to the Other is a worthy cornerstone of the good life, not only because it is an act of self-preservation, but because it is good in itself.

This prejudice, while obviously at odds with the background of contemporary technological culture, is one that has been explored by many philosophers and religious thinkers. It is a claim that, in many ways, substitutes metaphysics for pragmatism. Let us consider, for instance, Krestan and Bepko's (1990) reconstitution of codependence, in which they argue that it bears witness to the "struggle between the self's integrity and its need for relatedness." Such a formulation as this gives rise to all manner of pragmatic possibility, to the various techniques of self that allow it to negotiate its way through this dialectic of "need." But to understand "relatedness" as a "need" is already to place it under the purview of the subject, something that the sole author/self must procure in the same way as food or shelter. There are alternate understandings of this "need," such as Levinas's (1961/1979), which see us as called into being by the Other. This being called, he argues, is a "metaphysical Desire," which must be differentiated from what we call "need."

Desire is the desire for the absolutely other. Besides the hunger one sat-
isfies, the thirst one quenches, and the senses one allays, metaphysics
desires the other beyond satisfactions, where no gesture by the body to
diminish the aspiration is possible, where it is not possible to sketch out
any known caress nor invent any new caress. A desire without satisfaction which, precisely, *understands* the remoteness, the alterity, and the
exteriority of the other. (p. 34)

By offering this understanding, Levinas safeguards against the concealing of the Other that I have argued gives rise to nihilism. A similar
approach to the problem of otherness in psychotherapy is suggested by
Friedman (1976), following Buber (1966), when he points out the folly of
understanding "wholeness" as self-containment, and argues that human
being must be understood as, first and foremost, a capacity for response to
the Other. But these approaches resist the nihilism embedded in the notion
of the individual we have explored here only by invoking an entirely different understanding of the good life—the life lived when the "desiring
being is mortal and the Desired invisible" (Levinas, 1961/1979, p. 34).
This, of course, is a far cry from the codependence literature, which suggests that desire for a Mercedes is much like desire for another person.

The prejudice I am discussing here posits a category of the Other
that simply cannot be reduced to the self, or brought under the purview
of the subject who "needs" it in such a way as to be woven into its own
story. If this prejudice limits the practical utility of my analysis, this may
only indicate the impoverishment of a practical world thoroughly suf-
fused with the ontology of the calculable. But I would further argue
that my prejudice toward the restoration of a notion of an inviolable,
irreducible Other that is a necessary constituent of the self has its uses.
To see these practical implications, let me turn back to the larger context
in which, as I argued at the outset, the codependence literature is
embedded: the world of psychotherapy in general.

Kovel (1991) has articulated the basis for a practical application of
the restoration of the category of the Other. He describes the various
ways in which otherness has been erased by what he calls Ego.

We would not see Ego, then, in the rosy light afforded by ego psychology, as
the good cop who keeps the local toughs under control; we see ego as a law
enforcer, all right, but regard the law as having a major role in the production
of crime. . . . By not recognizing the Other, Ego demonizes the Other. (p. 229)

Kovel calls this "criminal law" logos, and he opposes it to the Other
which is, he argues, lived out in soul. And here the stage is set for the
reentry of the Other into the world which erases it.

> Soul confronts logos through a critique which does not deconstruct the text so much as reveal the hidden history of Otherness contained within it—the lost desire, the repressed speech, the hidden transformational capacity. . . . [C]ritique regathers and differentiates what had been split, becoming the work of soul in the realm of language. If texts lie, it is not as a code that reveals yet another text, but in reference to a historical truth. . . . Critique is emancipatory in spirit, because it releases spirit-power thwarted by domination. It is the "truth that will make you free." (p. 231)

Obviously, I submit this book as critique, in the sense that Kovel intends: as a revealing of the history of otherness contained (but concealed) in the codependence texts. And it is only through the prejudice by which I claim that there is a history of otherness to be revealed that I can make this critique. I also think that some of the questions I have raised about psychotherapy in general can be addressed through this prejudice. For psychotherapy can also be understood as what Kovel calls critique, but only if it is a practice which specifies its moral ground (see Kovel, 1981, for an examination of the possibilities of psychoanalysis as critique). After all, what is a therapist if not an Other who inserts him- or herself on a patient's horizon in such a way as to call him or her into a new self-understanding? And how is this done if not through the recollection of the patient's "history of otherness" that is revealed through transference? Theorists of psychotherapy have not been ignorant of this possibility of the practice. Indeed, the therapist as the interlocutory Other, coconstituting the patient's self, is an intuition basic to such diverse therapeutic systems as those of Rogers (1961), Winnicott (1958), and Kohut (1971, 1978).

But let us briefly consider one of these examples. Kohut's effect on modern therapeutic—or at least psychoanalytic—practice has been profound. He recognized the shift in pathology from the so-called hysterical or conversion disorders of Freud's day to the so-called self disorders, primarily "narcissistic personality disorder." Kohut describes a praxis in which the therapist comes out from behind the shield of analytic silence and anonymity in order to be an Other for the patient. The therapist does this by providing a recognition of the patient's otherness through a technique Kohut calls "mirroring." This, he suggests, helps the patient to overcome his or her narcissism by providing him or her with an Other against whom the patient does not have to be defended. As a result, the patient is able to regard the therapist as truly Other, that is, as a person in his or her own right, rather than as another image in the narcissist's mirror. The therapist becomes real, and the patient-therapist dyad becomes an "us" that confirms existence in a way that all of the illusions of narcissism could never do.

In this kind of praxis, then, the self is conceived as a social being, one shaped in the crucible of relationship; therapy becomes the milieu of change by virtue of its ability both to provide a critique of the patient's history of Otherness and to help restore an openness to the Other. But here we might ask the question that I have posed to the codependence literature: toward what kind of good life is this to move the patient? Kohut's answer to this—his moral grounding—is something called "healthy narcissism," a love of self that is no longer a response to inadequate parenting, not the hostile grandiosity of the wounded infant, but the mature acceptance of self for what it is. Mature self-love, not love of the Other, is the salvation of the self; the therapist's calling the patient into being was only a step along the road to the patient's ability to do this for him or herself. Indeed, for Kohut (1978), love of the Other, seeking confirmation of existence in the "us," is precisely the problem, for it reflects

> [t]he deeply engrained value system of the Occident . . . [which] extols altruism and concern for others and disparages egotism and concern for oneself. (p. 619)

Critique, in the sense that Kovel intends, stops here, short of an uncovering of *why* concern for the Other is a problem (or even an analysis of whether or not it is truly the case that we Westerners extol altruism and disparage egotism). Instead, what Kohut provides is a claim about "human nature," namely, that we are meant to be self-loving creatures and that our problems emerge when we fail to learn to love ourselves adequately.

> We should not deny our ambitions, our wish to dominate, our wish to shine and our yearning to merge with omnipotent figures. . . . If we learn to acknowledge the legitimacy of these narcissistic forces . . . we shall be able to transform our archaic grandiosity and exhibitionism into realistic self-esteem and into pleasure with ourselves, and our yearning to be at one with the omnipotent self-object into the socially useful, adaptive and joyful capacity to be enthusiastic. . . . (p. 620)

The good toward which the empathic therapeutic relationship aspires is adaptation and social usefulness, and it is best secured through the possession of "realistic self-esteem." As Kovel (1981) observes in a critique of Kohut similar to the present one, this grounding of Kohut's praxis brings "the radical discourse of Freud to the level of the moral philosophy of Dr. Norman Vincent Peale: a psychology for winners." (p. 267).

Because of its naturalistic presentation of "healthy narcissism," it fails to tell us how much self-esteem is "realistic" for people who have brought about and live in such a world as ours. It takes that world as given, and understands it as an appropriate place for us to adapt to and to enjoy, regardless of its horrors.

This notion of adaptation may be a useful formulation, particularly from the point of view of the institutions to which the healthy narcissist adapts and the people whose power is derived from the strength of those institutions. But it fails as critique because it fails to specify its moral ground, and it thus cannot recount the hidden history of otherness that lurks behind the notions of "healthy narcissism," "self-esteem," and "adaptation." Of course, Kohut cannot go proxy for all of therapeutic practice, any more than the codependence literature can. But this analysis can point us in a pragmatic direction, for it gives us questions that, particularly in light of the foregoing argument, can and must be asked of our therapeutic practices: are they moral discourses, and if so, what understanding of the good life do they point to? What strong evaluations are invoked in the course of psychotherapy, and what ontology of the human do they affirm? And is this a "good" understanding, or is it more concealing of the horizon, more obliteration of otherness? If it is a concealing, what does this mean about our psychotherapeutic practices, and how might they be reoriented so as to be capable of critique? What kinds of psychotherapy reliably recount the hidden history of otherness? Some of these questions could begin to be answered by a hermeneutic analysis of the transcripts of psychotherapy sessions, as well as of the various texts which comprise the theoretical basis of psychotherapeutic practice. Such an analysis could use the method I have used here, or some other interpretive framework that is similarly capable of illuminating the moral concerns embedded in texts.

A similar question can be asked of Twelve-Step programs. The multitude of groups following one version or another of the Twelve Steps is undeniably helpful to people trying to overcome addictions. In chapter 5, I argued that the codependence literature construes the Twelve Steps as guides to a community that is really a noncommunity, and the "Higher Power" as an Other that is not really other. But, as I noted in that chapter, this is not the only possible reading of the Twelve Steps; indeed, it is possible to read them as facilitating just the kind of self-transcendence that seems to be eclipsed by the codependence literature. By focusing on texts alone, and not on the experience of people who are in Twelve-Step groups, this book cannot claim to have the final word on the good life that is actually lived by those who participate in the groups. Further research can clarify precisely how the Twelve Steps are taken up in the everyday lives of those who are "recovering." This book makes clear that such research, however, cannot be content to ask naive questions about "effectiveness," but rather must be concerned with the critical questions of how that effectiveness affects and is affected by the ontology of concealed otherness. Research projects that seek to account for the understanding and experience of otherness on the part of Twelve-Step group participants, or to uncover the extent to which Twelve-Step programs function as critique, would be most interesting and useful.

Another implication of this study concerns the question of words like "abuse." I single this word out as an instance of a particularly nettlesome kind of jargon. We all think we know what we mean when we talk about "abuse," but this book indicates that we may not. To leave this word, and others like it (for instance, "addiction," "recovery," "dysfunctional," and so on), undefined is to invite a noncritical acceptance of practices that ought at least to be subject to critique.

We might see an instance of this by turning back to the codependence texts' understanding of "abuse" as both an important etiological factor in codependence and an ongoing experience in the codependent's life. It seems, however, that "abuse" is construed as any experience in which the person is commanded to leave his or her narrative dominion. It is certainly the case that a father's sexual contact with his daughter brings her out of the narrative of a child and into that of an adult in a way that we cannot help but see as destructive. But what of a person's getting caught up in something beyond herself, something that commands her to abandon her narrative in an experience of rapture? In a world of tightly bounded, sole authoring selves, there may be no room for "abuse," but there is also no place for the ecstatic, no room for the ambiguous and commanding experiences which, at least according to Rilke, offer "proof of existence." These are marginalized, called "abuse" or "addiction."

This understanding of "abuse" is, unfortunately, *not* too vague to be meaningless, nor is it advanced only by the codependence literature. Rather, it has become woven into our social fabric in a way that, as much as it might protect people, also deepens the nihilism I have been addressing here. To call something or someone "abusive" in a psychological discourse is to invoke a moralistic language, but to hide its moral dimension behind a "scientific" claim. "Abuse," understood as the command to give up sole authorship, then appears not as a particular characterization of a person or a practice; rather, it speaks with the authority of the scientific, reducing what are undoubtedly important moral questions to medical/legal questions. This understanding obliterates the history and community that holds these practices to be heinous; it reduces thought and action to technique. It thus loses its potential as critique, and instead threatens to give legitimacy to what I am claiming is a nihilistic understanding of being, as well as to the power structures that proceed from that ontology.

One way to glimpse the problems inherent in the abuse of the notion of "abuse" is to look at the current understanding of "substance abuse." A lack of "sobriety" is viewed with increasing suspicion in this country, and not just in the codependence literature. I doubt that this is only because of the possibility of addiction and the misery it brings. If this were the concern, then treatment would be more of a focus than enforcement, and, of course, the reverse is currently the case. All drugs (at least all illegal ones), and all ways of using them, are construed as instruments of "abuse," and all users are subject to suspicion, if not outright denunciation. The revelation that he once used marijuana caused Douglas Ginsburg to withdraw his name from nomination to the Supreme Court. The last presidential campaign saw candidates parsing the fine points of "smoking" and "inhaling," and the legality of offshore drug use. There is no indication that any of these public figures was "addicted" to or "abusing" marijuana. Indeed, it was only the question of mere use that came before the public, and in the case of Bill Clinton, it was apparently enough to know that he had not enjoyed his "youthful experiment." From this, we might deduce that it is the possibility that these public figures had altered their consciousnesses, that they had willingly abandoned narrative dominion, that makes them appear unfit for office. We are to be "clean and sober," "say no to drugs," and "D.A.R.E. to keep kids off drugs."

This prejudice makes "abuse" out of all instances of the use of mind-altering agents ingested from "outside the person." Moreover, it raises the spectre of "addiction" in any experience that diminishes one's narrative authority. It overlooks the possibility, documented by thoughtful people, (e.g., Watts, 1973; Grinspoon and Bakalar, 1979) that precisely by means of their taking one out of one's narrative dominion, drugs, at least psychedelic drugs, "can induce a genuine mystical or religious experience" (Ring, 1988, p. 139). This experience can bring a person to an experience that changes his or her comportment with others in ways that seem refreshing in light of the codependence literature.

> The striking changes in the subject's *hierarchy of life values* observed after psychedelic sessions . . . [included] a realization of the absurdity and futility of exaggerated ambitions, attachment to money, status, fame, and power. . . . (Grof and Halifax, 1977, p. 127, emphasis in original)

It is not my intent to advocate widespread drug use, or reform of the drug laws; I wish only to point out that this understanding of "abuse," promulgated by discourses that advocate sole authorship, is a central jus- tification for what might be viewed as a foolish public policy. Moreover, it speaks of the decreasing opportunity for people to abandon the nar- rative dominion that I have argued is a crucial problem of our times.

I would argue that this notion of "abuse" is not by any means lim- ited to the codependence literature; it is widespread in our culture and in its therapeutic practices. But this does not mean that actual experi- ences of abuse are simply artifacts of that discourse. Rather, I think it is important for research to be done to determine which experiences of being commanded to abandon sole authorship are "abusive" and which are not, and why. This kind of research, of course, would require a def- inition of "abusive"; it would require researchers to state in what way a certain experience is "bad" for a person, and so to clarify what under- standing of "good" is encoded in that "bad." It is just this kind of clari- fication that I think is crucial to a psychotherapeutic practice that acknowledges its own inescapable moral dimensions, and in itself would justify the research. This kind of research could help understand and carve out a language, and therefore a space, for taking up moral con- cerns in our psychotherapeutic discourses. And this language might, in turn, give us a way to understand a "de-centered self," a person who can abandon sole authorship as a matter of pursuing the good life, who manages to include in his or her narrative the possibility that the story will tell him or her rather than vice versa.

To create a narrative space for this kind of self, as I think Lacan (1966/1977), in a highly impenetrable way, attempts to do, is one way for psychotherapy to counter the nihilism that seems inevitably to seep into its practices. Wyschogrod (1990) has offered an account of the nar- ratives of what she calls "saints," in which she argues that these stories speak of the best antidote to nihilism: the dissolution of the self-interest that modern discourses like the codependence literature tell us is the cornerstone of the good life. Modern therapeutic practice, by and large, seems to lack such a narrative space—worse, it appears, at least in instances like the codependence literature, to pathologize those who would enter it.

By criticizing the ontology of sole authorship, I do not mean to suggest that we should engage in some kind of "endarkenment," and somehow return to an ontology—and an agony—like Othello's, in which the individual is barely distinguishable from his or her background. This is, of course, impossible in any case. More important, the fact that we can question our horizons, that we have come upon an understanding of being which makes significant such considerations as the dignity of the individual, is by no means an entirely bad thing (see Taylor, 1989, pp. 456-521). But neither is it entirely a good thing. It is not impossible to resist the nihilism that Heidegger argues shows up in our understanding of the self as sole author. But it is certainly not possible to resist an understanding which cannot emerge as something to debate in the first place. The unquestioning use of jargon, which in turn discloses an unquestioning acceptance of an ontology which must be questioned, can only lead to further concealment. And psychotherapy, which starts when we close the door, can too easily become a location of this concealment, a furthering of certain understandings and practices that may help account for at least some of the distress that brings our patients into the clinic in the first place. By the same token, psychotherapy could undoubtedly be a practice in which those understandings *are* questioned, in which reference is made to more than just the patient's sense of well-being, to other considerations of what makes for a good life. It may be a means to a renunciation of the excesses of individualism, or in some other way a truly critical process.

But this can certainly not happen unless we put into play the question of what good life we are, implicitly or explicitly, urging our patients to aspire toward. Otherwise, therapy easily becomes just another technology enhancing sole authorship, and remains open to scathing, and largely well-placed, critiques like those of Bellah et al. (1985), Rose (1990), and Hillman and Ventura (1992). How, if at all, do we therapists suggest that our patients understand their involvement in the social and political worlds? What kinds of commitments do we urge them toward? How do these urgings contribute to, or work to resist, the mounting social, political, and environmental problems we face, and the hyper-individualism which seems so crucial to those problems? It is, as Hillman (1992) points out, not sufficient to say, "First get inside yourself, find out who you are, get yourself straightened out, then go out in the world . . ." (p. 99). We cannot pretend that closing the door of the therapist's office somehow closes the door on that "world." Indeed, we must come to see how that "world" is carried into the office, not only by the patient, but also by the therapist, by the understanding of the good life which must underlie his or her interventions. And we must question that understanding in order to see what kind of world we are advocating, whether we know it or not, when we urge our patients to aspire toward a particular selfhood.

Appendix A

The Twelve Steps of Codependents Anonymous (from Beattie, 1990b, p. 270):

1. We admitted we were powerless over others—that our lives had become unmanageable.

2. Came to believe that a power greater than ourselves could restore us to sanity.

3. Made a decision to turn our will and our lives over to the care of God as we understood God.

4. Made a searching and fearless moral inventory of ourselves.

5. Admitted to God, to ourselves, and to another human being the exact nature of our wrongs.

6. Were entirely ready to have God remove all these defects of character.

7. Humbly asked God to remove our shortcomings.

8. Made a list of all persons we had harmed, and became willing to make amends to them all.

9. Made direct amends to such people wherever possible, except when to do so would injure them or others.

10. Continued to take personal inventory and when we were wrong, promptly admitted it.

11. Sought through prayer and meditation to improve our conscious contact with God as we understood God, praying only for knowl-

edge of God's will for us and the power to carry that out.

12. Having had a spiritual awakening as the result of these steps, we tried to carry this message to other codependents, and to practice these principles in all our affairs.

Appendix B

Books with the "codepen . . ." root in their titles or subtitles read in an initial survey of the literature:

Beattie, M. (1987j. *Co-dependent no more: How to stop controlling others and start caring for yourself.* San Francisco: Harper & Row.

Beattie, M. (1989). *Beyond codependency and getting better all the time.* San Francisco: Harper & Row.

Beattie, M. (l990a). *The language of letting go: Daily meditations for code-pendents.* San Francisco: HarperCollins.

(l990b). *Codependents guide to the twelve steps.* New York: Prentice-Hall Press.

Becker, R. (1989). *Addicted to misery: The other side of codependency.* Deerfield Beach, FL: Health Communications, Inc.

Becnell, B. C. (1991). *The co-dependent parent: Free yourself by freeing your child.* San Francisco: HarperCollins.

Bundesen, L. (1991). *GodDependency: finding freedom from codependency and discovering spiritual self-reliance.* New York: Crossroad Publishing Company.

Cruse, J. (1989). *Painful affairs: Looking for love through addiction and codependency.* Deerfield Beach, FL: Health Communications, Inc.

DesRoches, B. *Reclaiming your self: The codependent's recovery plan.* New York: Dell.

Health Communications, Inc. (1984). *Codependency.* Deerfield Beach, FL: Author.

259

Hemfelt, R., and Warren, P. (1990). *Kids who carry our pain: Breaking the cycle of codependency for the next generation.* Houston, TX: Nelson Thomas Publishers.

Kellogg, T. (1990). *Broken toys, broken dreams: Understanding & healing codependency, compulsive behaviors, & family.* Amherst, MA: BRAT Publishers.

Kritsberg, W. (1990). *Healing together: A guide to intimacy and recovery for co-dependent couples.* Deerfield Beach, FL: Health Communications, Inc.

Mastrich, J., and Birnes, B. (1990). *Strong enough for two: How to overcome codependence and other enabling behavior and take control of your life.* New York: Collier Books.

Meier, P., Minirth, F., Hemfelt, R., and Hawkins, D. (1989). *Love is a choice: Recovery for codependent relationships.* Houston, TX: Nelson Thomas Publishers.

Mellody, P. (1989). *Facing codependence: What it is, where it comes from, how it sabotages our lives.* San Francisco: Harper and Row.

Mellody, P., and Miller, A. W. (1989). *Breaking free: A recovery workbook for facing codependence.* San Francisco: HarperCollins.

Ricketson, S. C. (1989). *The dilemma of love: Healing codependent relationships at different stages of life.* Deerfield Beach, FL: Health Communications, Inc.

Schaef, A. W. (1986). *Co-dependence: Misunderstood mistreated.* San Francisco: Harper and Row.

Schaeffer, B. (1991). *Loving me, loving you: Balancing love and power in a codependent world.* San Francisco: HarperCollins.

Stuart, M. S. (1987). *In sickness and in health: The codependent marriage.* Deerfield Beach, FL: Health Communications, Inc.

Subby, R. (1987). *Lost in the shuffle: The co-dependent reality.* Deerfield Beach, FL: Health Communications, Inc.

Wegscheider-Cruse, S. (1988). *Choicemaking for codependents, adult children and spirituality seekers.* Deerfield Beach, FL: Health Communications, Inc.

Wegscheider-Cruse, S. (1989). *The miracle of recovery: Healing for addicts, adult children and codependents.* Deerfield Beach, FL: Health Communications, Inc.

Wegscheider-Cruse, S., and Cruse, J. (1990). *Understanding codependency.* Deerfield Beach, FL: Health Communications, Inc.

Weinhold, B., and Weinhold, J. (1989). *Breaking free of the co-dependency trap.* Walpole, NH: Stillpoint Publishing.

Weiss, L., and Weiss, J. B. (1989). *Recovery from co-dependency: It's never too late to have a happy childhood.* Deerfield Beach, FL: Health Communications, Inc.

Notes

CHAPTER 1. CODEPENDENCE IN CONTEXT

1. The example of nuclear weapons, and the challenge it poses to psychotherapists' "value-free" pretense, has not gone unnoticed by the profession (see, e.g., Lifton and Falk, 1982; Mack and Redmond, 1989). Mack has suggested that standard analytic method can be brought to bear on the fears and misgivings people report to their therapists about nuclear weapons, and that working through these feelings might well lead to action. But much of the psychological literature on the threat of nuclear war addresses the problem of "psychic numbing," a collection of defenses and resistances that has the effect of erasing awareness of the threat, and, indeed, of the existence of nuclear weapons (Mack, 1984; Lifton, 1979, 1982; Lifton and Falk, 1982), and suggests that the problem is unlikely to surface in people's consciousnesses. As a counter to this "numbing," Mack and Redmond (1989) suggest that a therapist might understand a silence such as I observed between Mark and me as a manifestation of this numbing, as a "resistance attached to the perception of such great dangers in the outside world" (p. 352). Understood this way, Mark's silence about such a pressing issue itself becomes something to be interrogated, for, as Mack and Redmond say,

> . . . the nonacknowledgement of a global reality of such import, like the nonmentioning in a family of a terrible fact like a parent's fatal illness or the ongoing abuse of a child, may itself have a reality-distorting, pathogenic power. (Mack and Redmond, 1989, p. 352)

This would indicate that I should interpret the silence of someone like Mark as pathological, that any normal, healthy person would be concerned about the nuclear threat, and that as therapist it is my job to explore this "resistance." Perhaps this is so, but this ends psychotherapy's claim to being "value-free," to deriving values only from within the patient's experience. I would be interrogating this aspect of the everyday not because Mark presented it to me, but because his failure to do so struck me as reflecting a social practice that *I* think is problematic. We can perhaps all (or most of us—there are cogent apologists for the morality of deterrence theory) agree that nuclear weapons are dangerous, and even bad. But what is the basis of this claim? Is it in service of "mental health" or some moral vision or both or neither? And how are we therapists to know at what point a client's silence about a political practice is "resistance" and at what point it simply reflects a deeply held belief that happens to be at variance to the therapist's? The possible confusion of the moral and the medical raises the spectre of therapists using their presumed expertise in "mental health" in order to coerce their clients to adopt the therapists' own moral beliefs. This, of course, is a totalitarian's tactic; it amounts to declaring insane people who don't agree with a given ideology, and was the basis of the psychiatric imprisonment of political dissidents in the former Soviet Union.

   I do not mean to suggest that Mack is seeking to dominate his clients in this fashion. He has a heartfelt belief, which I share, that the proliferation of nuclear weapons is a bad thing. But the necessary implication of injecting this belief into the clinical setting is that, at least in this case, an external consideration must provide the magnetic north of psychotherapy's moral compass. For the problem with nuclear weapons is surely *not* that they are mentally unhealthy. The problem is that they might destroy us all, and that they squander resources and endanger the environment even if they fulfill their paradoxical function of existing in order never to be used. This is a good reason to advocate against their deployment, but it runs counter to the psychotherapeutic imperative to derive value from within each individual. And it is hard to know if my potential intervention with Mark regarding his work is really "therapeutic," or simply a way for me to inject my own "political" opinions into our work in such a way as to make him "feel bad" about himself (or feel that he is "mentally unhealthy") for doing something of which I do not approve. I can discuss these issues with him, but then the question arises of whether or not, now that I have abandoned the inner as a moral compass, I am still doing therapy. This question will remain unanswered until psychotherapy specifies its moral vision, which it cannot do so long as it pretends to the "value freedom" that is implicit in the endeavor to find moral orientation primarily within ourselves.

CHAPTER 2. THE CAT'S GRIN

   1. Ricoeur extends his definition of "text" to all of meaningful human action, and this claim underlies his understanding of psychoanalysis as providing a hermeneutic of human action. By citing Ricoeur here, I am not adopting Ricoeur's expansive definition (although I largely agree with it). "Reading" and "text," for my purposes, are to be understood in their everyday sense

CHAPTER 3. THE CONTOURS OF THE
CODEPENDENCE GENRE

1. Peele and Brodsky's (1975) account is held to be the ur-sprung of the expansion of the addiction model from the realm of entanglements with drugs and alcohol into the realm of entanglements with other people (see, e.g., Weinhold and Weinhold, 1989). Peele's account here is part of a critique that stops short of recanting his earlier work, but instead argues against those who, he believes, have misappropriated his theories.

> In discussing sexual addictions and compulsive love afairs, I am obligated to mention my own role in the movement. I wrote . . . the book *Love and Addiction* . . . which most works on love and sexual addictions use as a primary source. I concentrated on two goals in *Love and Addiction*. First, I wanted to make clear that drug addiction is not a medical disease, since it has the same compulsive profile as many behaviors we regard as quite ordinary and nonbiological, like love affairs. My aim there was turned on its head when subsequent writers agreed that compulsive love and sex were like drug addictions; therefore they were *also* diseases. Second, *Love and Addiction* was a social commentary on how our society defines and patterns intimate relationships. But all of this social dimension has been removed, and the attention to love addiction has been channeled in the direction of regarding it as an individual, treatable psychopathology. (Peele, 1989, p. 140)

2. For purposes of textual flow, these books will hereafter be referred to with the following abbreviations:

Beattie (1987): CNM
Beattie (1989): BC
Mellody, Miller, and Miller (1989): FC
Schaef (1986): CD

Also, according to its cover, *Facing Codependence* is authored by "Pia Mellody, with Andrea Wells Miller and J. Keith Miller." But it is written in the first person singular, and, while the relative contribution of each author is not made clear, the narrative voice is clearly Mellody's. So I will refer to this book as if it had been written by Pia Mellody alone.

CHAPTER 7. THE CODEPENDENCE LITERATURE
AS AN INSTANCE OF NIHILISM

1. It may strike the reader as anachronistic to get at what I am calling a problem of modernity with a "pre-modern" writer such as Shakespeare. But

the modern understanding of the self did not, of course, arise at a particular moment; the importance of self-reflection, of the self's finding its own direction in the world, can be seen much earlier, as, for instance, in Augustine's *Confessions*. And Shakespeare was aware of, and interested in, this possibility of self; indeed, according to Bloom (1991), this understanding on the part of Shakespeare was an important aspect of his genius.

> The principal insight I have had in teaching and writing about Shakespeare is that there isn't anyone before Shakespeare who actually gives you a representation of characters or human figures speaking out loud, whether to themselves or to others or both, and then brooding out loud, whether to themselves or to others or both, on what they themselves have said. And then, in the course of pondering, undergoing a serious or vital change—becoming a different kind of character or personality, and even a different kind of mind. We take that utterly for granted in representation. But it doesn't exist before Shakespeare. . . . The ability to do that, and to persuade one that this is a natural mode of representation, is purely Shakespearean. We are now so contained by it that we can't see its originality anymore. But the originality of it is bewildering. (pp. 29-30)

Even if we don't agree with the sweeping assertion Bloom is making here, Bloom's point is not diminished: Shakespeare gives us reflective "selves," people who already see themselves as capable of reflection upon their immersion in a world of others. This possibility was something Shakespeare was aware of, and thus can be seen as standing in the background of his creation of Iago and Othello.

    2. Taylor's claim here begs for an empirical analysis. He is arguing something about "the self" that is contentious, leaving out the possibility of a self which somehow constitutes itself outside of any "web of interlocution." My own prejudice is clearly congruent with Taylor's here, and one interesting source of empirical support for this statement is in the various accounts of feral children. Malson (1972), writing a commentary on Itard's (1802/1972) account of the Wild Boy of Aveyron (the subject of Francois Truffaut's film *Wild Child*), notes that the lesson of feral children might be stated in this fashion.

> If one studies the similarities between men one will find that what they have in common is a structure of possibilities, or rather of probabilities, which are realized in some specific social context. Before his encounter with others, man is nothing but a notional quality as thin and insubstantial as mist. To acquire his substance, he requires a milieu—the presence of others. (p. 10)

Now clearly, a number of leaps must be made from "substance" to "self," but Malson at least points us in Taylor's direction: "Victor" is nothing, or at least nothing human (and therefore by implication incapable of having or being a self), without a web of interlocution. Indeed, Victor was without language, and remained this way throughout his life.

Another account of a feral child comes to us more recently, and is chronicled by Rymer (1992). A child in southern California was largely deprived of human contact until she was discovered by the social services bureaucracy at the age of twelve (in 1970). In Rymer's account, the child (who is called Genie, and was, like Victor, without language) was largely unaware of the presence of other people around her. "She seemed hardly able to differentiate between various visitors. Some observers referred to her as ghostlike" (p. 54). "She treated everything, including people, as objects" (p. 64). Interestingly, Rymer ties this lack of awareness to the development of a sense of self. He recounts a time during which "she made hitting gestures" at a girl who was in the same hospital ward. This was considered a breakthrough, because

> . . . finally, Genie had turned some anger outward, aiming it at a source of frustration. She was upset with the new girl because she was wearing a dress from the hospital laundry which Genie had formerly worn; the episode was the first indication that Genie was developing a sense of self. (p. 65)

This "breakthrough" came because Genie had become aware of her involvement with others. She had ceased to see herself as an entirely isolated monad, and entered into a web of interlocution, even if that was only in the "language" of the angry gesture.

More needs to be said about this important claim, but these examples do help to show the plausibility of Taylor's contention that we cannot have what is considered most human—a self—until we are immersed in, and take up a relationship with, some community of others.

3. The dialectical structure of Rieff's work must be noted here. In speaking of the triumph of the therapeutic, Rieff is particularly championing Freud's psychoanalysis. With Freud, Rieff believes that religious faith is a hindrance to humankind, that it is only by facing our "true" existential condition (that there is no God, and therefore no reason to be bound to "positive communities") that we can progress. Rieff is therefore concerned to criticize some therapeutic systems, like Jung's, which do not abandon faith. For Rieff, such therapies help us to avoid the truth, while psychoanalysis ensures that we will never do so. In the reading of Rieff that follows, I am concerned primarily with the therapeutic system that he believes is best suited to a world without faith.

CHAPTER 8. CONCLUSION:
A RECONSTITUTION OF CODEPENDENCE

1. Of course, Freud had in mind a very different kind of trauma than is generally discussed in the codependence literature. He was primarily concerned with the arousal in the child of psychic states that were forbidden by his family

and society at large. These "fantasies," according to Freud, could as easily be aroused by actual events in the child's life as by imaginative interpretations of otherwise innocuous occurrences. For Freud, the difference was close to nil because what was important was the intrapsychic conflict. And, as Schorske (1981) contends, the effect of this leveling is to withdraw critical attention from the world of actual events (see also Masson, 1984). The codependence literature, on the other hand, is concerned with what "actually happens," with discovering and "recovering" from the traumas that were inflicted by parents and others. In a sense, the codependence literature restores an awareness of the social world which Freud obliterated. But it does so without restoring the critique that Schorske also argues Freud erased. The texts work primarily to show the way in which the "external" world has "contaminated" the self. Considerations of politics and society reenter the picture only long enough for the "recovering" person to see how urgent it is to establish narrative dominion over them.

Bibliography

Adkins, A. W. H. (1970). *From the many to the one*. Ithaca, NY: Cornell University Press.

Al-Anon (1981). *Al-Anon's twelve steps and twelve traditions*. New York: Author.

Arendt, H. (1965). *Eichmann in Jerusalem*. New York: Penguin Books.

Barclay, M. (1990). *Utopia/dystopia/atopia: A dissertation on psychopathology and utopian thinking*. Unpublished doctoral dissertation, Saybrook Institute Graduate School and Research Center, San Francisco.

Bateson, G. (1972). *Steps to an ecology of mind*. New York: Ballantine Books.

Baumeister, R. F. (1987). How the self became a problem: A psychological review of historical research. *Journal of Personality and Social Psychology* 52(1): 163-76.

Beattie, M. (1987). *Co-dependent no more: How to stop controlling others and start caring for yourself*. San Francisco: Harper & Row.

———. (1989). *Beyond codependency and getting better all the time*. San Francisco: Harper & Row.

———. (1990a). *The language of letting go: Daily meditations for codependents*. San Francisco: HarperCollins.

———. (1990b). *Codependents guide to the twelve steps*. New York: Prentice-Hall Press.

Becnell, B. C. (1991). *The co-dependent parent: Free yourself by freeing your child*. San Francisco: HarperCollins.

Bellah, R., Madsen, R., Sullivan, W., Swidler, A., and Tipton, S. M. (1985). *Habits of the heart: Individualism and commitment in American life*. New York: Harper & Row.

269

Berlin, I. (1991). *The crooked timber of humanity: Chapters in the history of ideas*. New York: Alfred Knopf.

Black, C. (1981). *"It will never happen to me!"*. New York: Ballantine Books.

Bleicher, J. (1980). *Contemporary hermeneutics: Hermeneutics as method, philosophy, and critique*. London: Routledge & Kegan Paul.

Bloom, H. (1991, August). Shakespeare's Freud. Interview from the Spring 1991 issue of *The Paris Review*, republished in *Harper's*, pp. 29-30.

Borgmann, A. (1984). *Technology and the character of contemporary life*. Chicago: University of Chicago Press.

Bowen, M. (1976). *Family therapy in clinical practice*. New York: Jason Aronson.

Bradhsaw, J. (1988a). *Bradshaw on: The family*. Deerfield Beach, FL: Health Communications, Inc.

———. (1988b). *Healing the shame that binds you*. Deerfield Beach, FL: Health Communications, Inc.

———. (1989a). Foreword. In B. Weinhold and J. Weinhold, *Breaking free of the co-dependency trap* (pp. xiii-xiv). Walpole, NH: Stillpoint Publishing.

———. (1989b). Foreword. In L. Weiss and J. B. Weiss, *Recovery from codependency: It's never too late to reclaim your childhood* (pp. xiii-xiv). Deerfield Beach, FL: Health Communications, Inc.

Buber, M. (1966). *The way of response*. New York: Schocken Books.

Bundesen, L. (1991). *GodDependency: Finding freedom from codependency and discovering spiritual self-reliance*. New York: Crossroad Publishing Company.

Caputo, J. D. (1989). Disseminating originary ethics and the ethics of dissemination. In A. B. Dallery and C. Scott (Eds.), *The question of the other*. Albany: State University of New York Press.

Cassell, C. (1984). *Swept away: Why women confuse love and sex . . . and how they can have both*. New York: Bantam Books.

Cermak, T. L. (1986). Diagnostic criteria for codependency. *Journal of Psychoactive Drugs* 18(1): 15-20.

Cocks, G. (1985). *Psychotherapy in the Third Reich*. Oxford: Oxford University Press.

Cowan, C., and Kinder, M. (1985). *Smart women, foolish choices*. New York: Clarkson N. Potter, Inc.

Cruse, J. (1989). *Painful affairs: Looking for love through addiction and codependency*. Deerfield Beach, FL: Health Communications, Inc.

Cuming, R. D. (1956). Introduction: The trial and death of Socrates. In Plato, *Euthyphro, apology, crito, phaedo* (pp. vii-xv). Indianapolis, IN: Bobbs-Merrill.

Cushman, P. (1990). The empty self. *American Psychologist 45*: 715-31.

Dallmayr, F. R. (1984). Introduction. In M. Theunissen, *The Other* (C. Macann, Trans.). Cambridge, MA: MIT Press.

Dawkins, R. (1976). *The selfish gene*. Oxford: Oxford University Press.

DesRoches, B. (1990). *Reclaiming your self: The codependent's recovery plan*. New York: Dell.

Dodds, E. R. (1951). *The Greeks and the irrational*. Berkeley: University of California Press.

Dreyfus, H. (1981). Knowledge and human values: A genealogy of nihilism. *Teachers College Record 82*: 507-20.

Dworkin, R. M. (1989, September 28). The future of abortion. *The New York Review of Books*, pp. 47-52.

Edwards, P. (1979). *Heidegger on death*. La Salle, IL: The Hegeler Institute.

Eliot, T. S. (1917/1971). The love song of J. Alfred Prufrock. In *The complete poems and plays 1909-1950*, pp. 3-8. San Diego: Harcourt Brace Jovanovich.

Farias, V. (1989). *Heidegger and nazism*. Philadelphia: Temple University Press.

Ferry, L., and Renaut, A. (1990). *Heidegger and modernity* (F. Philip, Trans.). Chicago: University of Chicago Press.

Forest, J. J. (1987). Effects on self-actualization of paperbacks about psychological self-help. *Psychological Reports 60*: 1243-46.

————. (1988). Exploring more on the effects of psychological self-help paperbacks. *Psychological Reports 63*: 891-94.

Forward, S., and Torres, J. (1987). *Men who hate women and the women who love them*. New York: Bantam Books.

Foucault, M. (1980). *Power/Knowledge: Selected interviews and other writings 1972-1977* (C. Gordon, L. Marshall, J. Mepham, and K. Soper, Trans.; C. Gordon, Ed.). New York: Pantheon Books.

————. (1983). The subject and power. Afterword to Dreyfus, H. L., and Rabinow, P., *Michel Foucault: Beyond structuralism and hermeneutics* (pp. 208-28). Chicago: University of Chicago Press.

————. (1986). *The care of the self* (R. Hurley, Trans.). New York: Pantheon Books (original work published in 1984).

————. (1987). *Mental illness and psychology* (A. Sheridan, Trans.). Berkeley: University of California Press (original work published in 1954).

Freud, S. (1910). Leonardo da Vinci and a memory of his childhood. In *The standard edition of the complete psychological works of Sigmund Freud* (J. Strachey, Ed. and Trans.), Volume 11, pp. 63-138. London: Hogarth Press.

————. (1923). A seventeenth-century demonological neurosis. In *The standard edition of the complete psychological works of Sigmund Freud* (J. Strachey, Ed. and Trans.), Volume 19, pp. 73-107. London: Hogarth Press.

————. (1950). Letter 71. Universality of the Oedipus complex. In *The standard edition of the complete psychological works of Sigmund Freud* (J. Strachey, Ed. and Trans.), Volume 1, pp. 263-65. London: Hogarth Press (letter written in 1897).

————. (1950). *Totem and Taboo* (J. Strachey, Trans.). New York: W. W. Norton and Company (original work published in 1912).

————. (1961). *Beyond the pleasure principle* (J. Strachey, Trans.). New York: W. W. Norton & Company (original work published in 1920).

————. (1966). *The psychopathology of everyday life* (A. Tyson, Trans.). London: Ernest Benn Limited (original work published in 1901).

Friedman, M. (1976). Aiming at the self: A paradox. *Journal of Humanistic Psychology 16*: 2, 5-34.

Friel, J., and Friel, L. (1990). *An adult child's guide to what's "normal."* Pompano Beach, FL: Health Communications, Inc.

Friel, J., and Subby, R. (1984). Co-dependency. In *Co-dependence* (pp. 31-46). Deerfield Beach, FL: Health Communications, Inc.

Frost, R. (1949). *The complete poems of Robert Frost.* New York: Holt, Rinehart, and Winston.

Fuller, R. C. (1982). *Mesmerism and the American cure of souls.* Philadelphia: University of Pennsylvania Press.

Gadamer, H.-G. (1981). On the scope and function of hermeneutical reflection. In D. E. Linge (Ed. and Trans.), *Philosophical Hermeneutics* (pp.18-44). Berkeley: University of California Press (original work published in 1967).

Gergen, K. J. (1991). *The saturated self: Dilemmas of identity in contemporary life.* New York: Basic Books.

Gierymski, T., and Williams, T. (1986). Codependency. *Journal of Psychoactive Drugs 18*(1): 7-14.

Gomberg, E. L. (1989). On terms used and abused: The concept of "codependency." *Drugs and Society 3*(3-4): 113-32.

Greenberg, G. (1989). Naming the silence: Toward an understanding of psychic numbing. Unpublished manuscript.

Grinspoon, L., and Bakalar, J. (1979). *Psychedelic drugs reconsidered.* New York: Basic Books.

Grof, S., and Halifax, J. (1977). *The human encounter with death.* New York: Dutton.

Haaken, J. (1990). A critical analysis of the co-dependence construct. *Psychiatry* *53*: 396-405

Habermas, J. (1973/1980). The hermeneutic claim to universality. In J. Bleicher (Ed. and Trans.), *Contemporary hermeneutics.* London: Routledge and Kegan Paul.

Hales, S. (1986). Rethinking the business of psychology. *Journal for the Theory of Social Behaviour 16*: 57-76.

Health Communications, Inc. (1984). *Co-dependency.* Deerfield Beach, FL: Author.

———. (1990). *Discover recovery! Fall 1990 consumer catalog.* (Available from Health Communications, Inc., 3201 S.W 15th Street, Deerfield Beach, FL 33442-8190)

Heidegger, M. (1962). *Being and time* (J. Macquarrie and E. Robinson, Trans.). New York: Harper and Row (original work published in 1926).

———. (1977). The question concerning technology. In William Lovitt (Ed. and Trans.), *The question concerning technology and other essays* (pp. 3-35). New York: Harper & Row (original work published in 1954).

———. (1977a). The age of the world picture. In W. Lovitt (Ed. and Trans.), *The question concerning technology and other essays* (pp. 115-54). New York: Harper & Row (original work published in 1952).

———. (1977b). The word of Nietzsche: God is dead. In W. Lovitt (Ed. and Trans.), *The question concerning technology and other essays* (pp. 53-112). New York: Harper & Row (original work published in 1952).

Henderson, B. (1983). Self-help books emphasizing transpersonal psychology: Are they ethical? *The Journal of Transpersonal Psychology 15*: 169-71.

Hillman, J. (1992, January/February). Therapy keeps us from changing the world: An interview with James Hillman. *The Utne Reader*, pp. 98-99.

Hillman, J., and Ventura, M. (1992). *We've had a hundred years of psychotherapy and the world's getting worse.* San Francisco: HarperCollins.

Hitchens, C. (1990, July 30). Minority report. *The Nation*, p. 102.

Hochschild, A. *The managed heart: Commercialization of human feeling.* Berkeley: University of California Press.

Hunter, R. (1990). *A box of rain.* New York: Viking Press.

Ihde, D. (1979). *Technics and praxis.* Boston: D. Reidel

Interface Foundation, Inc. (1991). [Winter 1991 catalog of course offerings.] (Available from Interface, P.O. Box 860, Watertown, MA 02172)

Itard, J. (1972). *The wild boy of Aveyron.* New York: New Left Books (original work published in 1802).

Kaminer, W. (1990, Feb. 11). Chances are you're codependent too. *The New York Times Book Review*, pp. 1, 26-27.

———. (1992). *I'm dysfunctional, you're dysfunctional.* Reading, MA: Addison-Wesely.

Kant, I. (1969). *Foundations of the metaphysics of morals* (L. W. Beck, Trans.). New York: Macmillan (original work published in 1795).

Kohut, H. (1971) *The analysis of the self: A systematic approach to the psychoanalytic treatment of narcissistic personality disorders.* New York: International Universities press.

———. (1978). *The search for the self.* New York: International Universities Press.

Kovel, J. (1981). *The age of desire.* New York: Pantheon Books.

———. (1991). *History and Spirit.* Boston: Beacon Press.

Krestan, J. A., and Bepko, C. (1990). Codependency: The social reconstruction of female experience. *Smith College Studies in Social Work 60*: 216-32.

Kritsberg, W. (1990). *Healing together: A guide to intimacy and recovery for co-dependent couples.* Deerfield Beach, FL: Health Communications, Inc.

Lacan, J. (1977). *Ecrits: A selection* (A. Sheridan, Trans.). New York: W. W. Norton & Company (original work published in 1966).

Lasch, C. (1979). *The culture of narcissism: American life in an age of diminishing expectations.* New York: W. W. Norton.

Levinas, E. (1979). *Totality and infinity: An essay on exteriority* (A. Lingis, Trans.). The Hague: Martinus Nijhoff Publishers (original work published in 1961).

Liberman, K. (1989). Decentering the self: Two perspectives from philosophical anthropology. In A. R. Dallery and C. E. Scott (Eds.), *The question of the other.* Albany: State University of New York Press.

Lifton, R. J. (1979). *The broken connection.* New York: Simon and Schuster.

————. (1982). Beyond psychic numbing: A call to awareness. *American Journal of Orthopsychiatry 52*: 619-29.

Lifton, R. J., and Falk, R. (1982). *Indefensible weapons: The political and psychological case against nuclearism.* New York: Basic Books.

MacIntyre, A. (1984). *After virtue: A study in moral theory.* Notre Dame, IN: University of Notre Dame Press.

Mack, J. E. (1984). Resistances to knowing in the nuclear age. *Harvard Educational Review 54, 3*: 260-70.

Mack, J. E., and Redmond, J. C. (1989). On being a psychoanalyst in the nuclear age. *Journal of Humanistic Psychology 29*, 3: 338-55.

Malson, L. (1972). *Wolf children and the problem of human nature* (E. Fawcett, P. Ayrton, and J. White, Trans.). New York: New Left Press.

Maslow, A. (1962). *Toward a psychology of being.* Princeton, NJ: D. Van Nostrand Co., Inc.

Masson, J. M. (1984). *The assault on the truth: Freud's suppression of the seduction theory.* New York: Penguin Books.

Meier, P., Minirth, F., Hemfelt, R., and Hawkins, D. (1989). *Love is a choice: Recovery for codependent relationships.* Houston, TX: Nelson Thomas Publishers.

Mellody, P., and Miller, A.W. (1989). *Breaking free: A recovery workbook for facing codependence.* San Francisco: HarperCollins.

Mellody, P., Miller, A. W., and Miller, J. K. (1989). *Facing codependence: What it is, where it comes from, how it sabotages our lives.* San Francisco: Harper and Row.

Miller, A. (1981). *The drama of the gifted child* (R. Ward, Trans.). New York: Basic Books (original work published in 1979; original title in English was *Prisoners of childhood*).

Norwood, R. (1985). *Women who love too much.* New York: Pocket Books.

Omega Institute for Holistic Studies. (1991). [Summer 1991 catalog.] (Available from Omega Institute, Lake Drive, RD 2 Box 377, Rhinebeck, NY 12572)

Omer, H., and Da Verona, M. (1991). Dr. Iago's treatment of Iago. *American Journal of Psychotherapy 45*: 99-112.

Oxford English Dictionary. (1971). Oxford: Oxford University Press.

Packer, M. J., and Addison, R. B. (1989). Overview. In M. J. Packer and R. B. Addison (Eds.), *Entering the circle: Hermeneutic investigation in psychology.* Albany: State University of New York Press.

Paul, J., and Paul, M. (1983). *Do I have to give up me to be loved by you?* Minneapolis: CompCare Publications.

Peale, N. V. (1956). *The power of positive thinking.* New York: Fawcett Crest (original work published in 1952).

Peele, S. (1989). *The diseasing of America: Addiction treatment out of control.* Lexington, MA: Lexington Books.

Peele, S., and Brodsky, A. (1975). *Love and addiction.* New York: Taplinger Publishing.

Potter-Efron, R., and Potter-Efron, P. (1989). *Letting go of shame.* San Francisco: Harper & Row.

Rabinow, P. (1984). Introduction. In P. Rabinow (Ed.), *The Foucault reader* (pp. 3-29). New York: Pantheon Books.

Rapping, E. (1990, March 5). Hooked on a Feeling. *The Nation,* pp. 316-19.

Ricketson, S. C. (1989). *Dilemma of love: Healing co-dependent relationships at different stages of life.* Deerfield Beach, FL: Health Communications, Inc.

Ricoeur, P. (1970). *Freud and philosophy: An essay on interpretation* (D. Savage, Trans.). New Haven: Yale University Press.

———. (1981). The model of the text: Meaningful action considered as a text. In J. B. Thompson (Ed. and Trans.), *Hermeneutics & the human sciences* (pp. 197-221). Cambridge, UK: Cambridge University Press (original work published in 1971).

———. (1981). The hermeneutical function of distanciation. In J. B. Thompson (Ed. and Trans.), *Hermeneutics & the human sciences* (pp. 131-45). Cambridge, UK: Cambridge University Press (original work published in 1973).

Rieff, P. (1966). *The triumph of the therapeutic.* New York: Harper & Row.

Rilke, R. M. (1987). *The Duino Elegies* (R. Hunter, Trans.). Eugene, OR: Hulogos'i Communications, Inc. (original work published in 1922).

Ring, K. (1988). Paradise is paradise: Reflections on psychedelic drugs, mystical experience, and the near-death experience. *Journal of Near-death Studies* 6(3): 138-48.

Rogers, C. (1961). *On becoming a person.* Boston: Houghton Mifflin.

Rose, N. (1990). *Governing the soul: The shaping of the private self.* London: Routledge.

Rosen, G. M. (1976). The development and use of nonprescription behavior therapies. *American Psychologist 31*: 142-47.

————. (1981). Guidelines for the review of do-it-yourself books. *Contemporary Psychology 26*: 189-91.

Rymer, R. (1992, April 13). A silent childhood, part 1. *The New Yorker*, pp. 41-81.

Sampson, E. E. (1981). Cognitive psychology as ideology. *American Psychologist 36*: 730-43.

————. (1985). The decentralization of identity: Toward a revised concept of personal and social order. *American Psychologist 40*: 1203-11.

Saper, Z., and Forest, J. (1987). Personality variables and interest in self-help books. *Psychological Reports 60*: 563-66.

Satir, V. (1974). *Conjoint family therapy: Your many faces.* Palo Alto: Science & Behavior Press.

Schaef, A. W. (1986). *Co-dependence: Misunderstood mistreated.* San Francisco: Harper and Row.

————. (1987). *When society becomes an addict.* San Francisco: Harper and Row.

————. (1991). Intimacy and Codependence. Workshop description in *The Omega Institute Catalog*, p. 42. Rhinebeck, NY: The Omega Institute.

Schaeffer, B. (1991). *Loving me, loving you: Balancing love and power in a codependent world.* San Francisco: HarperCollins.

Schorske, C. E. (1981). *Fin-de-siecle Vienna: Politics and culture.* New York: Vintage Books.

Sloterdijk, P. (1987). *Critique of cynical reason* (M. Eldred, Trans.). Minneapolis: University of Minnesota Press (original work published in 1983).

Smith, A. (1988). *Grandchildren of alcoholics.* Deerfield Beach, FL: Health Communications, Inc.

Starker, S. (1988a). Psychologists and self-help books: Attitudes and prescriptive practices of clinicians. *American Journal of Psychotherapy 42*: 448-55.

————. (1988b). Do-it-yourself therapy: The prescription of self-help books by psychologists. *Psychotherapy 25*: 142-46.

Stewart, J. B. (1991). *Den of thieves.* New York: Simon and Schuster.

Stigliano, A. (1989). Hermeneutical practice. *Saybrook Review 7*: 47-69.

Straub, G., and Gershon, D. (1990). The empowerment workshop. Workshop description in *Interface Catalog* (Winter 1991), p. 13. Watertown, MA: Interface.

Subby, R. (1987). *Lost in the shuffle: The co-dependent reality.* Deerfield Beach, FL: Health Communications, Inc.

Taylor, C. (1979). Interpretation and the sciences of man. In P. Rabinow and W. M. Sullivan (Eds.), *Interpretive social science: A reader* (pp. 25-72). Berkeley: University of California Press.

———. (1985). *Human agency and language.* Cambridge, UK: Cambridge University Press.

———. (1989). *Sources of the self: The making of the modern identity.* Cambridge, MA: Harvard University Press.

Theunissen, M. (1984). *The other: Studies in the social ontology of Husserl, Heidegger, Sartre, and Buber* (C. Macann, Trans.). Cambridge, MA: MIT Press (original work published in 1977).

Thompson, M. G. (1986). *The death of desire.* New York: New York University Press.

Tocqueville, A. de (1990). *Democracy in America* (Volume 2). New York: Vintage Books (original work published in 1840).

van Wormer, K. (1989). Co-dependency: Implications for women and therapy. *Women & Therapy 8*(4): 51-62.

Watts, A. (1973). *In my own way.* New York: Vintage Books.

Wegscheider-Cruse, S. (1984). Co-dependency: The therapeutic void. In *Co-dependence* (pp. 1-4). Deerfield Beach, FL: Health Communications, Inc.

———. (1988). *Choicemaking for codependents, adult children and spirituality seekers.* Deerfield Beach, FL: Health Communications, Inc.

Weinhold, B., and Weinhold, J. (1989). *Breaking free of the co-dependency trap.* Walpole, NH: Stillpoint Publishing.

Weiss, L., and Weiss, J. B. (1989). *Recovery from co-dependency: It's never too late to reclaim your childhood.* Deerfield Beach, FL: Health Communications, Inc.

Whitfield, C. (1991). *Codependence: Healing the human condition.* Pompano Beach, FL: Health Communications, Inc.

Winnicott, D. W. (1958). *Collected papers: Through pediatrics to psychoanalysis.* London: Tavistock.

Woititz, J. (1983). *Adult children of alcoholics.* Deerfield Beach, FL: Health Communications, Inc.

Wolin, R. (1990). *The politics of being.* New York: Columbia University Press.

Wyschogrod, E. (1985). *Spirit in ashes: Hegel, Heidegger and man-made mass death.* New Haven: Yale University Press.

———. (1990). *Saints and post-modernism.* Chicago: University of Chicago Press.

Index

abortion, 202-3
abuse, (codependence literature concept of), 155, 161-4, 169, 243, 253-5. *See also* addiction; child abuse; substance abuse; victim status
addiction, 1, 69, 76, 81, 126, 143
  and choice, 81-2
  and codependence, 126, 137-8
  as a disease, 2, 69
  def initions of, 69, 142
  pervasiveness of, 2, 69
  to love ("relationship addiction"), 75-6, 137-8, 265
Adkins, A. W. H., 30-1
adult children of alcoholics (ACOA's), 242
  books about, 70-74
  characteristics of, 71-72
affirmations, 139-40
Al-Anon, 70-1
animal magnetism. *See* mesmerism
Arendt, Hannah, 213
articulacy (in moral narratives), 106-7, 112, 208-10
Aufklarer, the, 192-3, 200-1
authenticity, 20, 80
autonomy, 162
  and "abuse," 162
  and authority, 192-3, 201-2
  and boundaries, 231, 241

and community, 53, 129, 191, 193-4
and freedom of choice, 80-2
and "recovery," 73-4, 82
and respect and obligation, 159-161
and the categorical imperative, 201-2
and the "dysfunctional family," 79-82
and the Higher Power, 176-7
and the Other, 219, 242
as "mental health," 73-4, 182
defined, 120
in "dysfunctional families," 79-82
in the Enlightenment, 190-6, 200-1

being and doing, split between, 167, 184-5
being-with-others, 179, 184-5, 189-90, 194, 223
Bellah, Robert, 45, 62, 65, 207, 215, 256
Bepko, C., 47-9, 53-4, 87, 244, 248
Black, C., 71-4, 84
Bloom, H., 266
Boesky, I., 14, 24, 35
boundaries, 8, 79, 208
  and autonomy, 231, 241
  and intimacy, 155-8

boundaries *(continued)*
  and respect and obligation, 154-8,
    167-9
  and self-esteem, 156
  and the "Higher Power," 173-4
  as an ontology, 168
  defined, 154-5
  in codependence, 47, 124, 126-7,
    205
Bradshaw, J., 4, 78-84, 89-91, 137
Brodsky, A., 265

Caputo, J. D., 221
categorical imperative, 194, 201-2,
    205, 209
Cheryl (case study), 16-23
child abuse, 25-6, 155, 160-4
  See also abuse (codependence liter-
    ature concept of); victim status
choice, freedom of, 80-82, 89, 158,
    212, 231
Clinton, B., 254
codependence
  and addiction, 126, 137-8
  and altruism, 128, 243-4
  and "external referenting," 126-8
  and parenting, 163
  and physical illness, 128, 244
  and psychotherapy, 6, 27-9, 237-8
  and rapture, 242-4
  and religion, 174-5
  and the "cycle of abuse," 163
  and women, 8, 49
  as a disease, 11-2, 51-2, 88-9, 102,
    129, 105-6, 188
  as a strong evaluation, 106
  as a weak evaluation, 102
  boundaries in, 47, 124, 126-7, 205
  characteristics of, 123-9, 151, 243-4
  claimed universality of, 1-4, 11-13,
    48, 82
  and the "addictive society," 89,
    127
  as a meme, 3-4
  as an ontological problem, 128-
    32

controversy about, in the code-
    pendence literature, 91-2
  "controlling" behavior in, 159-60
  definitions of, 3, 11, 47, 91-93
  feminist view of, 48-51, 244
  horizon in, 169-70
  in mental health professionals,
    126, 243-4
  interpretation as an aspect of, 121,
    127, 141-2, 168-9
  ontological breakdown signified
    by, 238-42, 246
  reconstitution of, 237-48
codependence literature, authority
    of, 50, 63
  concealment of, 121, 114-5, 129-30
  and coauthorship, 115, 119,
    134
  and homogeneity, 94-5
  and horizon, 171
  and moral persuasion, 113
  and moral relativism, 204
  and strong evaluation, 105, 121
  as a concealing of the Other,
    119-20
  political dimensions, 211-2
codependence literature, the
  and incommensurability, 206
  and psychotherapy, 27-9, 237-8
  and the recovery genre, 3-4, 6, 70
  and the "triumph of the therapeu-
    tic," 206, 217
  and women, 8, 49-51
  as a cultural inscription, 37, 47, 51
  as a document of contemporary
    self-understanding, 28-9
  as a genre, 48, 83-5
  as a horizon, 243
  as a "mirror," 122-3, 133
  as a moral discourse, 100-16
  as a narrative space, 111-16, 171,
    183
  as a proxy for the "recovery"
    genre, 3-4
  as an embodiment of the rupture
    between self and Other, 189-90

codependence literature, the
(*continued*)
conflicts of claims within, 88-94
constituent texts, 84-5
critiques of, 48-50
dangers of, 247
"effectiveness" of, 91-93, 235
exemplary texts of, 96-7
Freudian theory in, 240
historical development of, 7, 67-83
homogeneity of, 6, 28, 68, 85-96
implicit moral theory of, 191-2,
    204, 207-8
lack of moral distinctions in, 109-10
moral orientation in, 113-4
narrative induction of, 123-9
naturalist epistemology of, 7, 93-4,
    105, 109-11, 114-5, 166, 184,
    188
on addiction, 51
on coauthorship, 115
on conformity, 50
on intimacy, 156-9
on moral orientation, 63
"oughts" in, 99-108
popularity of, 12, 29, 111, 182,
    187-8
pragmatism in, 235
proliferation of, 95-6
sales of, 64, 96
strong evaluation in, 100-7
suitability for hermeneutic analy-
    sis of, 6-7, 12, 62-5
vast claims of, 12, 48, 217
weak evaluation in, 101-3
widespread applicability of, 128,
    130-1
constitutive vs. life goods, 191
Cushman, Philip, 65, 121, 131, 211
"cycle of abuse," 163-4, 241

Dallmayr, F., 189
Dasein, 220-224
Descartes, R., 193, 222, 225
dignity (axis of moral space), 132-145
    and community, 135
and narrative, 134-5, 139-40
and privacy, 132-44
and relationships, 137-8
and respect and obligation, 136-7,
    147, 149-50, 158, 160
and self-esteem, 133-5
and the Inner Child, 139-40
as a right, 135
as the eclipse of the Other, 137-42,
    144, 145
definition, 132-3
economic metaphors for, 136-7,
    140-2
machine metaphors for, 142-4
Dodds, E. R., 30
Dreyfus, H. 199, 222
driving, 183-4
drug abuse. *See* substance abuse
drugs (illegal), 69, 126, 142, 254-5
Dworkin, R., 202
"dysfunctional family," the, 71, 76-84,
    114
and autonomy, 79-82
and choice, 80-82
and "cycle of abuse," 163
and the self as sole author, 79-83
characteristics of, 76-8
compared with "functional fami-
    lies," 79
homogeneity of, 4, 81
ontological dimensions of, 240
parenting rules in, 78-9
pervasiveness of, 4, 78
"recovery" from, 82-3

ego psychology, 249-52
Eliot, T. S., 230, 245, 246
empirical sciences, 5, 44, 55-7, 108-9
empiricism, 108-10, 114
    See also codependence literature,
        naturalist epistemology of
"empty self," the, 217, 222, 247
Enlightenment, the, 190, 207, 219-20
"false self," 80
family, the, 238-42
    See also "dysfunctional family"

Fatal Attraction (film), 75
feral children, 266-7
Foucault, Michel, 60, 102, 210-12
free-market capitalism, 59, 137, 183, 245
Freud, S., 21, 31, 77, 126, 206, 251, 267-8
  concept of self of, 29-30, 239-40
Friedman, Maurice, 148, 249
Frost, Robert, 167-9
full life (axis of moral space), 169-80
  See also "Higher Power"
Fuller, R. C., 40-42

Gadamer, H.-G., 57-59
Genie (feral child), 267
Ginsburg, D., 254
God
  question of the existence of, 193, 222, 228, 267
  See also Higher Power; spirituality
good life, the
  and authority, 193-5
  and ethical action, 191-2
  and incommensurability, 205
  and "mental health, " 207-8, 250-2
  and metanarrative, 199
  and psychotherapy, 21-5, 256
  and "recovery," 106-7
  and relationships, 117-8, 180-1
  and responsibility for others, 183-4
  and self-esteem, 12
  and selfhood, 107, 110
  and strong evaluation, 103-6
  and the de-centered self, 255
  and the priority of the Other, 249
  as the eclipse of the Other, 118-9, 184-5, 187
  as the object of moral philosophy, 100
  in *Othello*, 197
  public vs. private definitions of, 21-3
  Twelve-Step programs as, 252-3
goods vs. rights, 100-1, 162
"greenhouse effect," the, 26

Haaken, J., 49-50, 52, 54
Habermas, J., 57, 61
HarperCollins, Publishers, 96
Health Communications, Inc., 69, 83, 96
"healthy narcissism," 250-2
Heidegger, Martin, 67, 219-32, 256
  and hermeneutics, 58-59
  and National Socialism, 58, 227, 234-5
  language of, 220
  on Parmenides, 222-3
  on Plato, 222
  on representation, 225
  on "subjecthood," 231-2
  on the death of God, 228
  on the Enlightenment, 219-20
  on the "great age of the Greeks," 223-5
  on "the world picture," 226-8
  on values, 228
hermeneutic circle, 54
hermeneutics, 4-8, 52-62, 121
  and authority, 54, 57
  and empirical sciences, 5, 55-7
  and Heidegger, 58-9
  and prejudice, 53-4, 57, 234
  and self-help books, 54-62
  and texts, 54-62
  and the codependence literature, 7, 12, 62-5
  and the self, 55-6
  critical, 57-9
  limitations of, 57
hermeneutics, ontological, 52, 57-60
  and critical hermeneutics, 57, 59
  and Heidegger, 59
  and pragmatism, 235-6
  and the self, 61
  limitations of, 59, 61-2, 234-6
"Higher Power," the, 148, 171-80
  and boundaries, 173-4
  and false idols, 173
  and self-esteem, 175-6
  and shame, 173
  and sole authorship, 175

and traditional religions, 174-5, 176-7
as a divine within, 174-7
as a horizon, 173-5
as an Other, 174-80
necessity of surrendering to, 173-4
Hillman, J., 65, 246, 256
Holocaust, the. *See* National Socialism
homelessness, 13, 183
homeostasis, 144
horizon, 189-90
  and codependence, 169-70
  and "recovery," 173, 180
  and spirituality, 172, 175
  as an "in here," 230-1
  concealment of, in the codependence literature, 171
  defined, 170-1
  "Higher Power" as a version of, 173-5
  inescapable otherness of, 169-71
  loss of, 207, 228
  See also codependence literature, authority of
Husserl, E., 44
hyperindividualism, 45

Iago, 189, 199, 202-4, 214-5, 227
incest, 253
incommensurability (of moral narratives), 202-6, 219-21
Inner Child, 139-40, 229, 240, 243
intimacy, 137-8, 153-9

Kaminer, W., 38, 48, 50-1, 63-4, 87, 95
Kant, I., 194, 200-1, 205, 218
Kohut, H., 250-2
Kovel, J . 34-5, 249-52
Krestan, J. A., 47-9, 53-4, 87, 244, 248

Lacan, J., 255
Levinas, E., 248
Lifton, R. J., 182, 263

MacIntyre, A., 62-3, 131, 190, 194, 202-4, 207, 219-20, 228, 248

Mack, J. E., 263-4
Mark (case study), 23-5
mass-death technology, 182-4, 263-4. *See also* nuclear weapons
Masson, J. M., 268
maturity, 79-80, 104, 110, 114, 170, 182, 251
memes, 2, 5, 164
"mental health," 14-5, 207-8, 214, 250-2
mesmerism, 40-44
metanarrative, 193, 197, 199, 201, 203, 205
metaphysical ethics, 190, 195, 198, 204-5
modern self. *See* self as sole author
modernity, 191, 221, 235
moral orientation, 62-3, 112-4, 264
moral space
  and reading, 121
  and selfhood, 112-6
  as a narrative space, 112-6, 197-8
  as a space of questions, 112-3, 121-2
  axes of, 118-9, 132

narcissistic personality disorder, 250-2
narrative, 64, 113-4, 198, 201
  and dignity, 134-5, 139-40
  and empiricism, 114
  and strong evaluation, 113
  and the self, 113, 236
  moral dimensions, 62-3, 112-6, 197-8, 208
  need for thematic unity in, 131
  ontological dimensions, 223
narrative authority. *See* sole authorship
National Socialism, 58, 60, 213, 216, 227, 234-5
natural sciences. *See* empirical sciences; empiricism; codependence literature, naturalist epistemology of
nihilism, 8, 64, 188-90, 202, 218-32, 245

nihilism *(continued)*
    and "abuse," 253-4
    and incommensurability, 204
    and *Othello*, 198
    and psychotherapy, 206, 213-4, 256
    and "recovery," 7, 60-1, 188, 229-
        30, 232, 247
    and relationships, 219
    and the "therapeutic," 206
    definitions of, 60, 188
    of sole authorship, 190, 229, 247
    of the self as sole author, 7-8, 198-
        9, 219, 234
    ontology of, 219-28
North, O., 204
nuclear weapons, 23-5, 183-4, 263-5

obligation, 23, 136. *See also* respect
        and obligation (axis of moral
        space)
Oedipus complex, 239-40
ontological hermeneutics. *See*
    hermeneutics, ontological
Othello, 189, 199, 201-2, 205, 207,
    214-5, 227
Othello (Shakespeare), 189, 196-8,
    212-4
Other, the, problem of
    and "abuse," 162
    and Dasein, 224
    and dignity, 143-4
    and ego psychology, 249-52
    and horizon, 170
    and respect and obligation, 148-
        51, 159-60, 164, 169
    and selfhood, 34-5, 237
    and sole authorship, 167, 184-90,
        228, 231-2, 244-6
    and the good life, 118-9, 184-5,
        187
    and the "Higher Power," 174-80
    and the self as sole author, 32-4,
        113, 119, 138, 149, 155, 190,
        221-3, 229, 238
    and victim status, 164
    Heidegger on, 220-32

Parmenides, 222-3
Peale, Norman Vincent, 39, 251
Peele, S., 64, 69, 70, 88, 265
Plato, 222, 225
"positive communities," 206-8, 267
practical reason, 201
prosperity, 178-80, 183
"psychic numbing," 263-4
psychodynamic theory, 53, 250-2
"psychological man," 206-10
psychotherapy, 61, 249-50, 252, 255-6
    and authenticity, 20
    and codependence, 6, 27-9, 237-8
    and nihilism, 206, 213-4, 256
    and nuclear weapons, 263-4
    and obligations, 20-3
    and *Othello*, 214-5
    and "recovery," 6, 64
    and "self disorders," 250-2
    and the good life, 21-5
    and the self as sole author, 15-29
    as critique, 250-2
    as moral articulation, 208-10
    as secular spiritual practice, 209-
        11
    authority of, 23
    lack of moral distinctions in, 22-7

Rapping, E ., 51
reading. *See* texts, appropriation of
"recovery," 1-4
    and addiction, 69
    and autonomy, 73-4, 82
    and freedom of choice, 82, 212
    and horizon, 173, 180
    and intersubjectivity, 142
    and narrative authority, 247
    and oppression, 245
    and "personal power," 153-4
    and politics, 240
    and prosperity, 183, 212
    and psychotherapy, 6, 64
    and rational thinking, 92
    and relationships, 117-9, 148
    and respect and obligation, 159-60
    and rights, 135

and self-love, 237
and the "Higher Power," 169-80
and the "real self," 81
as a meme, 2, 5
as a publishing genre, 3, 6, 68-83
as a strong evaluation, 104-5
as redemption, 181
as the good life, 106-7
defined, 1
from "dysfunctional families,"
  82-3
moral dimensions of, 2, 3, 100,
  207
nihilism of, 7, 60-1, 188, 229-30,
  232, 247
pervasiveness of, 1, 64, 69
spiritual dimensions, 172
universal need for, 1, 69
relativism, 195
"religious man," 206
respect and obligation (axis of moral
  space), 148-67
and boundaries, 154-8, 167-9
and dignity, 136-7, 147, 149-50,
  151-8, 160
and "recovery," 159-60
and self-esteem, 152-3
and self-interest, 153, 154
and sole authorship, 136, 152,
  158-64
and the problem of the Other,
  148-51, 159-60, 164, 169
and Twelve-Step programs, 165-7
as a serendipity of self-love, 163-4
as "pathological," 149
codependent's understanding of,
  151
dangers posed to the codependent
  by, 151, 154
defined, 149-51
economic metaphors for, 152-3,
  158-9
for children, 160-4
foreign policy metaphors for,
  156-7
geographic metaphors for, 154-8

machine metaphors for, 153-4
strong evaluations inherent in, 167
responsibility for others, 159-60, 167,
  183-4, 245
Ricoeur, P., 3, 54-7, 60, 62-3, 121,
  264-5
Rieff, P., 206-19, 267
rights, 135-7, 181
Rilke, R. M., 242-3
Rose, N., 211-12, 215, 256
Rosen, G. M., 42

Sampson, E., 45, 208, 211
Satir, V., 80-1
Schorske, C., 31, 239-40, 268
self as sole author (modern conception of self)
and boundaries, 155
and coauthorship, 241
and community, 13-15, 33, 35,
  136-7, 208, 218
and Descartes, 32
and intimacy, 156
and metanarrative, 205
and psychotherapy, 15-29, 32
and the "dysfunctional family," 79-
  83
and the Other, 32-4, 113, 119,
  138, 190, 221-3, 229, 238
and universal morality, 195
and "webs of interlocution," 203-4
as a machine, 142-4
as indigenous psychology of
  Western culture, 208
as prior to the Other, 149, 155
critiques of, 45-6
historical development of, 13-15,
  31-3, 182, 189, 190-196, 265-6
metaphors for, 168
moral dimensions, 6, 14, 16-26,
  61, 65, 100, 111, 118, 194, 201,
  209
nihilism of, 7-8, 198-9, 219, 234
political dimensions, 174
prejudices inherent in, 32
See also sole authorship

self, de-centered, 74, 76, 255
self, the, 29-33
  and addiction, 76
  and hermeneutics, 55-6, 61
  and the problem of the Other,
    34-5, 237
  in moral space, 112-6
  inescapably social nature of, 200,
    266-7
  premodern understandings of, 30-1
  social construction of, 12, 29-33,
    112
self-care. *See* self-esteem
self-esteem, 8, 27, 46, 214, 251
  and "abuse," 161-4
  and boundaries, 156
  and community, 137
  and dignity, 133-5
  and "healthy narcissism," 251-2
  and intimacy, 137-8, 153-4
  and others, 151-2, 167, 181, 184
  and respect and obligation, 152-3,
    163-4
  and shame, 184
  and sole authorship, 134, 137-8
  and the good life, 12
  and the Higher Power, 175-6
  and the Inner Child, 139-40
  as a moral distinction, 163, 167-8,
    188, 205-6, 209
  as a right, 135-7
  defined, 133
  in ACOA books, 72-3
  in "women who love too much,"
    75-7
  privacy of 136-7, 205, 214
self-help books, 6, 38-46, 54-62
  and academic psychology, 42-6
  and hermeneutics, 54-62
  "effectiveness" of, 43, 46
  empirical studies of, 43-4
  ethics of, 42-3
  popularity of, 44, 111
  practical vs. personal genres, 38
  prescription of by psychologists,
    42-4

self-understanding implicit in, 45-6
self-love. *See* self-esteem
shame, 27, 80
  and child abuse, 155, 161
  and prosperity, 178-80
  and self-esteem, 184
  and the Higher Power, 173
  and traditional religions, 175
Sloterdijk, P., 60
sole authorship
  and child abuse, 161
  and coauthorship, 119, 155
  and dignity, 134
  and free-market capitalism, 245
  and intersubjectivity, 142
  and oppression, 244-5
  and *Othello*, 189, 196-7
  and otherness, 119-20, 149, 181,
    244-7
  and parenting, 162-3
  and relationships, 152, 189
  and respect and obligation, 136,
    152, 158-64
  and self-esteem, 134, 137-8
  and the "Higher Power," 175
  and the problem of the Other,
    167, 184-90, 228, 231-2, 244-6
  as a basis of community, 165-7
  as a right, 135, 144
  as an ontology, 181-2
  defined, 148
  nihilism of, 190, 229, 247
  of children, 161-4
  political implications of, 183-5
spirituality, 169-80. *See also* "Higher
    Power," the; horizon
Starker, S., 42-6, 55
Stevens, W., 141
strong evaluation, 104-8, 112, 121,
    139, 147, 195, 213-4
  and articulacy, 107
  and dignity, 133
  and nihilism, 218
  and obligation, 150
  and *Othello*, 197-8
  and "recovery," 104-5

and respect and obligation, 167
as an inscription of the good life,
103-6
codependence as, 106
defined, 100, 104
in the codependence literature,
100-7
moral dimensions, 108-11
necessity of, for selfhood, 115
substance abuse, 142, 254
See also drugs (illegal); abuse
(codependence concept of)

Taylor, C.
and nihilism, 199-200
on articulacy of moral discourses,
106-7, 112, 208-9
on constitutive vs. life goods,
191-2
on dignity, 132
on moral orientation, 62-4
on "moral reactions," 195, 202
on naturalist epistemologies, 108,
110-11
on respect and obligation, 148
on rights, 134-5
on strong evaluation, 100-5, 108,
115
on the axes of moral space, 118-9
on the existence of God, 193
on the history of the modern self,
30-1, 190-2
on what makes a full life, 169-71
texts
and hermeneutics, 54-62
and the self, 60

and the "surplus of meaning," 56
appropriation of, 55-6, 63, 121
"therapeutic," the, 206-18
thinking, Heidegger's view of, 222-6
Third Step, the, 175
Tocqueville, A. de, 41, 210
Transactional Analysis, 90-1
transference, 22, 250
trauma theories, 238, 267-8
Triumph of the Therapeutic (Rieff),
206-18
Twelve-Step programs, 61, 164-7,
210, 213, 257-8
and "recovery," 165-6
as a narrative space, 214
community formed by, 165-6
good life in, 252-3
proliferation of, 70
respect and obligation in, 165-7
spiritual dimensions, 170
Twelve Steps for Codependents, 172,
257

universal morality, 195, 218

van Wormer, K., 48, 244
victim status, 164-5, 184-5, 242

weak evaluation, 102-3, 207
"webs of interlocution," 200-4, 223-4,
246, 266
Wild Child (film), 266-7
Woititz, J., 71-4
Women Who Love Too Much
(Norwood), 74-8
world-view, 203, 226-7, 242
Wyschogrod, E., 182, 234, 255